MISSION POSSIBLE

The True Story of Ukraine's Comprehensive Banking
Reform and Practical Manual for Other Nations

VALERIA GONTAREVA AND
YEVHEN STEPANIUK

authorHOUSE®

AuthorHouse™ UK
1663 Liberty Drive
Bloomington, IN 47403 USA
www.authorhouse.co.uk
Phone: UK TFN: 0800 0148641 (Toll Free inside the UK)
        UK Local: 02036 956322 (+44 20 3695 6322 from outside the UK)

Published by AuthorHouse   07/10/2020

ISBN: 978-1-7283-5383-8 (sc)
ISBN: 978-1-7283-5384-5 (hc)
ISBN: 978-1-7283-5382-1 (e)

Be brave, be curious and determined,
overcome the odds. It can be done!

Stephen Hawking

FOREWORD

THIS IS AN extraordinary book from an extraordinary person.

Valeria Gontareva, the former Governor of the National Bank of Ukraine, is well-known in global central banking and policy reformer circles, and in her country, and is her country is an admired reformer – except to vested and corrupt interest that her actions often targeted. She presided over the overhaul of the central bank and the financial sector in 2014-2017, at the height of the biggest crisis facing her country since independence, with a collapsed economy and war with its powerful neighbour.

During her tenure, Governor Gontareva had to draw up a strategy for and implement, macroeconomic stabilisation, a radical change in monetary policy, and banking sector reform in what most considered impossible circumstances. In the process, she had to nationalise or liquidate close to half of the country's banks, and completely restructure the central bank. A banker by training, she also proved to be a skilful politician, working with alliances at home and abroad to help reforms succeed.

This book is an insightful, candid and passionate account of her approach and policy experience. She has called it a "Practical Manual" for reforms – it is that but also much more: a historical record of reforms against all odds. It also testifies to her true leadership and deep dedication to her country and her fellow citizens, despite risks to her own and her family's safety. Governor Gontareva recently survived what was most likely an attempt on her life, and has defied several acts of intimidation to write this compelling book. For that we are most grateful.

The book was written in collaboration with Yevhen Stepaniuk, while Governor Gontareva was in residence at the London School of Economics and Political Science, where she is a Senior Policy Fellow at the Institute of Global Affairs at the the School of Public Policy. We are fortunate to have her participate in our Global Policy Lab, where she is well placed to help the next generation of leaders and policy makers launch their countries' hard road to reform.

Professor Erik Berglof,
Director, LSE Institute of Global Affairs
London, May 2020

GLOSSARY OF ACRONYMS

ALCO	Assets and Liabilities Management Committee
AMC	Asset Management Company
AML / CFT	Anti-Money Laundering and Countering Financing of Terrorism
API	Application Programming Interface
AQR	Asset Quality Review
ARC	Asset Resolution Company
ARC	Annual Report Competition
ATM	Automatic Teller Machine
AUD	Australian Dollar
B-1	Board -1 Level
BCBS	Basel Committee on Banking Supervision
BCP	Business Continuity Planning
BEPS	Base Erosion and Profit Shifting
BIS	Bank for International Settlements
BOP	Balance of Payments
BRRD	Bank Recovery and Resolution Directive
CAGR	Compound Annual Growth Rate
CAMELSO	Composite Rating of Capital, Asset Quality, Management, Earnings, Liquidity, Sensitivity to Market Risk, Operational Risk
CAR	Capital Adequacy Ratio
CB	Central Bank
CBDC	Central Bank Digital Currency
CCR	Central Credit Registry
CD	Certificate of Deposit
CEE	Central and Eastern Europe
CEO	Chief Executive Officer
CFC	Controlled Foreign Company
CFO	Chief Financial Officer

CHF	Swiss Franc
CMU	Cabinet of Ministers of Ukraine
CNY	Chinese Yuan
COREP	Common Reporting
CPI	Consumer Price Index
CRA	Comprehensive Risk Assessment
CRR/CRD IV	Capital Requirements Regulation and Directive IV
CRS	Common Reporting Standard
DGF	Deposit Guarantee Fund
EAD	Exposure at Default
EBITDA	Earnings before Interest, Taxes, Depreciation and Amortization
EBRD	European Bank for Reconstruction and Development
ECB	European Central Bank
EFF	Extended Fund Facility
EIB	European Investment Bank
ELA	Emergency Liquidity Assistance
ESRB	European Systemic Risk Board
EU	European Union
EUR	Euro
EWS	Early Warning System
FATCA	Foreign Account Tax Compliance Act
FATF	Financial Action Task Force
FCY	Foreign Currency
FDI	Foreign Direct Investment
FINREP	Financial Reporting
FinTech	Financial Technology
QPM	Quarterly Projection Model
FSC	Financial Stability Council
FX	Foreign Exchange
GAAR	General Anti-Abuse Rules
GBP	British Pound
GDP	Gross Domestic Product
GFC	Global Financial Crisis

G-SIB	Global Systemically Important Bank
IAIS	International Association of Insurance Supervisors
IBAN	International Bank Account Number
ICSD	International Central Securities Depository
IFC	International Finance Corporation
IFI	International Financial Institution
IFRS	International Financial Reporting Standard
IMF	International Monetary Fund
INSOL	International Federation of National Associations of Accountants and Lawyers
IOSCO	International Organization of Securities Commissions
IPO	Initial Public Offering
IR	Interest Rate
IT	Inflation Targeting
JPY	Japanese Yen
KYC	Know Your Customer
LCR	Liquidity Cover Ratio
LCY	Local Currency
LGD	Loss Given Default
M&A	Mergers and Acquisitions
MAP	Mutual Agreement Procedure
MFA	Macrofinancial Assistance
MLI	Multilateral Instrument (Multilateral Convention to Implement Tax Treaty Related Measures to Prevent Base Erosion and Profit Shifting)
MoF	Ministry of Finance
MONEYVAL	Committee of Experts on the Evaluation of Anti-Money Laundering Measures and the Financing of Terrorism
MPC	Monetary Policy Committee
M-t-M	Mark-to-Market
NBU	National Bank of Ukraine
NFSC	National Financial Services Commission
NDA	Net Domestic Assets
NIR	Net International Assets

NPL	Non-Performing Loan
NRC	National Reform Council
NSFR	Net Stable Funding Ratio
OECD	Organization for Economic Co-operation and Development
P&L	Profit and Loss Statement
P2P	Peer-to-Peer
PD	Probability of Default
PEP	Politically Exposed Person
PLZ	Polish Złoty
POS	Point of Sale
PSD2	Payment Services Directive 2
QE	Quantitative Easing
RAMP	Reserves Advisory and Management Partnership
RCSA	Risk and Control Self-Assessment
REER	Real Effective Exchange Rate
RIT	Reforms Implementation Toolkit
RPL	Related Party Lending
RTGS	Real-Time Gross Settlement
S&P	Standard & Poor's
SBA	Stand-by Arrangement
SDR	Special Drawing Rights
SEP	System of Electronic Payments
SEPA	Single Euro Payments Area
SIB	Systemically Important Bank
SME	Small and Medium-sized Enterprises
SOB	State-Owned Bank
SOE	State-Owned Enterprise
SPV	Special Purpose Vehicle
SREP	Supervisory Review and Evaluation Process
ST	Stress-Testing
TA	Technical Assistance
TLAC	Total Loss-Absorbing Capacity
UAH	Ukrainian Hryvnia

UBO	Ultimate Beneficial Owner
UBPR	Uniform Bank Performance Report
UK	United Kingdom
URA	Ukrainian Reform Architecture
USAID	United States Agency for International Development
USD, US$	United States Dollar
VAT	Value Added Tax
XML	Extensible Markup Language

CONTENTS

INTRODUCTION[1]

In October 2014, I held my first meeting as Governor of Ukraine's National Bank, with Stanley Fisher, then Vice-Chairman of the US Federal Reserve. As I described to Fisher the economic crisis in Ukraine, and all the macro-financial imbalances in our war-torn economy, I asked him how we could restore macroeconomic equilibrium. He told me that he had never had to deal with such incredibly complicated issues, and that our mission was impossible. Just three years later, the success of reforms we implemented during my tenure at the Bank was acknowledged by the IMF, who said that Ukraine's "powerful change in focus, structure, and staffing since 2014...is unprecedented in modern central banking."

This book is the story of how we accomplished "Mission Impossible". There are many countries in the world today that similarly require real reform of their financial and banking sectors. Some of them must entirely revamp their banking industry; others need only reform outdated elements of their systems. But what is clear is that every central bank and banking regulator in the world must adjust to our new reality, and become agile, modern institutions able to rapidly react to the challenges of our time.

An inherent feature of the new reality is the regular occurrence of "black swan" events. The COVID-19 pandemic, which began to spread in early 2020, when the manuscript was already finished, is a black swan for the entire global economy. The subsequent economic turmoil could be stemming from a number of simultaneous shocks starting from the weak domestic and external demand for goods and services, a major disruption in supply chains, and a reduction of trade flows to significant pressure on state budgets and tighter financial conditions.

---

[1] The authors would like to thank for comments by Erik Berglof and Piroska Mohacsi-Nagy, LSE IGA and the participants of a lectures and seminars at the LSE during 2019.

It could be a real-time test for banks across the globe and a vivid reminder of the pressing need for reforms that could strengthen the resiliency of the banking system to shocks.

Consequently, when considering reform, we must ask ourselves: What do we do first? Where do we begin? Moreover, my personal observations tell me that we are usually only ready to undertake radical reform when the situation is already critical and when the threats are not potential but real. That is to say – we undertake reform far too late. This usually means that we only undertake reform standing on the brink of an abyss. It means that we start with ailing economies, failing banking systems, and non-transparent, inefficient central banks. It means that only one step separates us from falling into the bottomless financial precipice of corruption and economic collapse.

I am not the most seasoned central banker in the world. My professional background, however, of more than 20 years of banking experience and dedication to finance and the economy, allowed me to institute the quick, painful, but ultimately effective and necessary reform of Ukraine's banking system. I was elected as the Governor of the National Bank of Ukraine (NBU) after "the Revolution of Dignity" in June 2014. I was immediately confronted with a perfect storm. We lost about 20% of our GDP because of the annexation of Crimea and war in the Donbass. Our enterprises ground to a halt and infrastructure in Donbass was completely destroyed. The balance of payments collapsed and the exchange rate, which mirrors the balance of payments, responded accordingly – not to mention the effect on persistent, unsustainable imbalances in all sectors of the domestic economy and the banking system that had accumulated over the twenty previous years in Ukraine. This included empty Treasury coffers, gaping holes worth billions in the books of state-owned enterprises (SOE), and a large number of non-viable banks.

A Mission Impossible task indeed – but we completed all major reforms of the financial and banking sectors in just three years: We moved to a flexible exchange rate regime and implemented the new monetary policy of inflation targeting; we cleaned up the banking system from insolvent banks and enhanced its resilience. Furthermore, we built a powerful, modern, independent Central Bank. We transformed the NBU completely: We rebuilt all internal processes and turned it into a completely reorganized institution, one with fully functioning supervisory, credit, financial stability, monetary policy and process management committees.

That is why I decided to write this Practical Manual to help other countries start comprehensive reforms of their own financial sectors. If you are reading this book, your country may already be facing sizable double deficits (budget and current account deficits). The corrosive effect of doing nothing or doing too little, too late or too long may already be eating away at your economy. The cost of inaction will extend far beyond monetary ramifications: In my country, as well as others around the world, prior delay and inaction eventually manifested as massive financial meltdowns and waves of social-political unrest.

There are a number of common challenges for regulators in a global system. The expansion of FinTech, cryptocurrencies, and artificial intelligence is impeding central banks both in advanced and developing economies. The same is true for the acute threats of cyber-security, de-offshorization, de-dollarization and other issues that have no borders in today's world.

Our experience in rethinking the role of financial monitoring, as well as our independently developed and successful toolkit for disclosing beneficial owners, can be useful to many developed European countries, which are now overwhelmed by a wave of money laundering scandals.

To overcome this perfect storm is no mean feat. As an aspiring reformer you may face a triple hit of depreciation, higher interest rates and volatile capital flows. More than that, you will encounter incredible resistance from the Old Guard, internal and external. You might face personal threats and sustained harassment, hybrid information war and fake news. Your enemies, always numerous, can and will campaign against you with all tools at their disposal, from lies to violence. And even after your resignation, you may face not just political persecution, but violence, terror, destruction and fear. I know. I suffered, and still suffer the threats and attacks from the corrupt vested interests I fought against in Ukraine.

But a nation's Central Bank is the guardian of the state against those who would use their private wealth and power to take advantage of it. The Central Bank is also like a surgeon who cuts out a malignant tumor of corruption to further the life and prosperity of the nation. The cornerstone of a robust, incorrigible financial sector that safeguards the lives and livelihoods of the country's citizens is an independent Central Bank, which underpins financial and price stability, laying the foundation not only for an advanced modern central bank but also for the country's market economy on the whole.

Don't balk. There is no time to waste. As Stephen Hawking counseled: "Be aware of the preciousness of time. Seize the moment. Act now."

Take the leap of faith! This Practical Manual will help.

CHAPTER 1

The Pre-Reform Environment

EFORMS CAN BE carried out at different times and in different manners. Many developing countries live in a permanent state of reform. However, probably in no country did deep reform take place under such adverse circumstances as the reform of the financial sector in Ukraine from 2014 to 2017. My experience spearheading this reform will be of interest and use to other reformers and to decision makers in many countries and across various sectors.

President John F Kennedy said in his State of the Union Address in 1962 that, "The time to repair the roof is when the sun is shining". But he did not say what to do when the roof was torn off to the extent that the walls and even the foundation of the house were destroyed.

At the time of my arrival at the National Bank in mid-2014, Ukraine's banking sector was at the epicenter of what is called in economic literature the "perfect storm": a simultaneous banking and currency crisis aggravated by external imbalances and an economic recession.

Indeed, Ukraine's full-blown financial crisis in 2014 partly resulted from economic policies of prior years, which had led to the accumulation of large macroeconomic imbalances. Due to the artificial maintenance of a fixed exchange rate, Ukraine's economy was losing external competitiveness, resulting in the rise of its current account deficit to over 10% of GDP and the depletion of foreign exchange reserves. The inconsistent monetary and fiscal policy, lack of energy sector reforms and debt dollarization (active borrowing in foreign currency in the domestic market and issuance of domestic sovereign bonds indexed to FX) increased the quasi-fiscal deficit component and vulnerability of the debt to the foreign exchange risk. We also faced a bank run, with the banking sector having lost about 35% of private individuals' deposits. It was just incredible.

At the same time, there was a war going on in the country. Before I joined the Central Bank, we had already lost Crimea, occupied by Russian forces in March 2014, which represented about 3% of our GDP and 5% of our population. On top of that, a real war started in our eastern regions in August 2014, when Russia began giving major military support to separatist rebels fighting the Ukrainian government. As a result of warfare in the industrial east Donbass, we lost another 10% of our territory, 15% of our GDP, and 30% of our export revenues. Important parts of our infrastructure and industrial capacities were physically destroyed. And we lost them all in one day. There was no period of time to adjust. Everything happened so quickly, within a few days. The loss of production capacities, together with the accumulated imbalances, represented an incredible hit to our banking sector and significantly impaired the macro-financial stability of the state.

Some background will contextualize what we were facing.

a) Macroeconomic Recession

First of all, when I was appointed as the Governor of the National Bank, the country was already at war with Russia, which was gaining momentum. Then, a series of flammable military events accompanied the entire first part of my tenure at the National Bank, and significantly influenced the market situation.

The annexation of Crimea, which took place in February-March 2014, was extremely painful for our society overall, but did not have catastrophic economic consequences, since the pre-2014 share of the Crimean Peninsula was only about 3% of GDP, and most of the transshipment of goods for export was carried out through the ports of the Black Sea, located on the mainland of Ukraine.

A much more significant factor was military action in the Donbass region, which began soon after the annexation of the Crimea. Ukraine's **eastern regions, namely Donetsk and Lugansk, which were the regions affected by the military conflict, had been critical in terms of attracting foreign currency to Ukraine.** In 2013, these two regions accounted for 15.7% of Ukraine's GDP and almost 25% of its industrial production. In addition, these two regions were largely export-oriented by specializing in key export industries: their share in total exports in 2013 was 24%, including 44.7% in metallurgy, 29.1% in chemicals, and 24.0% in machine building.

Thus, in a matter of months, Ukraine lost capacities that produced *more than 15% of Ukraine's GDP and about 30% of the country's industrial output*. Enterprises located in the occupied territories also provided about *30% of all export proceeds*. The escalation of military conflict at the beginning of 2015 caused further significant damage to infrastructure and termination of production activities by many enterprises in the Donetsk and Luhansk regions.

The economic recession deepened during 2014-2015. GDP contracted by 6.6% in 2014 and by 9.8% in 2015. The most complicated situation was in industry. **Disruption of production capacities and transport infrastructure** in the industrialized East, and breach of production interregional ties due to military unrest in the east, resulted in an industrial output decrease of 10.1% in 2014.

The decrease in exports was accompanied by a fall in the investment potential of the country due to increasing uncertainty, high political and economic risks, and capital outflows. There was a significant deterioration in market expectations along with a simultaneous increase in the demand for foreign currency, an increase in the deficit, and excessive volatility of the exchange rate.

Even our previous assumptions that a decline in domestic demand would be partly offset by net export contribution were no longer relevant because of lost production capacities in the East. As most metallurgical, chemical, machine-building plants in the hostility areas suspended production, transport infrastructure was largely crushed.

The second, no less important factor for the economy, was the loss of the Russian market for domestic products. Since Soviet times, Ukrainian industrial enterprises were tied to production chains with industries in Russia. Therefore, the loss of this market painfully affected Ukraine's industry. **Total exports of goods to Russia was cut in half, from 25% in 2010-2013 to 12.1% in 2015.** The overall turnover of goods with Russia was also halved in 2014 to USD 21 billion compared to USD 39 billion in 2010-2013, and continued to decline until it reached an historical low of USD 8.2 billion in 2016.

Since 2012, deterioration of trade relations with Russia has led to 3x lower overall exports (10x for foodstuffs, 4x for machinery and equipment). The situation was exacerbated by the **critical dependence of Ukraine on imports of energy from Russia**:

- In 2013, Ukraine imported 92% of its total gas imports from Russia and 51% of its total domestic consumption needs. The domestic production of natural gas was not sufficient to satisfy internal needs of industry and households.
- While imports of crude oil from Russia to Ukraine were at 0 in 2013, Ukraine's imports accounted for 73% of gasoline consumption and 84% of diesel fuel consumption in 2013. The majority of light oil products imported to Ukraine were made from Russian crude oil.
- In the power generation sector, especially nuclear power generation, Ukraine was highly dependent on Russia to the tune of 80% of purchasing nuclear fuel elements and 100% of nuclear fuel storage.

The impact of war was exacerbated by the **effect of accumulated macroeconomic imbalances, which led to a steep currency depreciation.** The fixed UAH/USD exchange rate, which had been maintained artificially at UAH 8 per 1 USD in 2010-2013 led to an extensive current account deficit, totaling over USD41bn in 2011-2013, or around 8% of GDP. In 2013 alone, the **current account deficit soared to nearly 9% of GDP** ($16.5 billion).

Due to the fixed exchange rate, along with the overvalued exchange rate, international reserves began decreasing in the 3rd quarter of 2011, and dwindled from US$38bn to US$20bn by the end of 2013. **During only the first 2 months of 2014, the country's international reserves declined by another 25% or USD 5bn** (from USD20bn to US$15bn), hitting the sustainability metrics. Indeed, in recent years alone, Ukraine spent US$23bn from its foreign currency (FCY) reserves to artificially maintain the fixed exchange rate. External debt to GDP also exceeded permissible metrics.

Exhibit 1. Current account balance in Ukraine (2010-2017), in US$bn and in % of GDP

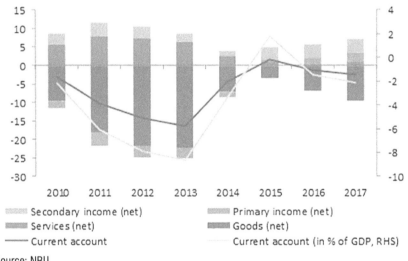

Source: NBU

Considering the export-oriented model of the economy, of which ferrous metals and metallurgical products accounted for about 20%, the loss of production capacity in the occupied territory immediately affected the foreign exchange market. Sharply reduced foreign exchange earnings put pressure on the UAH exchange rate: Within a matter of months, UAH had jumped to 30 per 1 USD, which meant an almost **4x**

devaluation of the national currency, with the figure for individual transactions exceeding UAH 40 per US dollar!

Combined with a capital outflow, the general balance of payments deficit soared to $13bn in 2014, thus leading to a decrease in international reserves to a critical level with **net international reserves turning negative** at US$3bn in 1H2015. By the end of 2014, based on balance of payment data and accounting for the schedule of payments on external debt liabilities, we estimated the **financing gap for 2015 would be nearly US$10bn**. External markets were completely closed for Ukraine, so the only source of financing was IMF credit.

Exhibit 2. External financing gap in 2015[2]

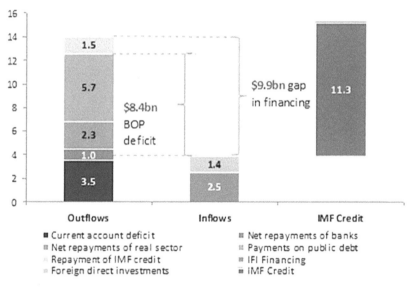

Source: NBU

Analysis of the balance-of-payments gap for 2015 showed two things: First, the current account remained negative. This was basically due to our inability to fully adjust through external trade because of the destruction of export capacities. In Ukraine's case, adjustments occur mainly through imports, or in other words, domestic demand.

---

[2] Macroeconomic forecast, December 2014

An erosion of Ukraine's industrial capacity that was generating the major share of export earnings made it infeasible to use devaluation to regain competitive advantage. Exports of goods projection was scaled down by US$4.2 billion in 2014, based on production suspension and crushed transport infrastructure in the military operations area and restrictions in trade with Russia. Even after a drastic devaluation of local currency in 2014, and taking into account lower than expected current transfers, the current account deficit was projected at US$6.8 billion or 5.3% of GDP. Based on a series of interviews, and factoring in the data for monthly export revenues of enterprises in the military area, we estimated a shortfall in export earnings of US$500-600 billion per month and we had no FCY reserves to support it.

Second, the financial account generated most of the gap. This was due to the inability of the sovereign to roll over debt and to low **rollover rates in the banking and corporate sectors, which plunged to 50%** in 2014 and to 26% in 2015.

The gap consisted of two elements: balance-of-payments gap for the given period, and additional FCY needed to boost reserves to the particular level associated with external stability. While the latter portion could be funded by IFIs or bilaterals, the former part was more systemic and needed to be addressed by relevant policies.

b) Public Finance: Debt and Deficit Explosion

In 2014, the budget deficit grew to 6% of GDP mainly because of debt service expenditures growth, which were affected by the UAH devaluation and an increase in defense expenditures caused by the military conflict. This conventional fiscal deficit was **intensified by a quasi-fiscal deficit** caused by the largest energy state holding, Naftogaz. This deficit was due to the fact that gas was sold to the population at prices significantly lower than market prices as a result of a political compromise, which created additional pressure on public finances.

The artificial retention of low gas prices for the population against the backdrop of the rising cost of imported gas led to an increase in the state holding company's deficit. In 2014, when Russia unilaterally raised the cost of imported gas by 80%, Naftogaz's **deficit exceeded UAH 100 billion (equivalent to USD 9.3 billion), which was one and a half times higher than the entire public budget deficit!** In addition, the company had to pay off arrears for imported gas and raise funds for the purchase of gas for servicing Ukrainian consumers in the next heating season. The company's gross debt at the end of 2014 amounted to UAH 61 billion (or US $3.9 billion). Considering the real inability to attract independent financing, the lion's share of the company's deficit was covered by financing from the state budget through the issuance of government bonds.

Additionally, the state Pension Fund persistently ran a deficit, on average 2% of GDP for 2008-2014, and was financed via loans from a single treasury account or direct financing from the state budget. **Thus, the broad public sector deficit** (together with Naftogaz) **approached 15% of GDP,** while the public debt, including the guaranteed debt, exceeded 70% of GDP.

Exhibit 3. Broad public sector deficit, UAH bn

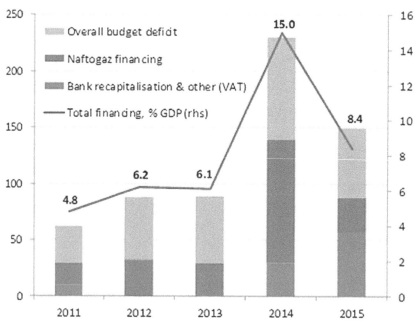

Source: NBU

At the time of my arrival at the central bank, **the treasury accounts of the state were close to zero,** which meant that at any moment the government might become unable to stay current on its payments!

Added to that was the **huge unexpected military expenditure caused by wartime, so it is no exaggeration to say** the country was on the brink of a financial abyss, and it was a question of the survival and existence of Ukraine. No doubt all of these factors led to the inevitable pressure on the central bank to finance the budget and quasi-fiscal deficit in order to avoid the destruction of the country.

c) Ineffective Banking Sector

The pervasiveness of numerous captive banks and financial pyramids had held back the development of Ukraine's financial market and aggravated distrust of its financial institutions for years. We realized that the banks had been ineffective and unprofitable during the previous 5 years, upon an initial examination of Ukraine's banking system after arriving.

The well-known saying that even if there was no war, it would have to be invented is apropos here. While **the systemic problems of the banking sector** that emerged suddenly in 2014 had not been visible before, they **were actually the result of accumulated imbalances and ineffective supervisory policy from several decades.** To the critics, I say: **the war in the East only exacerbated the problems of banks, but in no way caused their occurrence.**

Just take the **state-owned banks** -- even the most superficial analysis of their loan portfolios showed a **cross-section of the entire modern history of Ukraine**, and could serve as a mirror of elites' wrong-doings and vested interests. Just as one can see the history of the evolution of mankind from a soil section, so the state bank's balance sheets showed the history of the change of power in Ukraine in the preceding ten years: **each ruling team had given loans to their favorites with the help of political henchmen in the management of state-owned banks.** In the absence of independent supervisory boards, there was no proper control over the disbursement of loans to businesses affiliated with political elites, which after the change of power, settled down to non-performing assets. **Nearly USD 10 billion at the current exchange rate had been poured into state-owned banks from the state budget over the previous 10 years as additional capitalization.**

The banking system, which represented more than 85% of the financial sector's assets, had **structural weaknesses that increased its exposure to shocks** and was the result of regulatory forbearance and poor governance in the system.

The other key characteristics of the banking system were:

- *Large fragmentation.* The banking system was very fragmented with the 80 smallest banks (out of 180) having less than 5% market share.
- *Related-party lending.* Lending to the owner's business was the main activity for a large number of banks (a scheme in which the bank was a piece in a value chain of the corporate sector).
- *Non-transparent ownership.* The central bank did not know who the real owners of banks were due to existing requirements that banks were not forced to show their ultimate beneficial owners and the central bank could only see the names of offshore companies as bank owners.
- *Hidden NPLs.* The pre-2014 banking data testified to the inconsistency of the NPL recognition in bank books. A large share of loans, primarily issued to related parties, were acknowledged as performing, despite the fact that new loans were issued to service the previous loans.
- *Dollarization* of banks' assets and liabilities was nearly 50%.

Moreover, the banking sector in Ukraine had been hard hit by a combination of political, security, and exchange-rate pressures since the beginning of 2014. Internal shocks, mainly the military conflict in eastern Ukraine, negatively affected economic development, undermined the trust of consumers, and resulted in destabilization of the financial markets. Diminished economic activity and trade imbalances contributed to depreciation and accelerated inflation. The weakening of UAH had a devastating effect on the Ukrainian banking system.

This resulted in a deteriorating quality of bank credit portfolios calling for the balance sheet cleanup that started in 2014, and required additional capital increases from banks to create significant provisions against credit exposures. In 2014, provisioning became the main driver of the banking system losses. The situation with problem banks' balance sheets was further aggravated by the lack of effective protection of creditor and consumer rights, especially guarantees for property rights, and a fair judiciary system.

But the biggest problem was a run on the banks. By the end of September 2014, the banking system has lost about 24.5% of household deposits (US$13.3bn net of change in exchange rates). Foreign currency deposits slumped by 33.8% or US$7.9bn. The long-term deposit outflow played a lead role, declining by 35.7% since December of 2013, providing 77.7% of total household deposits' outflow.

Furthermore, households accelerated deposit withdrawals due to perceptions of FCY scarcity as well as a high precautionary demand for cash FCY holdings, which traditionally serve as a risk-free alternative to bank deposits in Ukraine.

Exhibit 4. Individual deposits in banks, 01.12.2013=100%

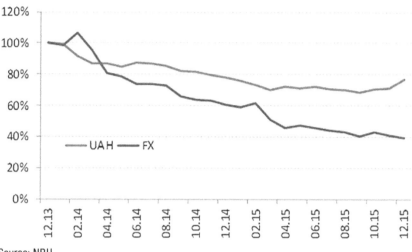

Source: NBU

It should be noted that pre-2015 in Ukraine, there were essentially no term deposits. According to the legislation in force at that time, funds deposited even for the long term could be demanded by the depositor at any moment.

As a result, **by 1Q2015, the banking system had lost nearly 30% of UAH and over 50% of FX household deposits**. UAH deposits started to recover only in June 2015 while FX outflows continued.

Consequently, the net demand for FX in the interbank market in 2014 amounted to almost USD 10 billion. In the cash FX market, the net demand from the population amounted to USD 2.4 billion due to high devaluation expectations. In total for 2014, the negative balance of FX interventions of the National Bank amounted to almost USD 12.3 billion, leading to the depletion of FX reserves.

CHAPTER 2

Our Rapid Response Measures

AS WAS CLEAR by the end of 2013, having a local currency pegged to the US dollar was suicidal for the economy and put Ukraine on the brink of an economic precipice. By the middle of 2014, we **switched to a flexible exchange rate.**

However, as pressure on the UAH exchange rate intensified in late 2014, we started to use **a mix of FX interventions and strict administrative measures,** including limits on deposit withdrawal and cash FX operations, **with an aim towards curbing panic-driven behavior** and preventing a flow of foreign currency outside the banking system. Using FX interventions, we also aimed to help the market to find an **equilibrium exchange rate** that could serve as a benchmark for restoring market balance.

We limited the withdrawal of deposits in foreign and national currencies. The refinancing of the National Bank could support the outflow of UAH deposits, but the dollar liquidity could not be met in the amount needed. We also limited the maximum amount of FCY cash purchase for private individuals[3] (see Chapter 5).

In parallel, we launched **currency auctions and targeted interventions to supply banks with FX cash** to meet the needs of banks' clients. More than USD 1.8 billion was sold for this purpose.

To avoid additional foreign exchange pressure, the NBU actually removed the largest buyer of foreign currency – Naftogaz -- from the interbank foreign exchange market, having provided the company with direct access

---

[3] NBU resolution #540 dated 29.08.2014

to foreign currency through **targeted interventions**. In the 1H2014, the National Bank sold USD 4.4bn (with more than 51% going to Naftogaz), and twice as much in the 2H2014 – USD 8.8bn (75% to Naftogaz).

To support the bank's liquidity under the outflow of individual deposits, we provided limited refinancing loans to banks to compensate for outflows of clients' deposits within the guaranteed sum of UAH 200,000, the disbursements of which were monitored by the curator of the National Bank. We updated the requirements for assessment of collateral for refinancing, introduced the practice of providing personal guarantees of shareholders, and attracted independent international appraisers to value assets pledged to the central bank as collateral. This was done in order **to tackle the perilous practice** pre-2014 of providing refinancing loans without adequate collateral, in particular upon illiquid assets that were overpriced multi-fold.

Taking into account the unprecedented burden on the Deposit Guarantee Fund (DGF) associated with the massive withdrawal of banks from the market, we took **measures to ensure the adequacy of funds available to the DGF and its liquidity.** In particular, the technical procedure for granting loans to the DGF was improved, and the options for the government's and central bank's support of the Fund were expanded. According to the Resolution of the Cabinet of Ministers, the Fund was authorized to receive a loan from the state in the form of cash or government bonds at an NBU key rate collateralized by future contributions to the Fund or government bonds. In order to support the liquidity of the DGF, the NBU agreed to accept government bonds as collateral in the amount of 100% of their book value, expanded the list of collaterals to include property rights for future receipts, and extended the terms of loans from 1 to 3 years[4].

In parallel, **we immediately started negotiations with the IMF**. According to the Memorandum of Economic and Financial Policies of April 22, 2014 (updated on August 29, 2014) the main state authorities (which were the President, the Prime Minister, the Minister of Finance,

---

[4] NBU resolution #587 dated 18.09.2014

and the NBU Governor) committed to fulfilling a financial sector reform program aimed at restoring macroeconomic stability, strengthening governance and transparency of economic policy, and restoring the path of sustainable economic growth.

The reform agenda in Ukraine was generously supported by the international community. An "umbrella" of external financial assistance up to $ 40 billion has been committed to Ukraine by the IMF and other international lenders for the next four years.

a) "Stop fiscal dominance!"

Quite a lot has already been written in the academic literature about the detrimental effect of fiscal dominance on financial stability in the country and the effectiveness of the monetary policy of the central bank. At the same time, in many countries the practice of domination of fiscal policy over the monetary policy objectives continues to take place, and in all likelihood, the risk of its occurrence is relevant even in those countries where it is not observed now.

The global spread of populism leads politicians to use monetary instruments to implement their political goals and promises. And if in the case of developed countries, fiscal policy easing is aimed at reviving economic activity, in most developing countries, it is aimed at fulfilling the basic social functions of the state. Non-functioning fiscal rules, seasoned with accommodative monetary policy, in developing countries always lead to a distortion of the economy -- the payback for which comes much earlier than we expect.

At the same time, **the problem of fiscal domination is one of the most difficult to solve.** Due to the *inertia of economic and political processes,* it cannot be solved in one sitting. We could not at once stop support of the stability of public finances, especially considering the country was at war and had enormous accumulated imbalances in its economy. But we immediately developed the road map with actions to be done to stop fiscal dominance. And we are proud that **in Ukraine we managed to resolve the issue in about a year and a half** (see Chapter 5).

Given the zero-treasury account, **the central bank was forced to meet the needs of the government and cover the deficit with the help of what I called Ukraine-style QE**, i.e., by monetizing government bonds. We were well aware of the destructiveness of this practice of fiscal domination, but we could not change it all at once. Otherwise, the country's security of energy supply and social stability would be endangered. Nearly 40% of government expenses were financed by borrowings. As a result, by the end of 2014, the volume of government bonds issued amounted to UAH 457.6 bn (US$35.5bn) with 69.5% of bonds owned by the NBU.

At the same time, given the excessive debt burden of the government, our actions aimed at resolving the problem of fiscal domination had both an external and an internal focus. Starting in 2014, we began to work out possible options, **modeling the situation with public finances for years to come**.

Restructuring Ukraine's external debt was one of the key milestones of the EFF Agreement with the IMF and other official creditors, and was the only effective solution to the problem of excessive debt burden in Ukraine to avoid default. Unfortunately, that happened only in April 2015. In 2014, the Stand-by IMF program obliged us to pay all debts to bondholders, official creditors, and even arrears to Gazprom.

In 2015, the Ukrainian Government worked with the Special Committee of Creditors to agree on conditions for the restructuring of the state and guarantee of the state debt in order to meet the objectives of the IMF Program:

- Savings on external payments for debt obligations of the public sector in the amount of US$15.3 billion for the period of the IMF program
- Ensuring the ratio of government debt and government-guaranteed debt to GDP at a level not exceeding 71% of GDP by 2020

- Maintaining the general requirements for servicing debt operations, on average, at 10% of GDP (maximum 12% of GDP per year) in 2019-2025

The restructuring of the $18 billion external debt, which included the restructuring of 11 issues of sovereign Eurobonds and 3 issues of Eurobonds guaranteed by the state, opened the possibility of Ukraine receiving $17.5 billion over the next four years according to the IMF Program. Together with financing from other lenders, that meant Ukraine could raise up to $40 billion in external financial assistance.

Lenders agreed to write-off 20% of the nominal amount of debt (about $ 3 billion) in exchange for Ukrainian GDP-linked warrants (value recovery instruments, or GDP-linked securities), which included payments based on real GDP growth.

- GDP-linked securities (value recovery instruments of GDP warrants) could generate payments from the Ukrainian government in 2021-2040 under the following conditions: (a) Ukraine's baseline year GDP rises to or above US$125.4bn; (b) real GDP growth the same year exceeds 3%; whereas, for the debut payment which could occur in 2021, the baseline year would be 2019, with the payment amount calculation in nominal GDP based in 2018 with inflation in 2019. At the same time, payments were capped at 1% of nominal GDP of the baseline year for five years.

Thanks to the deal, payment of US$8.5 billion of the principal amount of debt was deferred to after 2018. This reduced the debt burden on the Ukrainian economy in the short run, and thus allowed macroeconomic stability and maintenance of international reserves.

In general, the state-guaranteed and guaranteed state debt in dollar terms decreased by the end of 2015 by 6.2% to USD 65.5 billion, or about 80% of GDP, which corresponds to the path of gradual reduction of the debt burden. However, as Russia, which holds a US$3.0bn Eurobond due in December 2020, rejected the proposal, the old debt deal principal included only US$15.0bn.

In addition, due to a successful restructuring, Ukraine's sovereign ratings have been raised by leading rating agencies S&P, Fitch and Moody's from pre-defaults to levels B-, CCC, and Caa3 respectively.

The internal focus of NBU activities aimed at counteracting fiscal dominance was targeted at **reprofiling of government bonds in the NBU portfolio.** In order to avoid repeating the mistakes of the past in terms of fiscal domination, and to mitigate the debt burden on the government in the medium term, we started discussion with the Ministry of Finance on **reprofiling government bonds owned by the central bank**.

According to our calculations, the Ministry of Finance faced substantial payments for servicing and redeeming of government bonds in favor of the NBU, which could reach UAH 288bn in 2017-2019 (or more than 10% of budget revenues for the corresponding years), thus we decided to take preventive actions. In order to avoid default on the public debt, and not wishing to resume the harmful practice of monetization of t-bonds, we offered the Ministry of Finance to restructure the existing debt by exchanging government bonds from the NBU portfolio for **new government bonds with the redemption in the next 30 years linked to inflation rates**.

Though discussion started in late 2015, a final agreement was reached in October 2017. According to the agreement (and approved by the Government), bonds of par value of 219.6 bln UAH (out of 360.6 bln UAH in the NBU portfolio) reprofiled. Approximately UAH 145.2 billion of government bonds were converted into long-term hryvnia bonds of different maturity, with a yield linked to inflation, and about UAH 74.4 billion of t-bonds were converted into long-term hryvnia bonds of different maturity with fixed interest rates. The rest of the portfolio remained unchanged (with a fixed rate of return).

- New government bonds were issued for a period of 7 to 31 years. In total, there were 40 issues that had to be redeemed twice a year from 2025-2047 – on May 10 and November 10.

- The interest rate on government bonds to be redeemed from 2025 to 2035 was fixed in the range of 8.12% to 11.3% (with a coupon period of 6 months). The rate will decline from 11.3% per annum in 2025 to 9.78% in 2029 and 8.12% in 2035.
- For bonds to be redeemed from 2036 to 2047 (the coupon period is 12 months), the yield was set at 12-month CPI plus 2.2%. If there is a deflation, the rate of return would be 2.2%.
- The accumulated and unpaid coupon income on government bonds subject to exchange was paid to the NBU at the date of execution of the debt transaction.

Thus, with the help of the aforementioned debt operation, we were able not only to reduce the risk of refinancing public debt, but also to make the government vitally interested in lowering inflation, as this would allow it to pay less for its debt.

Together with the energy sector reform that led to an increase of tariffs on gas for households gradually reaching import parity and helping to restore the profitability of Naftogaz, **since 2016, fiscal dominance is no longer in place in Ukraine.**

b) Contingency planning

When implementing reforms, factors must be taken into account that are not under your control but are likely to be directed against change. In our case, the key factor beyond our control was the war in Eastern Ukraine. We also had to consider that panic events in the market, triggered by the withdrawal of another bank from the market, could have unpredictable consequences, embodied in a snowball event, crushing an entire financial system already in the process of cleaning and reloading.

Thus, it is important to have a backup plan (or Plan B). And we had one. Key employees of the National Bank, jointly with the expert support of the IMF mission team, developed a **Contingency Plan**, which provided for possible unconditional measures by the National Bank of Ukraine aimed at preventing capital flight from banks and stabilizing the banking system.

This Contingency Plan was supposed to be activated in the event of a lack of substantial liquidity and significant risk of deposits outflow with the possible risk to the viability of the credit institutions with chain effects that could lead to instability of the financial system and destabilizing consequences on the economy and country as a whole.

Our Contingency Plan for Ukraine in 2014 considered the experience of Cyprus's Ministry of Finance with adoption of a "Decree on the Enforcement of Restrictive Measures on Transactions in case of Emergency Law of 2013".

When contingency planning began, the Financial Stability Council was not established yet, there was a second government since the Revolution, and the military conflict was in active phase. Thus, the central bank was the only institution in the country able to keep a dispassionate mind and to act decisively in case of emergency, and only the central bank had the necessary instruments to calm disruption in the financial market.

The Contingency Plan implied the imposition of *temporary restrictive measures* to (a) address a situation of a massive or unsustainable withdrawal of deposits from one or more credit institutions or any other emergency liquidity situation such as a forthcoming lack of liquidity by a systemically important bank, and (b) prevent the depletion of the international reserves and/or a free-fall of the exchange rate as well as its adverse effect on the balance sheet of banks, corporations and households. The measures included restrictions on withdrawal of deposits in the local banks, reprogramming of term deposits, import restrictions, administrative measures on capital and some current transactions, and on the purchase, sale, export, import and transfer abroad of foreign exchange.

The restrictive measures were considered to be imposed for a limited time necessary to relieve the liquidity and exchange rate pressures until confidence would be restored through the implementation of confidence-building macroeconomic, structural and financial measures. The confidence building measures were aimed at ensuring stable macroeconomic conditions, stabilizing the foreign exchange market, strengthening the regulatory and supervisory environment, and restructuring and recapitalization of banks so as to restore profitability and solvency. The availability of funds for immediate bank recapitalization was critical in enhancing confidence and reassuring depositors that the authorities were using the time to address bank weaknesses and the "bad apples" were being removed from the banking system.

Since a tightening of the restrictive measures would undermine the credibility of the authorities' policies, the restrictive measures had to be *most constraining at the time of introduction.* The restrictive measures were structured in a way that it allowed a gradual easing as conditions permitted.

The restrictive measures were supposed to be removed as soon as conditions permitted. Authorities should be required to constantly monitor the development in deposit outflows, FX purchases and cross-border transfers and ease the restrictive measures gradually as soon as financial stability and macroeconomic conditions permit, with the final objective being the safe removal of all restrictive measures introduced either as part of an action plan or before to address foreign exchange and deposit outflows. The authorities should also be required to ensure that financial and nonfinancial sector entities and individuals comply with the restrictive measures to ensure their effectiveness while in effect. To this end, authorities should continuously monitor the implementation of the restrictive measures and impose sanctions as necessary to deter noncompliance.

Though the bank holiday has not been introduced in Ukraine, we acknowledged that if there was such a decision, the imposition of restrictive measures should have been done without delay and within the same day of the designated authority[5] recommendation. Depending on the trigger event, the decision had to be taken immediately and the bank holiday declared immediately and applied intra-day.

The enactment of the regulation/legislation, as appropriate, for the imposition of a bank holiday together with the comprehensive package of restrictive measures should be made as swiftly as possible. The authorities should verify in advance the necessary steps to impose the restrictive measures including the need for issuing, revoking or amending relevant legal instruments and the appropriate procedures.

The duration of the bank holiday should be decided by the designated authority but should not last for more than one or two days. If possible, it should be declared on the last business day of the week so that all necessary arrangements, including IT adjustments in the financial system, can be done over the weekend to avoid anxiety among depositors and market uncertainty.

We decided on the following restrictions on bank operations *during a bank holiday*:

- All banking transactions including those conducted electronically will be prohibited.
- The automatic teller machines (ATMs) will not be in operation.
- The systems of internet and telephone banking will not be in operation.
- A credit institution will not execute any outgoing payment orders, whether internal to a credit institution or across credit institutions in Ukraine or abroad, after issuance of notification by the designated authority.

---

[5] The reference to "designated authority" means to be interpreted to refer to the responsible agency which under the legislation is appropriately authorized to take/implement the relevant actions. In case of Ukraine we aimed at establishing of Financial Stability Council which would have the power to recommend to the central bank and government to introduce contingency measures. Though in other countries, the designated authority may differ depending on the type and nature of the measure that need to be taken. In certain cases. the designated authority may mean the collective actions of several agencies or bodies.

- No overdue interest will accrue on claims of any nature that fall due during the bank holiday, except external obligations.
- No cash or cashless transactions will be able to be made through any debit/credit/prepaid card except transactions abroad by those who are abroad at the time of introducing the restriction – and based on individual permission from the central bank.
- Payments relating to existing obligations of credit institutions to other financial institutions including repos, interbank deposits and derivative contracts will be executed.
- Banks will not be allowed to buy or sell assets/derivatives.
- Banks will keep incoming payments on account with the central bank and with respect to foreign exchange on foreign correspondent accounts.

With the assistance of an IMF Mission team, we developed a *detailed action plan for phasing-in and phasing out emergency measures*. While the timeline for phasing out measures was gradual and condition-based, the phasing-in action plan was aimed at ensuring that all necessary preparatory measures are put in place before the activation of contingency plan.

Triggers, based on balance of payments and financial stability considerations, were supposed to be activated if the majority of a set of agreed upon indicators were breached as a result of deterioration on FX and UAH deposit outflows, exchange rate depreciation, reduction in NBU's gross international reserves, and other relevant indicators. The measures presented below would have been introduced if the following triggers were activated:

Trigger 1: The contingency plan would be triggered if household deposit outflows exceed 30% from the reference point (27.01.2014).

Trigger 2: Bank liquidity: The contingency plan would be triggered if the overall liquidity ratio (combining UAH and FX liquidity) fell below or equal to 5 percent of deposits in banks that represent 25 percent of total deposits (household and corporate) in the group of the largest

35 banks. The liquidity was measured daily on a bank-by-bank basis for the largest 35 banks. Overall liquidity was defined as the sum of cash and cash equivalent, available funds in NBU accounts (excluding reserve requirements) plus correspondent accounts with well-known international banks (excluding encumbered accounts). Within the period under analysis liquidity support from NBU or interbank loans from state banks should show no more than zero growth.

Trigger 3: Exchange rate: The contingency plan would be triggered if the weighted average interbank market selling exchange rate of the Hryvnia against the US dollar depreciated relative to its level as of November 24 (UAH 15.34/US$1) by more than 10 percent on three business days over any seven-day period.

Trigger 4: NBU reserves: The contingency plan would be triggered if the level of NBU's gross reserves declined below $6.9 billion at any time, unless a substantial amount of external support was scheduled to arrive within 30 days of the tripping of this trigger.

Exhibit 5. Trigger events monitoring charts

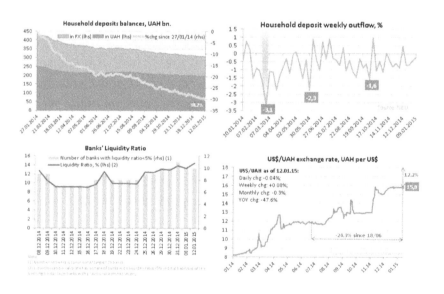

The relevant indicators were monitored on a *daily basis*. The objective was to be able to identify at an early stage whether a situation calling for activation of the contingency plan was developing. To this end, the early warning indicators that have been established as high frequency indicators were continuously monitored, and could trigger activation of the contingency plan.

In the event, on the 13th of January 2015, household deposit outflows breached the reference point level, dropping by 30.2% (-131.9 bn UAH), of which UAH deposits declined by 23% (-UAH58.0bn) and FX deposits declined by 39.9% (US$9.2bn at constant rate of 7.993/1US$). The monthly withdrawal was estimated at approximately UAH4.5 billion for UAH deposits and US$400-500million for FX deposits.

But even some of the early warning indicators that have breached thresholds were not breached all at once. Thus, we decided not to activate a Contingency Plan given the perspective of debt restructuring (see Chapter 2) and relying on the expected IMF support under the Stand-by Agreement.

While the Plan was never fully implemented, a *number of its actions were included in the list of currency restrictions introduced in 2014-2015* (see Chapter 5). At the same time, **it was extremely important to have a comprehensive backup plan** so that unforeseen events were not able to catch us off guard.

CHAPTER 3

Comprehensive Banking Reform:
Where to begin? What to do first?

THE ACCUMULATED IMBALANCES and significant shocks for the banking system that led to the perfect storm in early 2014 required the National Bank to take *immediate, unpopular but necessary reforms of the economic financial sector* and a *set of firm stabilization measures.* Developing a stable banking system that would serve as the stimulus for the economic growth was the key goal for the National Bank of Ukraine and involved structural changes in the banking system, strengthening its system stability and efficiency.

Sporadic reform efforts had been undertaken in Ukraine continuously over the prior decade, though they were never holistic and direct, probably because the real call for reforms only began around 2014, in the wake of the Revolution of Dignity.

I and other top managers from the private sector who came to lead reforms in different areas of Ukraine in 2014 (banking sector, public finances, infrastructure, energy sector, agriculture etc.) had similar questions in our minds:

- **Sequencing:** what to do first, how to achieve easy wins and pave the way for more complex reforms? Anyone who has ever done genuine reform understands that the main problem is how to implement the needed reforms. In other words, the most difficult part is how to get from point A (total disaster) to point Z (completely compliant with EU standards and regulations) in a realistic time horizon.
- **Alignment:** how to align the key stakeholders in the process (domestic and international)? Coordination is crucial. In the

process of implementing reforms, it is vital to have support from international partners and donors, and they must be properly coordinated.

- **Capacity in skills and resources:** what kind of financial and human resources are needed for the endeavor, and from where will they come? The most important ingredient in a recipe for successful reform is a **properly built architecture, with the right expertise, commitment and agility to deliver.**

I am convinced that *reforms are most effective when implemented fast, when the political conditions are right* – once democratic and reformist principles have been confirmed and dedicated pro-reformer teams have been put in place. But what truly makes or breaks reforms is whether the country has the capacity to implement those reforms, that is whether **a solid and a coherent infrastructure exists to support the efforts.**

In 2014, when I became the Governor of the National Bank of Ukraine, there was no such infrastructure -- we started our reforms from scratch. There was no strategy, no institutional capacity, no resources. We understood that in order to transform the system we needed fundamental and radical reforms, with a proper infrastructure in place.

We further understood that in order to transform the system we needed fundamental and radical reforms. As the banking system in Ukraine represented nearly 85% of the financial market, in fact, the National Bank of Ukraine was responsible for reforming the entire financial system.

a) The Comprehensive Program for the Development of the Financial Sector 2020

Set within the framework of the nationwide Ukraine 2020 Sustainable Development Strategy, *a Comprehensive Program for Financial Sector Development* ("Program 2020") was required to deal with the unprecedented systemic problems in the financial sector, which accumulated over decades, and the dysfunctional system of state regulation and supervision. Program 2020 allowed us to *systematize actions* needed for the transformation and regulation of the banking sector as well as to accurately *determine the possible paths and necessary resources* to achieve them.

A primary impetus for beginning reform in the financial sector was an Association Agreement with the European Union signed on 27 June 2014. We incorporated key elements of that agreement as well as the Memorandum of Cooperation Ukraine signed with the International Monetary Fund into Program 2020.

The Ukraine-EU Agreement resembled the plan that Eastern European countries adopted during EU accession. **Ukraine was not reinventing a Ukrainian bicycle, but rather implementing European principles and standards.**

Program 2020 was fully ***compliant with EU Directives*** on financial sector regulation as it was based on a thorough analysis of their requirements. All the stakeholders, the central bank, the Ministry of Finance, Securities and Financial Services Commissions, Deposit Guaranty Fund, banking associations, leaders of Parliament factions and civil society, were instrumental parts and beneficiaries of Program 2020. But the central bank, as a "white knight", started reforms first to preserve macro-financial stability of the country. Proper fulfillment of the central bank's functions to secure price and financial stability was a prerequisite for the development of financial system and economic growth in the country.

Program 2020 was not simply a set of long-term strategic slogans. It was a plan of concrete steps to achieve the ultimate goals of reforming the state's financial system - developing an effective financial system that is competitive globally. It listed ***all key reforms with clear deadlines and performance criteria***, and was accompanied by a system of ***regular monitoring***, which provides status information on implementation of program activities (in particular, problem areas) to the Steering

Committee, and a *clear delineation of leaders' and project managers' roles* within the specific streams.

We did not find any analogues of such a program anywhere in the world. Program 2020 was not the strategy of one regulator, but a strategy and a roadmap in one document for complex reform of the entire financial system.

Program 2020 was *approved by the National Reform Council* in May 2015, and then by each of the financial sector regulators responsible for banks, financial services, and securities market.

The *main objective of Program 2020* was to ensure functioning and development of the financial market through creation of a competitive environment in accordance with EU standards. It required building a fully-fledged, efficient, and effective financial market, creating market infrastructure, and strengthening the market's resilience to external threats.

The Program's objective must be achieved through implementation of multiple interrelated actions aimed at comprehensive reform of the financial sector.

The Program was guided by the following **Core Principles:**

- regulatory approximation to EU rules and regulations
- liberalization of financial markets
- ensuring a balance of economic interests through a competitive market environment
- independent and efficient regulators, with risk-based supervision
- transparency and high standards of information disclosure by both financial sector participants and regulators
- responsibility and confidence among the financial market participants and regulators
- integrity of the financial system, comprehensive protection of the rights of creditors, consumers and investors.

Keys to successful implementation of the Program included:

- reaching macroeconomic stabilization, as well as low and stable inflation (5% ± 1 pp of annual CPI change in the mid-term), eliminating imbalances in the external sector, and resuming economic growth;
- economic deregulation and tax reform to stimulate the inflow of local and foreign capital to the economy;
- observance of property rights and the principle of liability for wrongdoings and mismanagement by implementing judicial and law enforcement reform;
- building trust among customers of the financial market, protecting consumer rights, and improving their financial awareness.

The basic precondition for the successful implementation of the Program was *resolving problems from prior years and achieving macroeconomic stability.* In this area, the NBU took steps to reduce inflation, enhance a flexible exchange rate, and reduce foreign exchange market volatility, including development of exchange risk-hedging instruments and switching to inflation targeting.

The Program was planned in ***three main directions***:

A. Ensuring financial stability and development of financial markets and instruments through ensuring the sufficient level of banking system capitalization; addressing the accumulated banking sector imbalances; improving the quality of corporate governance; and developing the interbank market and its benchmark rates, as well as the local syndication market, bond market, government securities market, insurance companies and pension funds.

B. Developing institutional capacity of financial market regulators. In particular, by strengthening the independence and transformation of regulators through regulatory functions redistribution, better coordination among regulators of the financial market, and introduction of risk-oriented supervision in different market segments.

C. Protecting consumer and financial market investors' rights through implementation of actions aimed at improving consumer rights protections, establishing the institution of financial ombudsman, and establishing reliable systems of depositors' and investors' protection.

Exhibit 6. The structure of the Comprehensive Program for Financial Sector Development until 2020

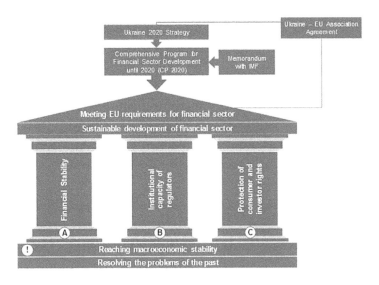

Within an implementation timeframe we identified **three main stages of the transformation of the financial system:**

Stage 1: Clean Up

Resolving the problems of the past meant cleaning up the financial system from insolvent and fraudulent participants. We undertook a resolution of insolvent financial institutions, conducting asset quality review (AQR) and stress-tests (ST) of banks, disclosure of UBOs and unwinding related-party lending and proper recapitalization of banks.

Stage 2: Reloading

Laying the foundations for sustainable development of the financial sector required restoring confidence in the market by enhancing corporate governance standards, introducing robust risk-based supervision and early-warning indicators, implementing international financial reporting standards (IFRS), and promoting transparency in reporting.

Stage 3: Sustainable Development

Developing the financial sector and restoring economic growth was designed to restart bank lending and capital market development thus contributing to economic growth. As of 2020, Ukraine has reached this stage of reform development.

All three stages of financial sector reform overlapped in time. For example, even during the first phase, we began to prepare the legislative changes necessary for restarting and developing of the financial sector.

The timetable of these stages shows how they overlapped and why.

Exhibit 7. Key stages for financial sector reform, 2015-2020

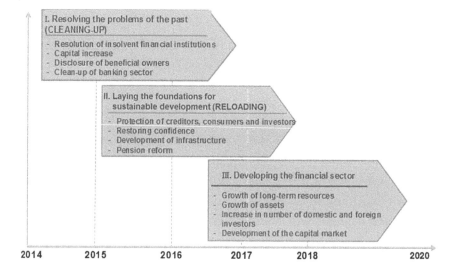

b) Reform Infrastructure and Toolkit: National Reform Council, Reform Steering Committee

Properly built reform architecture is an important element of its effectiveness. A holistic and coherent infrastructure is essential to energize and re-energize reform, to re-focus efforts on critical priorities and reform delivery, and to build sustainable capacity in the system.

The architecture of financial reform in Ukraine was headed by the **National Reform Council** (NRC), chaired by the President of Ukraine, and including the Prime Minister, Speaker of Parliament, Governor of NBU, Representative of Advisory Board, Ministers of the Government, Chairs of Parliament Committees, and representatives of civil society.

Its **main objectives** were:

- Making decisions on the direction and priorities of reforms;
- Ensuring consensus on reform implementation;
- Coordinating reforms;
- Monitoring implementation of reforms;
- Considering proposals on reform action plans.

The Reforms Executive Committee was the executive arm of the NRC responsible for developing an agenda for the NRC, ensuring implementation of NRC decisions, developing indicators of achievements of reform targets, and monitoring progress.

Each public sector (i.e., the central bank and ministries) established a **Reform Steering Committee**, which consisted of representatives of all stakeholders (including market participants) and was responsible for the development and implementation of the reform package in the respective area, supporting discussion and communication of reforms to public.

As NBU Governor, I was responsible for the financial sector reform and supervised the Financial Sector Reform Steering Committee (called the **Task Force for Financial Sector Reform**), which was a collegial body specially established to consolidate efforts and assist in formulating a common policy and approaches to the implementation of the financial sector reforms in Ukraine.

This body was established by order of the NBU Governor on 11 March 2015 following the decision by the National Reforms Council to assign responsibility for overseeing the implementation of the financial sector reform to the NBU Governor.

The Reform Task Force participants included top-representatives of:

- National Bank of Ukraine
- Financial market regulators
- Ministry of Finance of Ukraine
- Deposit Guarantee Fund
- Parliamentary Committee on Finance and Banking
- Administration of the President of Ukraine
- Professional associations and business community

Exhibit 8. Architecture of Financial Reform in Ukraine

Representatives from other ministries and agencies, as well as international institutions, were invited to participate in Task Force meetings, which were held on a regular basis.

On March 4, 2015, the first meeting of the Task Force on Financial Sector Reforms in Ukraine took place. During 2015 to 2018, the Task Force held 32 meetings where 85 issues related to the implementation of key financial sector reform projects were discussed and relevant decisions were taken. We also implemented the practice of inviting key experts on specific issues to Task Force meetings in order to consider their opinions and make better decisions.

Participation of top-executives of the involved stakeholders in the Steering Committee is extremely important. Since formally this body has no executive powers, its decisions are implemented with the help of administrative acts of the authorities. Thus, synchronization of stakeholder actions and executive discipline is ensured.

Reform Implementation Toolkit in Ukraine

Program 2020's objective had to be achieved through implementation of a number of interrelated actions aimed at a comprehensive reform of the financial sector.

In order to implement the Program and achieve its objective, we created project teams to implement planned activities in accordance with **international standards of project management**; sponsors and project leaders (51 projects, according to the project register) were identified.

We developed a monitoring and reporting system and a **Reform Scorecard** with a set of indicators to track the progress of financial sector reform projects, as shown below.

Exhibit 9. Financial sector reform dashboard (as of Dec 2016)

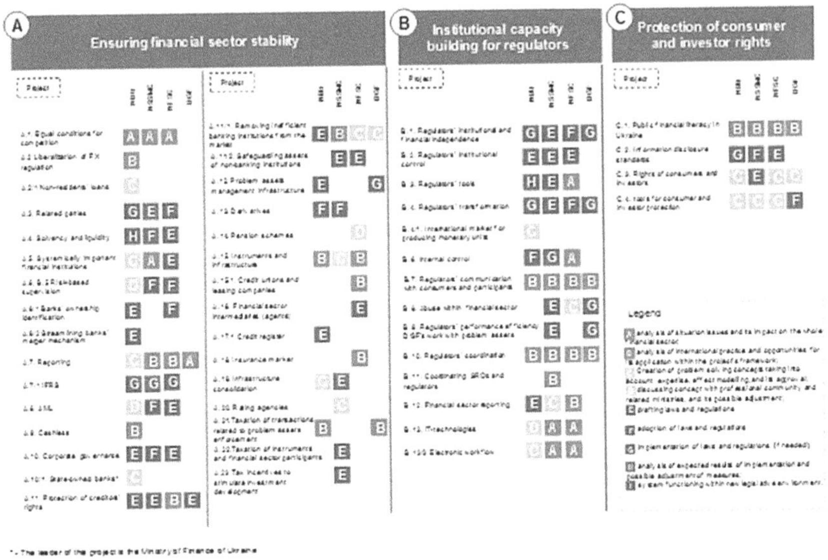

A Ensuring financial sector stability	B Institutional capacity building for regulators	C Protection of consumer and investor rights

* The leader of the project is the Ministry of Finance of Ukraine

c) Financial Stability Council

Apart from the general reform infrastructure and given the huge risks for financial stability, we established an additional **platform for the collaboration of public authorities in the area of financial stability**.

We acknowledged that a country's financial stability depends not only on banks but also on non-bank financial institutions. This meant we needed to ensure effective coordination between the NBU and other financial regulators on the implementation of macroprudential policy measures. To this end, the interdepartmental **Financial Stability Council (FSC)** was established on our initiative by Presidential decree in March 2015[6] and brought together all financial sector regulators, the Ministry of Finance, and the Deposit Guarantee Fund. Since then, the FSC's mandate has been to identify and mitigate risks in a timely manner that threaten the stability of the domestic banking and financial systems.

---

[6] Decree of the President of Ukraine of 24 March 2015 # 170/2015

According to the Decree, the members of FSC are:

Co-chairmen of the Council:

- Governor of the National Bank of Ukraine
- Minister of Finance of Ukraine

Council members:

- Chairman of the National Commission on Securities and Stock Market
- Chairman of the National Financial Services Commission
- Managing Director of the Deposit Guarantee Fund
- Deputy Governor of the National Bank of Ukraine
- Deputy Minister of Finance of Ukraine

The purpose of the FSC was to ensure timely detection and minimization of risks that threaten the stability of the banking and financial system. In order to achieve this goal, the FSC was tasked with:

- exchange of information and timely detection of current and potential external and internal threats and systemic risks to ensure financial stability and minimize their negative impact on the financial system;
- coordination of preventive measures and measures of rapid response (anti-crisis management) in the presence of signs of an unstable financial state of the banking system, as well as circumstances that threatened the stability of the banking and / or financial system.

We deliberately established the FSC as a platform for professional discussion on systemic risks, but not as a decision-making body or public authority. In other words, the FSC could neither compromise mandates of its member institutions nor interfere with activities of other public authorities. Instead, the decisions it takes are translated into actions by the executive acts of member institutions.

Institutions that are addressed must implement FSC recommendations or explain their reasons for not doing so. In line with Ukrainian law (On the National Bank of Ukraine), the FSC is authorized to recognize signs of risks to the stability of the national banking and/or financial system. This empowers the NBU to impose temporary restrictions in regulating and supervising banks. The FSC meets at least quarterly. The FSC publishes press releases after each meeting and compiles an annual report on its activities.

d) Coordination with donors

In order to achieve the objectives of Program 2020, the NBU implemented a cooperation program with the EU, IMF, World Bank, EBRD, EIB, BCBS, IOSCO, IAIS and other international financial institutions, associations and regulators in the field of financial markets and services. Since 2014 we have had about 50 technical assistance projects running with help from the international community, including the World Bank, the IMF, the EBRD and others.

Cooperation with the IMF remains our strategic task. We hold numerous meetings and conference calls with IMF management and the mission working in Ukraine, and feel prodigious support for our reforms. It was essential that the IMF and other IFIs, as well as international investors and the US Government, understood the importance of stabilizing the situation caused by the military conflict in the eastern part of Ukraine and curbing associated geopolitical risks.

It became clear to me that international assistance and strategic consultations happen sporadically in developing economies. However, in the process of implementing reforms, it is important to have coordinated and frequent support from international partners and donors. Their initial support of Ukraine during the turbulent period in 2014-2015 laid the foundation for our reforms.

During meetings with the IMF and World Bank, we offered to create a *single platform* for all the programs of financial assistance to Ukraine in order to enable streamlined coordination of all projects. The IMF, World Bank, EBRD, EIB, IFC and donor states became key participants of the platform.

Twice a year, the National Bank held ***coordination meetings with international partners and donors***. At these meetings, we demonstrated progress in implementing financial sector reform projects and transforming the central bank. At these meetings, heads of relevant departments of the NBU responsible for the reform projects also articulated their need for technical assistance, and representatives of international organizations could voice their readiness to meet those needs, based on the mandate of their institutions.

This coordination mechanism provided a clear distribution of roles: there was no duplication between technical assistance projects, which made it possible to more effectively use the available financial and expert resources. In early 2015, 47 out of 53 financial reform projects were receiving technical assistance.

To sum it up, our reforms did not happen by chance -- we were helped with a comprehensive infrastructure, dedicated teams, project management approach, and proper coordination of TA and donors.

In the next chapters, I will try to introduce you to the art of the impossible.

CHAPTER 4

The Necessary Legislative Prerequisites

THE FOLLOWING CHAPTERS will dig into the key milestones in implementing Ukraine's financial sector reform in general, and the institutional capacity of the National Bank in particular. However, all those changes would have been impossible without legislative support, first and foremost, the amendments that fixed the principles of independence of the central bank and its powers to use operational tools for independent monetary policy and bank supervision.

That is why from the very beginning of the reform, in fact, in parallel with the preparation of the reform strategy, we worked together with international partners (IMF, EU Commission, World Bank, etc.) to prepare the legislative ground for reform. With support of the IMF, we developed a set of draft laws aimed at strengthening central bank independence and providing the central bank with ammunition to clean up the banking sector and strengthen its resilience to market shocks.

In a crisis, both in the economy and public confidence, it was extremely important that these changes arose through cooperation programs with our international partners, and their adoption was a *precondition for the implementation of relevant cooperation programs*, such as Stand-by and EFF Arrangements with the IMF, and Macro-Financial Assistance with the EU.

Under the 2014 Stand-by Agreement (which was succeeded with an EFF Agreement in early 2015), *the modality for the succession of tranches was a clear commitment of the Ukrainian authorities to strengthen the NBU's governance and financial autonomy* to ensure adequate safeguards. Specifically, in consultation with Fund staff, the NBU had to prepare draft legislative amendments to the NBU Law to *strengthen the decision-making and oversight mandate* of the Council as well as the autonomy of its members and the Deputy Governors, transform the Board into a smaller Executive Committee, and authorize the Council to establish special reserves before the profit distribution. The personal autonomy of NBU Council members and Deputy Governors had to be strengthened by enhancing appointment and dismissal procedures, and by taking steps to mitigate conflict of interest.

The authorities also committed to discontinue the practice of the NBU making advanced (i.e., before completion of the NBU financial audit) profit transfers to the budget by adopting respective amendments to the Budget Code. The adoption of the relevant draft legislative amendments has been marked as *structural benchmarks* under the Stand-by/EFF programs.

After the necessary legislation was adopted in June 2015, we were able to launch a restructuring of the NBU organizational structure to ensure a clear organizational and operational separation of monetary policy formulation from monetary policy implementation function. In particular, to ensure that monetary policy decisions were unbiased and had strong analytical support, we set up a Monetary Policy Committee to advise the Board.

We considered the necessary set of legislative changes not only from the point-of-view of the present but also as a *strategic decision for many years ahead*, since the National Bank finally got an opportunity to pursue an independent monetary policy and increase the efficiency of its functioning as an institution. This legislation has also brought the National Bank in line with the best international standards for central banks.

The successful implementation of the policy conditions for Ukraine, and its continuous satisfactory track record in the ongoing IMF programme, was a prerequisite for the continuation of the *EU Macrofinancial Assistance (MFA)*. According to the MFA Agreements, financial backing was provided to the Ministry of Finance (with the central bank acting as a government agent) for up to 15 years with the interest rate equal to the EU's cost of borrowing (with AAA rating). Disbursement of the funds under MFA programmes were subject to satisfactory progress with policy conditions, and fall into four thematic areas, with financial sector issues being one of them.

Under the *first MFA programme* (EUR 610 million), legislation was required to ensure the implementation of the International Financial Reporting Standards among all financial market participants by end-2014. For the fourth tranche of the loan (EUR 250 million), we had to prepare a strategic long-term plan for the gradual approximation of financial sector regulation to the EU legislature in this area.

In order to receive financial assistance under the *second MFA program* (EUR 1 billion), the NBU had to prepare and adopt regulations for systemic banks as well as for disclosure of the ultimate owners of banks.

Thus in 2014-2015, the National Bank and international experts developed **a set of draft laws aimed at strengthening the independence and institutional capacity of NBU, enhancing prudential supervision, and improving the sustainability of the banking sector – all of which** were adopted by the Ukrainian Parliament.

On July 4, 2014, Parliament adopted the *'anti-crisis law'*, on the initiative of the National Bank, which (a) introduced a category of a *'systemically important bank'* and the right of the NBU to determine such banks, based on the size, degree of financial interconnections and activities of the bank; (b) increased the *minimum authorized capital* of the bank up to UAH 500 million; (c) gave the NBU the right to introduce a simplified procedure for carrying out procedures related to the *urgent capitalization* of banks in the event of a decrease in the total amount of deposits in the banking system by 5 or more percent for a period of up to six calendar months; (d) authorized the NBU to apply *measures to bank owners* or owners of significant participation in the bank in case of application of sanctions by foreign states / international organizations.

In June 2015, Parliament adopted the *Institutional Capacity of the National Bank of Ukraine* and respective amendments to the Budget Code in order to provide the following important innovations: (a) the mandate of the NBU was updated and clarified, (b) the powers of the NBU Council were expanded, (c) the functional and financial independence of the central bank and the personal independence of governing bodies' members were increased, (d) decision-making at the committee level was introduced. This set of legislative changes advanced the NBU to the operational standards of the best central banks.

In July 2016, Parliament took another important step by enhancing the *institutional capacity of the Deposit Guarantee Fund* with a law that expanded the functions of the NBU with the authority to pre-qualify persons who may be involved in withdrawal of insolvent banks from the market and to make a list of such persons.

The result of implementing these provisions was enhanced requirements for persons engaged in the liquidation of banks, which together with other provisions of the adopted law, provided an opportunity to increase the amount received by the Deposit Guarantee Fund from the sale of assets of insolvent banks, and kickstarted payments to depositors, which in turn, reduced social stress.

In March 2015, the NBU successfully passed through the Parliament progressive legislation that helped in *disclosing information about the real owners of banks*. The law prohibited the owners of failed banks to return to a banking business and to management positions in banks, increased bankers' responsibility for their activities, and threatened them with fines and imprisonment for misconduct and deliberate actions that brought a bank to bankruptcy. Among other things, this allowed the Deposit Guarantee Fund to recover funds from "bad" shareholders of failed banks more efficiently. This **law primarily strengthened responsibility of bank managers, beneficial owners of the bank**, and other owners of a qualifying holding in the bank when making decisions affecting the financial condition of the bank, as well as increased the efficiency of banking supervision to ensure the stability of the banking system and protection of the interests of banks' depositors and creditors.

The above-mentioned laws were put into the IMF Program, in which the "Financial Sector Policies" occupied almost half of the document. When asked why implementation of reforms in the financial sector was the most successful of all reforms in Ukraine, I always answer: because we planned them by ourselves! And we put into the IMF Memorandum all the necessary actions for the complex transformation of the banking industry and called them **prior actions or structural benchmarks**.

I should also note that in the area of responsibility of the National Bank, *we were always strongly committed to timely and full fulfilment of obligations stemming from agreements with international financial institutions.* Moreover, we deliberately strengthened the conditionality of these programs, which allowed us to more effectively overcome internal resistance to reforms and to ensure the adoption of necessary legislation.

One example of such resistance was the cornerstone law on strengthening the institutional capacity of the National Bank, which was adopted in June 2015, and enabled further financial sector reform. Without the support of IFIs, its adoption in Parliament would have been very problematic, given the many related and often vested interests in Parliament. Needless to say, the owners of many insolvent banks were members of Parliament, and many of them sat on the Parliamentary Banking Committee -- you can imagine the level of our confrontation.

In essence, given the huge opposition to strengthening the independence of the central bank and its institutional capacity in the Parliament, the IMF program served as a vehicle that allowed us to influence the decisions of other authorities in the country and to carry out reforms despite an extremely unstable political and social environment.

Nevertheless, we did all we could to support the legislative changes, including initiating the "financial days" in Parliament when only the draft laws of financial sector reform were put into the agenda. In this way, we succeeded in a number of important laws being adopted, particularly regarding the financial restructuring of enterprise debts, consumer lending, enforcement proceedings, and private enforcement agents.

CHAPTER 5

The first priority:
Macroeconomic stabilization

CONVENTIONAL WISDOM IS that to start any reform, you must begin with diagnostics of the current state of the system. This allows you to identify weaknesses and determine priorities and sequence of actions. Such a sequenced approach works fairly well in a fully functioning system, even when it has occasional flaws. But when the market collapses, piled-up imbalances begin to break through all kinds of thresholds, the country is in war, and uncertainty abounds, all activities must be started at once. **The first priority for us was macro-financial stability. The second was cleaning up the Ukrainian banking sector. And third was transformation of the central bank itself.**

Overcoming the crisis in Ukraine's economy was dependent on resolute and consolidated actions of all branches of power, as well as the support of the global community and international donors. **The National Bank of Ukraine considered the crisis as simultaneously a time for decisive actions leading to lasting reform.** Therefore, the regulator launched major reforms of both the overall banking system and the NBU as an institution.

Among our main achievements were a transfer to a flexible exchange rate, a radical change of bank refinancing approaches, a "clean-up" of the banking sector, facilitating its recovery, and NBU reform aimed at focusing on its main functions.

At first glance it may seem that these areas can be developed separately. However, in my experience, they are closely related to each other. _Macroeconomic stability cannot be created on the basis of an unstable, non-transparent and inefficient banking system. Similarly, it is not_ *possible to truly clean up the banking system without restructuring decision-making processes and strengthening the institutional capacity of the central bank itself.*

This chapter examines how we achieved our first priority, the difficulties of a switch from a USD peg to flexible exchange rate, FCY regulation, capital control and administrative measures. This very difficult time for us led to insights that can help other countries achieve reform less painfully and more efficiently.

a) In search of equilibrium

The transition to a flexible exchange rate was inevitable. However, after 20 years of a fixed rate, this process could not occur without difficulties. And the crisis developments in the economy only intensified the psychological complexity of the transition. We were ready to intervene on the interbank market in order to prevent panic, as Ukraine's financial sector has a long track record of irrational behavior, but we had limited resources for that.

Given those conditions, we attempted to use market instruments and regulatory mechanisms to level the influence of situational factors and to help the market find **an equilibrium exchange rate** that would respond to fundamental factors.

Our understanding of the need to find the fair value of the hryvnia was based on the fact that further irrational devaluation was unlikely to bring any additional benefits. As a result of the devaluation of the hryvnia, imports of goods had already decreased by 29% compared with 2013, and the overall trade deficit in goods had decreased from $ 22 billion to $7 billion (the lowest value since 2009), fully compensating for the losses from the trade war with Russia, military conflict in the East, and falling prices for commodities.

At the same time, the structure of imports had changed in the direction of much less sensitivity to changes in the price of intermediate consumption goods (tied into export chains), and critical import and basic consumption goods (energy, pharmaceuticals). For the further replacement of imports and the growth of exports, there was no need for further devaluation, but expansion of production capacity in capital investments, which was impossible given the ongoing military conflict and financial instability.

However, the economic losses from devaluation could have been significant. A further depreciation of hryvnia would have increased currency risks for a dollarized economy, in which loans in foreign currency accounted for almost half of the total loan portfolio. The sustainability of public debt could also be problematic, given two-thirds of foreign debt was denominated in foreign currency.

Therefore, we spent the second half of 2014 seeking out an equilibrium hryvnia exchange rate, which we tried to probe by currency auctions. Our calculations, based on analysis of fundamental factors, showed that an equilibrium exchange rate should have been about USD/UAH 13 to level the balance of payments (minus almost 40% of currency's value compared to the pre-crisis level, which was fixed for 5 years). However, a series of military meltdowns in the east of the country, and the initiated "cleaning" of the banking system, led **to irrational factors to begin taking over the fundamentals.**

The **indicative rate**, launched in September 2014, was automatically calculated by the trading system on the basis of information on bank transactions for the past day and acted as a guide for banks when they carried out operations in the foreign exchange market, and for their clients when submitting applications to buy or sell currencies.

Its introduction was a *temporary measure* aimed at stabilizing the panic sentiment of the population and preventing the erosion of the country's financial system. IMF experts provided us with support and technical assistance on this matter.

To reduce the distress on the cash segment of the foreign exchange market, the maximum amount of FX cash that could be sold by the bank to one person in one day was limited to no more than UAH 3k (or the equivalent of $200). The indicated restriction was also applied to the purchase of FX cash by individuals in order to repay obligations in foreign currency under credit agreements with banks.

In the meantime, in order to prevent currency outflows, the NBU also introduced additional anti-crisis restrictions on foreign exchange transactions related to imports without the supply of goods to the territory of Ukraine, the transfer of foreign currency by residents outside the country in order to redeem corporate rights from non-residents, and other transactions under the individual licenses of the NBU.

During this period, we were permanently present in the foreign exchange market with interventions, convinced that the crisis made it imperative that we maintain a regular supply of FX to the market. Otherwise, expectations of further devaluation would encourage businesses to refrain as long as possible from selling FX earnings expecting further devaluation of the local currency, thereby **creating a vicious circle and self-fulfilling expectations.**

In November 2014, following a meeting with CEOs of the country's largest banks, we decided to hold daily bid auctions of up to $3 million per day to support a supply of US dollars. At 11:00 am on each trading day, the NBU published the cut-off price and the weighted average auction rate, which later acted as an indicative hryvnia exchange rate to the US dollar and was published on the NBU website, as well as in the Thomson-Reuters information system.

An indicative rate was used to determine the FX rates of purchase and sale operations in the cash market as banks were allowed to set the FX rate at the cash desk with a deviation from the indicative FX rate of up to 5 percent.

As practice has later shown, the introduction of an indicative FX rate did not help to overcome the *multiplicity of FX rates* nor to unify courses on transactions in the official and gray markets. Some banks even found workarounds for making transactions at a rate that was more favorable for them, registering a transaction in the system at an indicative rate, and compensating the difference with the market FX rate using additional fees, cross rates to other foreign currencies and even cash settlements.

The existing gap between the interbank market rate and cash meant that banks simply refused to sell currency through the cashier. The "black" foreign exchange market flourished, as it was almost impossible to buy FX at a bank, but you could buy any amount of FX from non-bank currency exchanges or via the Internet.

It was not possible to tackle the deficit either by interventions conducted by the National Bank to support banks' cash sales, or by the threat of fines imposed on banks for refusing to sell the currency available at the cash office.

A personal case in point came at the end of a press conference in October 2014 when I unsuccessfully attempted to buy US dollars in cash at the cash desk of a nearby bank. Given the large gathering of journalists, this news began to spread rapidly in the media, reinforcing the already rather tense state of the public.

Another illustrative example was the restrictions on the withdrawal of foreign currency from bank accounts. By prohibiting early withdrawals and limiting the issuance of deposits in cash, we noticed an avalanche-like increase of certificates of deposit in banks' balance sheets, which were not subject to restrictions at that time. Depositors would buy short-term certificates of deposit, which made it possible to withdraw the entire amount of the deposit at once.

To put it in a nutshell, the FX auctions conducted since September 2014 and the indicative rate based on them helped to streamline the imminent exchange rate correction processes and gave the market more opportunities to switch to new levels of exchange rate equilibrium. But, like any other administrative tool, their effectiveness soon exhausted itself and ceased to contribute to finding the exchange rate equilibrium, and not reflecting customers' real demand for foreign currency.

However, holding auctions became very expensive for us -- in early January 2015, the volume of international reserves at the NBU's disposal decreased to $ 6.4 billion, which covered only 1.3 months of imports, or the amount it would take to service external debt and pay gas bills for an extra 4 to 6 months.

The lesson was that it was impossible to find a balance under conditions of a "free fall" in the exchange rate, driven by panic and periodic outbreaks of military operations in the country.

I ask myself now: could it have been possible to avoid spending reserves and immediately let the FX rate free float? The answer, in principle, is yes, we could have. But would we risk letting the market free-fall in that situation? The answer is, of course not. If the way out of the crisis was to let the financial system fall into a bottomless abyss, destroying institutional and social stability, there would be no turning back. Nor would we have been able to complete the rest of the reforms that have been already launched.

Thus, the main lesson was that we had to use draconic administrative measures and try to find an equilibrium as soon as possible. Otherwise the market would always find an opportunity to bypass the restrictions or just stand still while waiting.

Therefore, in February 2015, we decided to stop conducting daily currency auctions and calculating the indicative rate and switch to a flexible exchange rate regime both in the interbank and cash market, leaving the possibility for the NBU to occasionally enter the market on the buy or sell side to ease the transition from one level to another, rather than resist fundamental market forces.

On the day, we stopped daily interventions the USD/UAH market rate reached UAH 18 per USD. Over the next few weeks, it further devalued to UAH 25.5 / USD, thus equaling to the FX rate of the "gray market". As a result, the hryvnia lost almost 70% of its value compared with the pre-crisis period.

However, over time, this decision turned out to be the most appropriate one -- in the next 3 years, the hryvnia's exchange rate has avoided further devaluation and has remained fairly stable.

A significant *tightening of monetary policy* (from February to March 2015, we raised the key policy rate twice from 14.5% to 30% in order to contain spiking inflation and to absorb excessive hryvnia liquidity), and the introduction of restrictions on capital transactions, also played a significant role in stabilizing the exchange rate.

▶ **Lesson learned: to arrive at the desired destination, it is important to select the right vehicle**

I believe the decision to refer to the Stand-By facility was initially wrong, though it was orchestrated by the IMF. I had initially criticized the Stand-by arrangement (SBA) as the systemic macroeconomic and structural imbalances in Ukraine at that time should have been treated with an EFF facility.

Moreover, since the First Review under SBA, a number of downside risks, including an intensification of armed conflict in Eastern Ukraine, gas price tensions and continuing bank runs, have materialized to a much greater extent than was envisaged by the latest revision of the Program. This in turn led to a substantial worsening of the macroeconomic outlook and it limited the country's capacity to finance its balance of payment flows thus putting yearend-2014 Program targets in jeopardy.

Allowing **fiscal dominance was one of the main drawbacks of the SBA** (2014) which was designed in a way that made monetary policy goals subordinate to financing fiscal and quasi-fiscal imbalances. The monetary policy of NBU became a sacrificial lamb for the lack of needed structural changes in other policy areas.

The Program allowed large-scale fiscal dominance to undermine the objectives of monetary policy. Slow reforms in the energy sector resulted in an abnormal deficit of the state energy company, Naftogaz (5.7% of GDP). Under the Program conditions, the NBU had been pushed to finance Naftogaz's losses through monetization of government bonds. That inflated the NBU's balance sheet.

Monetary policy was in fact too loose and led to the accumulation of devaluation and inflation expectations and risks. Eventually, monetization of government securities contributed to a large-scale devaluation of the exchange rate and to inflation at the highest level in the last 13 years, of 43% in 2015.

The abovementioned risks intensified due to depletion of international reserves for servicing external debt payments and settling Naftogaz's arrears. The Program was based on an assumption of non-restructuring of government debt. But that assumption was incorrect, and restructuring state debt became unavoidable.

The SBA provisioned repayment of Naftogaz arrears using international reserves of the NBU. Additionally, the NBU covered gas imports larger than was initially assumed. At the end, reserves were almost completely lost (gross reserves fell to circa 5.5 bn USD and net reserves were -3 bn USD), and the NBU was facing increased turmoil on the FX market without proper ammunition.

Moreover, to boost its reserve position, the NBU was pushed by SBA to buy FX from the market. Those purchases destabilized the market due to the tiny FX supply at that moment.

At the same time, the SBA program obliged the NBU **not to intensify administrative measures** on the FX market. That slowed down NBU's reaction to negative developments on the FX market and proved to be a wrong requirement by the IMF.

Realization of the above-mentioned accumulated risks led to an uncontrolled devaluation of hryvnia in February to March 2015, and caused inflation to sky rocket (61% in April 2015).

Those outcomes *postponed transition of the NBU to the inflation-targeting framework* we had initially planned for 2015. Despite the announcement of IT transition in 2Q2015, the Program lacked sufficient focus on structural reforms in monetary policy area, needed for successful preparation for IT implementation.

I discussed these and other issues with the IMF Deputy MD, David Lipton, in Kyiv in October 2014, and he supported us. All these drawbacks were later confirmed by the IMF's Ex-Post Evaluation Program in March 2016.

At the same time, I must note that the SBA program, which opened in spring 2014, was been the first IMF Program since 1997, and has been consistently implemented, and was replaced in an orderly fashion within a year (2015) by the EFF program, which aimed at medium- and long-term balance-of-payments problems that require fundamental economic reforms.

Moreover, the next EFF program was the longest and most consistent in the history of cooperation between Ukraine and the IMF. Despite delays in the provision of separate tranches related to the failure to meet deadlines for conducting structural reforms outside the financial sector (land market, anti-corruption legislation, energy sector), it was completed and succeeded with the Stand-by Program in 2018.

Lesson learned: we could not pretend during the war time that we were in business as usual mode. Every Central Bank should prepare in advance a Contingency Plan that can be immediately implemented in the event of pre-defined triggers.

b) Capital flow measures, limited deposit restrictions

Capital controls to keep the FX market afloat were an unpleasant but essential measure for Ukraine as an emerging economy hit by military conflict. Those measures were irksome to business, but it was even more difficult for us to take the responsibility to put them in place.

But there was no other way. Capital outflow from the country occurred through all channels: junk papers, fake import contracts, reinsurance operations. Considering the "connectedness" of many foreign investments, capital outflow acquired the character of a snowball. And this happened against the background of a bank run and periodic intensified military actions in the east of the country. It was clear that *finding equilibrium in such conditions was the same as looking for a black cat in a dark room.*

The absence of other alternatives led us to the need to introduce draconian barriers to the outflow of capital. Further developments have shown that we did the right thing. With hindsight, I can say that those measures could have been introduced earlier, but in a situation of uncertainty, it is difficult to determine the very moment when there is no "way back".

We understood that rational behavior of an individual business in the current circumstances might lead to worse outcomes for the business community altogether. Restrictions introduced by the NBU to stabilize the foreign exchange market, thorough reviews of export and import agreements, and other temporary measures were aimed at keeping businesses and individuals from ill-advised decisions and at curbing herding behavior.

When we switched from the SBA to EFF program, we convinced the IMF to help us with the FCY Restriction Road Map as it became evident that in the absence of administrative measures the market would not find a balance. Worth noting were decisions taken with the active support of the IMF based on the Fund's extensive experience in helping countries come out of crises they have been facing. We intended to lift or moderate the restrictions as the foreign exchange and financial markets stabilized.

We introduced FX restrictions, which were unconventional among the policy decisions made by the NBU. The restrictions were initially launched in 2014 and included 100% and then 75% surrender requirement, the ban on repatriation of dividends, and rigorous verification of export and import contracts. Then, additional restrictions were launched in February to March 2015 in response to panic in the currency market, which intensified along with the escalation of the conflict in Eastern Ukraine.

One measure taken in February 2015 of special note was the introduction of the requirement to deposit local currency in a bank account three days before the transaction on FX purchase (t+3). This allowed our currency control division to manually analyze each transaction for substance. As a result, the foreign exchange market stopped for a few days, which we later called the *"golden breaker"*, which allowed us to halt the panic in the market and take a breath.

The FX restrictions were introduced synchronically for cash operations, interbank transactions and some current account transactions.

For FX cash operations:

- FX cash transfers abroad by individuals for non-trade purposes (w/o supporting documentation) were allowed in an amount not exceeding UAH 15,000 (~US$1000) within one banking day
- Withdrawal of FX cash or investment metals from clients' accounts through cashier's offices and ATMs was limited to an equivalent of UAH 3,000 (~US$200) per day per customer

For FX operations of banks:

- NBU approval was needed to make advance payments exceeding US$50,000
- A letter of credit was required for import contracts exceeding US$500,000 issued by AA (investment grade) foreign banks
- Purchase of non-cash FX and banking metals for the banks' own purposes was limited
- Foreign contracts exceeding US$25,000 (later raised to US$50,000) were subject to a price examination by banks to verify compliance with market prices
- Purchase of FX on behalf of a client was prohibited if the amount of FX on the client's accounts with bank exceeded US$10,000 (later raised to US$25,000)

- Extension of UAH loans to a customer was prohibited if the customer's remaining balance of FX account was pledged as collateral for such loan
- Purchase of FX was banned if it was financed by obtaining a loan in UAH

Export-Import operations:

- 100% surrender was required for FX proceeds from abroad
- Repatriation of dividends abroad was prohibited
- Advance payments in FX under import contracts exceeding US$50,000 was served on T+3 basis
- Export FX proceeds had to be brought back to the country within 90 days

Moreover, in order to partially fill the financing gap, we also looked into options for curbing inessential imports. Together with the Cabinet of Ministers, we explored the possibility of adopting a guarantee scheme for all bank deposits to prevent a bank run. Both items required a discussion with IMF staff on the issues of timing and modalities of its implementation based on international practices.

Of note, a major part of foreign investments (both in form of direct investments and corporate debt finance) had been coming for years from related parties (so-called **round-tripping of capital,** which refers to channeling abroad cash earned locally by the residents and its subsequent return to the local economy in the form of foreign investments in equity or debt instruments).

Historically, due to factors related to the deficiencies of the rule of law, a weak judicial system, and enforcement mechanisms (all those things are outside mandate of the central bank), as well as the lack of structural reforms in the country until 2013, most of the business was structured through foreign, mainly low-tax, jurisdictions. On the one hand, this provided the beneficiary owners with a certain level of protection outside the Ukrainian legal framework; on the other hand, it allowed use of flaws in the international tax system in order to withdraw capital from the country and subsequent return for specific needs.

It should also be noted that the formal, rigid currency regulation system stimulated business to hoard cash outside the country, in essence, anticipating the future needs of business.

The volume of **round-tripping transactions** during 2010-2018 was estimated at US$8.4bn, which represented 22% of direct investments inflow (US$38.2bn). The largest share of round-tripping transactions was observed during 2010-2013 (on average 33% of the total FDI inflow). During the crisis in 2014-2015, there was a net outflow of funds from Ukraine due to transactions with related parties.

Exhibit 10. Round tripping of FDI net inflow to Ukraine in 2010-2017

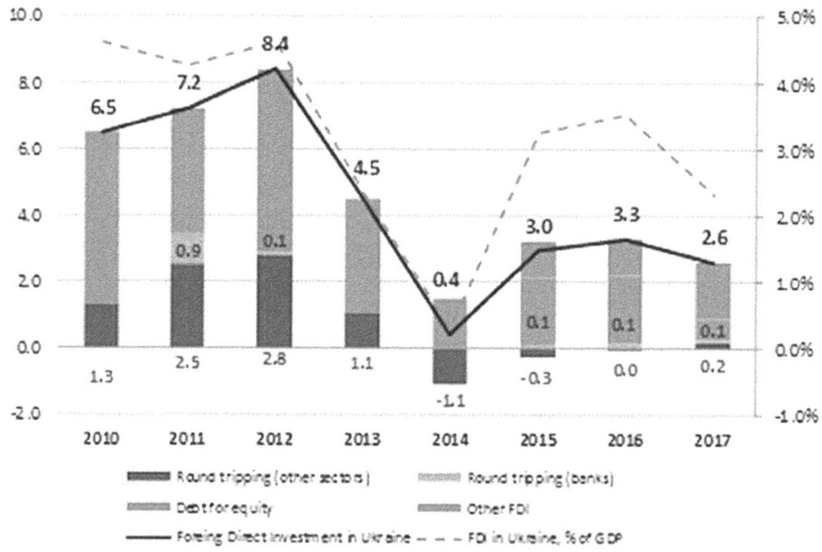

Source: NBU

Unprecedentedly high by global benchmarks, this level of dependence on the dynamics of capital flows on operations of related parties was an additional motivator for us to apply measures related to curbing capital outflows from Ukraine.

Of course, restrictions were not popular among the business community or the population. However, they helped stop the panic in the currency market, reduce volatility of foreign currency supply, limit the demand on foreign currency, and prevent unproductive capital outflow from Ukraine.

The stabilization of the FX market allowed the NBU to begin gradual removal of administrative restrictions. In April 2015, the National Bank had developed and agreed with the International Monetary Fund a **roadmap for the gradual withdrawal of temporary currency restrictions, which was not time-based, but condition-based**. Also, we started to work on the operational plan for the liberalization of the entire FX regulation system in Ukraine. A working group has since carried out an analysis of the regulatory framework and of the experience of other transition economies in this area and has designed a currency regulation target model for Ukraine.

The NBU was determined to gradually rescind administrative measures at a pace consistent with macroeconomic and financial stability. We started the liberalization process with current account operations and foreign direct investment inflow.

Implementation of each stage of the **liberalization was linked to certain conditions**, including macroeconomic stability, fiscal consolidation, improvement and dynamic development of the banking system, and the accumulation of sufficient international reserves. The plan for removal of administrative restrictions was introduced in 2014-2015, preliminarily designed with the IMF, and later integrated into the more broad-scale roadmap for gradual liberalization conditioned upon sustained improvement of FX and money markets. But *it took more than 3 years to eliminate most of the restrictions* (see Chapter 7). Even after adoption of the new Currency Act, several restrictions remained in action since the macroeconomic prerequisites required for further easing were not met.

The stabilization of the FX market together with an elimination of fiscal dominance was the precondition for the National Bank to shift to *inflation targeting*.

CHAPTER 6

New monetary policy framework

EV TOLSTOY FAMOUSLY said that "all happy families are alike but each unhappy family is unhappy in its own way". In the banking industry, the opposite is true: most developing countries suffer from similar distress.

The monetary policy regime of the National Bank until 2014 was similar to many examples of developing countries: pegging the national currency to the US dollar, the dependence of internal FX market on the global commodity prices, the inefficiency of interest rate instruments, and severe but ineffective restrictions on capital transactions.

In macroeconomic theory, this is a classic reflection of the *"impossible trinity"*, and until 2014, the National Bank of Ukraine chose the option of sacrificing the independence of monetary policy and economic growth in favor of a fixed exchange rate and ineffective market.

As a result, for decades, the Ukrainian economy had suffered from variable and unpredictable inflation, which lowered confidence in the hryvnia while causing high credit and deposit interest rates, high dollarization level and, as a result, an unstable economic environment, which hampered economic growth.

This was the outcome of a fixed exchange rate policy, which caused macroeconomic imbalances accumulation and turned out to be incapable either to ensure stable and low inflation rates or to support economic growth. Moreover, the pegged exchange rate arrangement made public expectations more sensitive to exchange rate fluctuations. Correspondingly, this created an incentive for economic agents to take excessive risks, thereby limiting possibilities for the exchange rate to buffer against external shocks.

Moreover, strict restrictions on the movement of capital were strong obstacles for attraction FDI to the country.

The maintenance of a fixed exchange rate against the backdrop of high inflation, contributed to a **significant deviation in the real rate of the national currency from its equilibrium value.** The subsequent return of the FX rate to equilibrium formerly happened via large-scale devaluations that took place in 1999-2000, 2009-2010 and 2014-2015.

There was also **fiscal domination**, which allowed the government, state-owned banks and state-owned companies to cover their deficit by issuing debt securities, which were later settled in the portfolio of the National Bank.

The large magnitude of price changes created an unfavorable environment for attracting long-term investments into the economy, since investors focus on short-term operations. Thus, high and unstable inflation was adversely affecting economic growth.

I did not see any alternative for Ukraine as a small open economy but to switch to a flexible exchange rate and inflation-targeting monetary regime synchronized with a more active use of interest rate instruments and a gradual liberalization of FX controls.

Therefore, in early 2015 we started the transition to **Inflation Targeting (IT)**. In this decision, we were supported by the IMF.

The **pre-conditions** necessary for such a transition were the following:

- flexible exchange rate
- price stability as the main goal of monetary policy
- instrumental independence of the central bank
- no fiscal dominance

The aim of the NBU was to gradually shift public attention from the exchange rate movements to the inflation rate. In our view, this could be done only by developing consistent, transparent monetary policy aimed at price stability.

Moreover, the focus of the NBU on ensuring price stability implies a floating exchange rate regime where exchange rate fluctuations serve as the main buffer against the impact of external shocks on the economy. This means that, as negative external shocks arise (e.g., the demand for the Ukrainian exports declines or terms of trade deteriorate), a moderate hryvnia depreciation will enable Ukrainian exports to preserve competitiveness and will mitigate any adverse impact on output and employment. If positive shocks arise, hryvnia appreciation will avert economic overheating and high inflation.

In truth, the **most difficult part** of Ukraine's transition to IT was **switching to the flexible exchange rate** since it wasn't expected to be as difficult as it came to be when the conflict in the Eastern Ukraine escalated. When that happened, the economic situation in Ukraine became very difficult. It was a triple crisis, or a perfect storm. Due to accumulated macroeconomic imbalances, unsustainable external position, and further confidence and terms-of-trade shocks, the devaluation of our currency was huge and inflation exceeded 60% in April 2015. Definitely, it was not easy time for monetary policy, but we needed to go through such a painful adjustment. What we learned was that **after the decision is taken, do not stop half-way.** Or in the words of Winston Churchill: "If you are going through hell, keep going."

The transition to a flexible exchange rate also became one of the key prerequisites that allowed Ukraine to access external support from the international financial institutions and to receive the IMF Board approval of a two-year Stand-by program. For our country and for the world as a whole, it was a strong signal of support both from a political and economic point of view. As a result, in 2014, Ukraine received IMF credit resources in the amount of approximately USD 4.6 billion and additionally raised the equivalent of nearly USD 4.7 billion from foreign markets and bilateral financial agreements. These measures allowed Ukraine to fully meet its sovereign obligations in a timely manner even under the difficult conditions of a decline in production and foreign economic activity.

Although the inflation targeting monetary regime had only been launched for the beginning of 2016, the NBU's monetary policy in 2015 was quite effective. In April 2016, inflation, which peaked above 60% in mid-2015, had moderated to single digits.

This can be a lesson for many other developing countries that are hesitant to move to IT for fear of flexible exchange rates. In the economic literature, this is called *"Fear of Floating"*. Each country's set of reasons for this reluctance is different. But in almost all cases, the question rests on the ability and willingness of the central bank to conduct an independent policy and to consistently eliminate reasons that impede it.

Like many countries with a long history of pegging the national currency to a hard equivalent, we also evaluated the potential risks of **losing the exchange rate nominal anchor as an element of macroeconomic policy** and financial discipline. We realized the balance-sheet risks that it would have on banks and the real sector, which have significant exposure in foreign currency, as well as on undeveloped capital markets, which do not offer sufficient tools to hedge currency risks.

Nevertheless, in Ukraine's case, the choice was simplified by the practical **absence of alternatives**. Given the reduction of the level of international reserves to a critical level, their complete exhaustion could have led to uncontrollable consequences of devaluation.

Therefore, in seriously planning the transition to full-scale inflation targeting, we **first had to stabilize the price situation**, and **second, we had to get rid of the fiscal dominance** in monetary policy that had taken place in the past.

Looking back, the transition to IT can be divided into **three main stages**:

- Stage I. Setting up technical preconditions (pre-2015)
- Stage II. Setting up institutional preconditions (1H2015)
- Stage III. Implementing the IT regime (2015 – 2016)

In 2014 – 2015, activities of the National Bank of Ukraine were aimed at eliminating outcomes of the crisis arising from macroeconomic imbalances that had accumulated in previous years and from the military conflict in the east of the country. The impact of these factors caused inflation to peak in April 2015.

Under such conditions, the main task of the National Bank of Ukraine was to halt the upward inflationary trend. This was made possible because of tight monetary policy of the National Bank of Ukraine, prudent fiscal policy and stabilization of inflation expectations. The inflation rate followed a steady declining trend, and by the end of 2015, stood at 43.3%.

Before switching to a full-fledged inflation targeting, monetary policy had been based on a monetary-targeting regime. According to the IMF program, the NBU used net domestic assets (NDA) and net international assets (NIR) as operational targets and monetary base as an indicative target.

The National Bank of Ukraine moved to inflation targeting in the beginning of 2016. Until that time, preparations continued to create all the crucial pre-conditions necessary for its implementation. During the first stage (until 2015), the NBU prepared *technical preconditions* for the adoption of inflation targeting. In particular, macroeconomic models were built and a quarterly forecast cycle was designed as part of these efforts.

During the second stage (in the first half of 2015), the regulator established *institutional preconditions*, including independence of the National Bank of Ukraine with respect to instruments used to reach its goals, eliminating fiscal dominance, and modification of the monetary policy decision-making process.

With a view to ensuring the transparency of monetary policy during the transition period to a new regime, the NBU published the **Roadmap for Implementation of Inflation Targeting, which** outlined steps the central bank was taking to create all the pre-conditions necessary for successful operation of inflation targeting in Ukraine. In particular, steps were needed to ensure efficient coordination with the NBU Council, the Government, the IMF, and the State Statistics Service of Ukraine. The NBU also committed to press ahead with efforts to bring its instruments, mechanisms, and procedures into line with the inflation targeting standards. At the same time, the NBU started providing stronger analytical support to the monetary policy decision-making process and took steps to enhance public awareness and understanding of the central bank's monetary policy.

The NBU also played a role in ensuring legislation entrenched the institutional independence of the central bank. On the initiative of the NBU, in June 2015 the Parliament adopted amendments to the Law on the National Bank, to strengthen the independence of monetary policy and institutional capacity of the central bank.

In August 2015, the Board of the National Bank of Ukraine approved a **Monetary Policy Strategy for 2016-2020**. Before the formation of the Council of the National Bank of Ukraine, this Monetary Policy Strategy was a working guideline of the NBU Board for monetary policy implementation. This was the first document to announce irrevocable quantitative inflation targets and the implementation of the inflation targeting regime in Ukraine.

In 2016, monetary policy of the National Bank of Ukraine was aimed at achieving the inflation target of 12% +/- 3 ppts announced in 2015 for 2016 year-end. Accordingly, the National Bank of Ukraine pursued monetary policy intended to:

- Preserve the hryvnia's intrinsic value via relatively high interest rates (tight monetary policy), while gradually lowering the key policy rate as inflationary risks abated
- Smooth excessive hryvnia exchange rate volatility via foreign exchange interventions, though without counteracting the persistent trend towards exchange rate appreciation or depreciation in different periods depending on economic fundamentals
- Avoid fiscal dominance, e.g., financing fiscal and quasi-fiscal needs by issuing money.

Eventually, consumer prices steadily declined to 12.4% in December 2016, which brought inflation in line with the target (12% ± 3 ppts). Keeping inflation within the target range should contribute to a decline in inflation expectations and stabilization of the macroeconomic situation in Ukraine.

To summarize, the NBU followed **five basic principles of monetary policy**:

- Unconditional priority of price stability compared to other goals and objectives (the inflation target was irrevocable)
- Adherence to a floating exchange rate (NBU FX interventions were made only in order to replenish international reserves or to prevent excessive exchange rate fluctuations)
- Proactive and forward-looking approach in decision-making (forecast-based decisions to ensure anchored inflation expectations)
- Transparency of policy decisions (which required regular and detailed explanations of the NBU decisions and actions)
- Institutional, financial, and operational independence of the NBU (monetary policy instruments were not used for any objectives that threatened price stability).

Exhibit 11. New principles of monetary policy were developed to achieve low and stable inflation

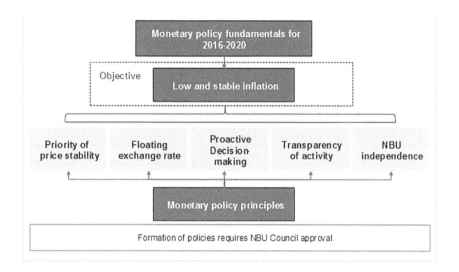

Upon its formation in December 2016, the Council of the National Bank of Ukraine approved **Monetary Policy Guidelines for 2017 and the Medium Term**. This decision affirmed consistency of the monetary policy, a firm commitment to meet quantitative inflation targets, and enforcement of the inflation targeting regime the Board of the National Bank of Ukraine had declared in August 2015.

The Monetary Policy Guidelines for 2017 and the Medium Term confirmed both **the medium-term inflation target of 5% ± 1 ppt** and the trajectory of inflation required to achieve this medium-term target:

- 8% ± 2 ppts as of the end of 2017
- 6% ± 2 ppts as of the end of 2018
- 5% ± 1 ppt as of the end of 2019 and forward

We considered that rate of inflation optimal for Ukraine in the mid-term with the rationale being that belonging to the group of developing economies, the Ukrainian economy lags behind developed economies in a number of economic indicators, such as labor productivity and GDP per capita. This means that Ukraine's large economic potential can be realized if reforms are carried out successfully to achieve higher productivity.

Higher productivity, in turn, means higher a cost of labor and higher prices, which also have to catch up with developed economies. Although **we set an optimal rate of inflation at 5%** for **the mid-term**, as soon as Ukraine catches up to developed economies in terms of productivity and GDP per capita, the target rate of inflation may be lowered to the EU level (2%).

Eventually, we considered a gradual reduction of inflation to maximize the trade-off between the long-term loss of potential GDP and employment due to high inflation, and the short-term cyclical loss of economic growth due to disinflationary policy.

Exhibit 12. Inflation targets for 2016-2020 in Ukraine

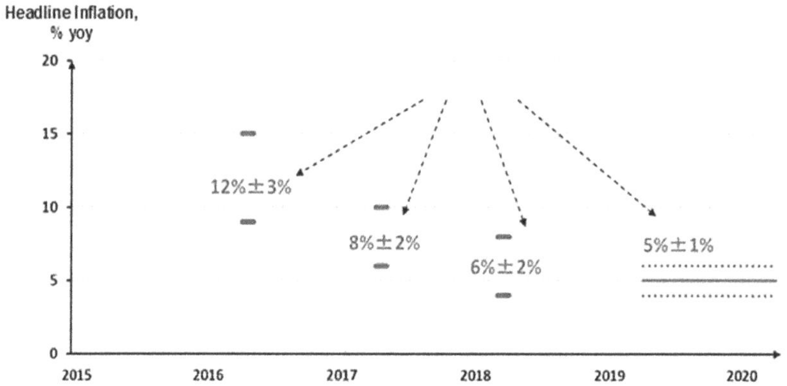

Approval of the Monetary Policy Guidelines for 2017 and the medium term were made by the NBU Council in December of 2016, and the de jure formalized inflation targeting regime was adoption in Ukraine.

One of the key priorities of the NBU was **to improve the efficiency of the monetary transmission mechanism.** To achieve this goal, we had to develop the government securities and derivatives markets, liberalize foreign exchange controls, and reload the banking sector.

These measures helped to enhance the central bank's ability to influence inflation developments in Ukraine.

In April 2016, we streamlined the **operational design of interest rate policy** in order to strengthen the role of its key policy rate:

- The **key policy rate** was defined as the interest rate on main NBU operations (liquidity providing or absorbing), which at that time, was the interest rate on 14-day certificates of deposits.
- Symmetric and fixed band for overnight standing facilities around the key policy rate were introduced.

These actions have allowed the NBU to achieve its inflation objectives primarily by adjusting the key policy interest rate, with other monetary policy instruments playing a supportive role.

Exhibit 13. The new operational design under the inflation targeting regime in Ukraine

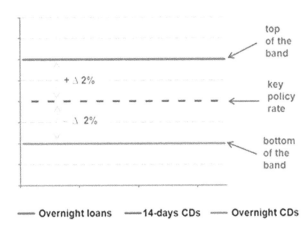

At the same time, the NBU streamlined procedures and liquidity management instruments. Since then, we have adopted the interest rate framework common for inflation-targeting central banks.

Interest rate (IR) pass-through has strengthened due to NBU efforts to enhance the role of key rate. Prior to 2015, the interest rate channel of monetary transmission mechanism was quite weak as the key policy rate played a rather symbolic role in the money market. However, since 2015, IR pass-through has improved significantly, particularly after the NBU switched to a new operational design of its interest rate policy.

Exhibit 14. NBU Policy Rates and Ukrainian Index of Interbank Rates, % pa

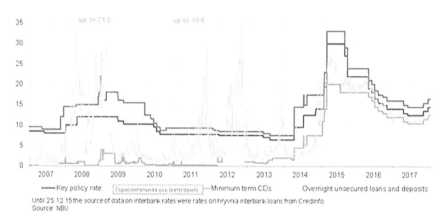

Until 25.12.15 the source of data on interbank rates were rates on hryvnia interbank loans from Credinfo
Source: NBU

To build the **yield curve**, we worked with the Ministry of Finance to line up the territory for fixed income instruments: up to 90 days was the territory of the NBU, while 90 days up to three years was the territory of the Ministry of Finance. We assumed that with the development of the securities market, the term structure of government bonds would be extended, and then the yield curve would increase to 5 to 7 years.

Given the liquidity surplus, we built our yield curve for NBU deposit certificates, starting with overnight and continuing for a period of 14 days, and up to 3 months.

Fair value of T-bills and building a yield curve

In order to increase the transparency of the central bank's decisions on refinancing of banks upon the security of government bonds, as well as to minimize central bank's own losses from the realization of interest rate risk, foreign exchange risk and liquidity risk, the National Bank started calculating the **fair value of government bonds in** 2015.

I was surprised to learn that only 10% of central banks use IFRS standards and do a proper mark-to-market valuation of their portfolio. I truly believe that all central banks should do so, especially if they have been using unconventional monetary policies in the wake of the Global Financial Crisis. As we know, all burdens of the last financial crisis were put on the shoulders of Ministries of Finance through the incredible surge in public debt and on central banks through extension of their balance sheets. I believe that a central bank with a large balance sheet and without proper M-t-M valuation is not a good idea. I am absolutely against ideas that the central bank is a storage place for bad and non-liquid assets.

The main rule of any central bank is not to deceive ourselves, society or market participants. Fiscal costs are not just direct expenses of the budget and deterioration of countries' financial ratios, but also a deterioration of the central bank's balance sheet and P&L. Society should know and understand this point in order to avoid moral hazard and similar mistakes in the future.

We have approved the fair value measurement methodology for government bonds[7] in accordance with the International Financial Reporting Standard 13 "Fair Value Measurement". This methodology was based on zero-coupon yield curves by groups of T-bills as a graphical interpretation of the yield of homogeneous zero-coupon government bonds with different periods to maturity.

Since we adopted this methodology, the fair value of government bonds has been used by the central bank:

- for presentation of government bonds held by the central bank at fair value in accordance with IFRS
- to disclose the fair value of government bonds in reporting

---

[7] NBU Board Resolution No. 732 dated 26.10.2015 (updated)

- to assess the adequacy of collateral for transactions with banks and the Deposit Guarantee Fund
- as a benchmark for market transactions with government bonds

In addition, the NBU began accepting government bonds as collateral at fair value for the following operations:

- refinancing of banks
- direct repo with banks
- cash storage contracts
- supporting liquidity of the Deposit Guarantee Fund

To this end, we approved the methodology for calculating *adjustment coefficients for T-bills* that can be accepted by the National Bank as collateral in accordance with NBU Resolution on liquidity support of banks[8].

As of December 2015, the National Bank's website began daily publishing information about the fair value of T-bills along with the adjustment coefficients. The NBU also launched the publication of zero-coupon yield curves of government bonds using the Nelson-Siegel parametric model. This model theoretically allows building a curve of any shape that occurs in practice. Each addition in the spot rate function influences a specific segment of the yield curve (short, medium, and long term) that adds to the flexibility of the model. Adopting this model was justified because it was well suited to describe the time structure of rates in an environment of underdeveloped financial markets, when the number of securities traded in the market is low, as is often the case in developing countries. A respective yield curve provides a smooth curve shape that can be used in macroeconomic research and for evaluating financial instruments.

In 2015, when inflation reached 45% and the NBU key rate was 30%, our long-term yield curve looked like a dream. But it is very important to build a long-term yield curve along which all market participants will

---

[8] NBU Board Resolution No. 615 dated 17,09.2015

work. Then, the central bank should commit to making this dream a reality by using all available monetary policy instruments.

The disclosure of information on the fair value of T-bills increased the confidence of banks in the decisions of the regulator, including those related to banks' liquidity support. Banks were able to use the same information to manage their liquidity, taking into account the provisions of the central bank's regulations.

Continuing to refine the model of assessing the fair value of government bonds held by the central bank or accepted as collateral for refinancing loans, the NBU has begun switching to the Svensson parametric model in 2018 for constructing a zero-yield curve for local currency government bonds[9].

The bank took this action because validation of the Nelson-Siegel model showed deterioration in the accuracy of market yield estimates for UAH government bonds for 2018. Therefore, the National Bank analyzed alternative models for constructing a zero-coupon yield curve and chose a Svensson model. The results of testing the Svensson model for 2018 data confirmed its compliance with current market conditions. This parametric model showed the smallest deviation in the model's yield compared to yields determined on the secondary market transactions, both for the most liquid government bonds with a residual maturity of up to 6 months, and for medium-term government bonds with a maturity of three to five years.

The switch to the Svensson model took place in 2019 after necessary automation was completed on the National Bank's software. Since April 2019, the National Bank has used the indicative fair value of government bonds determined by the new methodology when calculating the amount of collateral provided by banks for refinancing loans and cash storage contracts. This indicator is also shown in Bloomberg and Refinitiv (Reuters) trading systems and serves as a benchmark for investors. After

---

[9] NBU Board Decision No. 627 dated 20.09.2018

switching to the Svensson model, the National Bank has continued to publish zero-coupon yield curves for UAH bonds using the Nelson-Siegel parametric model.

a) Monetary policy decision-making bodies

Once prepared for the new monetary policy regime, we put an end to the dominance of fiscal policy over monetary and introduced all necessary internal procedures. Namely, we established the **Monetary Policy Committee**, introduced a decision-making process by the NBU Board in accordance with the announced schedule, started publishing a quarterly **inflation report,** and **established systemic communications of monetary policy decisions.**

With the legislative changes and internal organizational arrangements in force, the NBU's main decision-making bodies were the NBU Council, the NBU Board, the Monetary Policy Committee, and the key departments involved in formulating and implementing monetary policy.

The NBU Council was responsible for strategic-level decision-making that involved developing the Monetary Policy Guidelines, overseeing monetary policy implementation, and drafting proposals on changes thereto.

The NBU Board, in accordance with the Monetary Policy Guidelines, ensured implementation of monetary policy using appropriate monetary policy instruments and other means of banking regulation, organized execution of other functions, as provided by the Law on the National Bank of Ukraine, and managed the NBU's activities. Monetary policy decisions were taken by the NBU Board at special meetings held on a pre-announced schedule and published on the NBU's official website.

The Monetary Policy Committee (MPC) was established at the National Bank of Ukraine within the framework of the regulator's transformation and transfer to the inflation targeting regime. Establishing the MPC facilitated the systematization of monetary policy decision-making according to international practices and strengthened central bank public communications. The Monetary Policy Committee is an advisory body established to provide a forum for the exchange of information and opinions on monetary policy formulation, and implementation to ensure price stability.

The main tasks of the Committee are to study and deliberate on the following issues:

- Formulating the principles of, and implementing monetary policy to meet, the goals and objectives set out in the applicable laws and the Monetary Policy Guidelines
- Setting monetary policy goals and objectives
- Using monetary policy instruments to meet set targets

MPC meetings are held prior to NBU Board's meetings on monetary policy. If required, extraordinary meetings may also be convened.

Composition of the Monetary Policy Committee

The Head of the MPC is the NBU Governor.

The Deputy Head of the MPC is the NBU Deputy Governor, responsible for monetary policy and financial stability.

The members of the MPC are:

- the NBU Deputy Governors
- Director of the Open Market Operations Department
- Director of the Monetary Policy and Economic Analysis Department
- Director of the Financial Stability Department
- Director of the Statistics and Reporting Department

The monetary policy decision-making process at the National Bank of Ukraine comprises five key stages:

i. Preparation of proposals on monetary policy decisions, with relevant analysis by NBU staff

ii. The silence period on monetary policy

iii. Meetings of the Monetary Policy Committee

iv. Meetings of the Board of the National Bank on monetary policy issues

v. Announcement and communication of monetary policy decisions

I. Preparation of proposals on monetary policy decisions by NBU staff

A week prior to the meetings of the MPC and the NBU Board on monetary policy issues, a working meeting of the heads of the NBU departments involved in formulating and implementing monetary policy takes place.

At this meeting, the participants outline a range of issues to be included in the agenda of the meetings of the MPC and the NBU Board on monetary policy issues, and identify the analytical materials used as an input for monetary policy decision-making.

Presentation materials prepared by the departments contain the macroeconomic forecast, a broad assessment of the economic situation and monetary indicators, the identification of possible risks to financial stability, as well as proposals on changes to the monetary policy framework.

II. The silence period on monetary policy

The NBU maintains a so-called 7-day silence period on monetary policy (also called a quiet period) before making and unveiling a monetary policy decision. This period begins on the last Thursday that precedes the Board's monetary policy meeting, and ends at 2:00 p.m. on the day of the meeting -- the same time that the Board makes public its monetary policy action on the NBU's official website.

During this period, the NBU Board members and other members of the Monetary Policy Committee, along with the rest of NBU employees, must not discuss monetary policy issues with mass media, banks, experts, investors, and other stakeholders – whether on or off the record. The silence period also implies that mass media may not publish NBU representatives' interviews, comments, or other public materials prepared before the silence period went into effect that contain statements pertaining to monetary policy.

The silence period, which is common practice among inflation-targeting central banks, is intended to prevent public speculation around an upcoming monetary policy decision of the NBU, as they may have an ambiguous effect on the expectations of financial market participants, increase uncertainty, and trigger excessive market volatility.

III. Meetings of the Monetary Policy Committee

Meetings of the Monetary Policy Committee play a key role in the monetary policy decision-making process, as the MPC serves as a forum for discussions, the exchange of opinions, and reaching consensus.

The MPC meetings take place on the eve of the meetings of the Board of the National Bank on monetary policy issues. The meetings are attended by the members of the NBU Board, and directors of the departments involved in the monetary policy decision making process.

At such meetings, representatives from these departments present technical contributions prepared by staff on the macroeconomic forecast, outlook for future developments in the money and foreign exchange markets, financial stability; and they share the results of the assessment and expertise with the members of the NBU Board.

At the MPC meetings, the Committee members also discuss the key strategic and analytical documents produced by the NBU, notably proposals with regard to the Monetary Policy Guidelines and the Inflation Report.

IV. Meetings of the Board of the National Bank on monetary policy issues

Meetings of the Board of the National Bank on monetary policy issues take place in accordance with a pre-announced schedule (meetings are scheduled from 10:00 a.m. to 12:00 p.m.). At the meetings, the Board members contemplate proposals from the NBU staff on the need to modify the monetary and foreign exchange policy framework, proposals with regard to the main parameters of operations with assets and liabilities for the purpose of current banking system liquidity regulation, and other issues included in the MPC meeting agenda.

Following a discussion of the proposals from the staff, monetary policy decisions are taken through an open vote and by a majority vote of the Board members present at the meeting.

V. Announcement and communication of monetary policy decisions

Two hours after the NBU Board ends its monetary policy meeting, i.e., at 2 p.m., the NBU issues a press release on its official website outlining the NBU Board's monetary policy decisions. Simultaneously, the NBU Governor gives a press briefing to announce and explain the decision made by the NBU Board.

b) Communications on monetary policy issues

Today, the central bank's communications with the public play a crucial role in the conduct of monetary policy. On the one hand, they enable the public to monitor the activities of the central bank. On the other hand, the transparency of activities of the central bank enhances confidence in its actions, thus having a positive influence on the expectations of businesses and households.

In order to enhance public confidence in the central bank's decisions, we rebuilt our monetary policy communications in line with the best international practices by delivering *regular and proactive monetary policy communications* (press releases, press briefings, Inflation Reports, minutes) and allowing *broad public access to data.*

We started publishing the **Inflation Report** in 2015, and it became a key element of the communication policy and a flagship publication of the central bank. This document explains the rationale behind recent monetary policy decisions and contains measures to be taken to achieve monetary policy objectives based on the macroeconomic analysis and forecast.

The publication of the Inflation Report is aimed at enhancing the transparency, predictability and confidence in the National Bank by explaining to the general public the inflation determinants, the goals pursued by the regulator and the respective instruments used to achieve these goals. This analytical document provides the foundation for monetary policy decisions aimed at maintaining price stability over the medium term. It provides a **comprehensive analysis of the economic situation with a focus on current and projected inflation developments**, contains the macroeconomic forecast, and the assessment of the main risks to its baseline scenario.

The Inflation Report is published **on a quarterly basis,** one week after the Monetary Policy Committee meeting at which, apart from the monetary policy decisions, an updated macroeconomic forecast is considered and approved. The regular publication of the Inflation Report contributes to strengthening the independence of the National Bank by enabling it to express its opinion on the macroeconomic development, and to raising financial literacy among the public.

Along with an Inflation Report, we launched *regular public events with different target groups* (experts, businesses, students, etc.), which became a regular part of what is called a 'routine' cycle on monetary policy decision-making.

We also started to use **forward guidance** in the press releases on the key policy rate explaining the factors that may affect the next decision of the national bank. That helped to enhance communications with the expert community and the general public.

c) Analytical capacity, data mining, research, and reporting

As mentioned earlier, under the fixed exchange rate regime that was prevalent pre-2014, the role of interest rates was subdued by FX policy instruments. Since the key interest rate had almost no practical value, the central bank did not need to develop its analytical potential and improve the quality of its forecast.

But the situation radically changed with the transition to the inflation targeting regime, in which the accuracy of the *central bank's forecast is the key to a successful policy aimed at anchoring inflation expectations.*

Thus, with a reasonable understanding of the complexity of the task, we set a goal **to achieve excellence in our analytics and research.**

In order to arrive at more precise and reliable forecasts, we substantially improved our **modeling toolkit** used for forecasting of macroeconomic variables and scenario analysis. In particular, we introduced:

- A new set of nowcasting and short-term forecasting models for CPI and GDP, including web scraping of retail prices, and GDP near-term forecasting system based on monthly sectoral data and survey results
- A core semi-structural macroeconomic model (FQPM), which provides us with a new forecasting toolkit, including tools for current economic analysis, analysis of policy alternatives, combining empirical data, expert judgments and short-term forecasts into the middle-term forecast, and assessing forecast uncertainty (with confidence intervals and risks of scenarios)
- Additional models to model fiscal stance, REER equilibrium, money growth and a Global Simulation Model among others

A *model of non-performing loans* was developed as well. The model allows us to evaluate changes in the level of non-performing loans for certain types of loan portfolios (in national and foreign currencies for individuals and entities), depending on the forecast of macroeconomic variables. The results obtained with the model were used in particular during the diagnostic survey of the 35 largest banks in 2014.

This new analytical toolkit allowed us to **update the central bank's reporting system** and to provide historical analysis and forecast comparisons, which contributed to more prudent decisions on monetary policy issues.

The "Statistics" section of the official NBU website has been constantly updated and filled with relevant information. In particular, the set of indicators in the "Macroeconomics" section was significantly expanded, with current presentation of basic indicators of economic development of Ukraine. We standardized publishing the monetary and financial reports and launched a regional aspect. (These reports were previously submitted by regional offices of the NBU to regional state administrations and statistical offices.)

In 2015, we completed the transition to the compilation of external sector statistics in accordance with the requirements of the sixth edition of the regulations of the balance of payments and international investment position (IMF, 2009). Operational and ultimate data of monetary and financial statistics was unified for the purpose of comparison and compliance with standards.

Survey of business expectations

The regime of targeting monetary inflation is often called **"the regime targeting inflation expectations", which** means that the way economic entities interpret actions of the central bank influences the quality of decisions taken by them, and consequently, the economic system efficiency in general.

Qualitative feedback from economic entities forms the basis of understanding the way the economy interprets decisions of the NBU, as well as changes in business expectations. Thus, in conducting the business expectations survey, and publishing results on the official NBU website quarterly, we have implemented new web survey methods that have allowed us to centralize this function at the central office as well. These innovations have strengthened bilateral communications of the NBU and agents of economic activity, raising awareness of the influence of monetary policy on economic development and inflation processes.

An equally important step was *strengthening our capacities in macroeconomic research.*

At the beginning of research capacity reform in the NBU, we aimed to enhance the role of research to meet regulator needs in major functional areas; improve the quality of research products; develop human capital in the NBU; and improve the NBU public image within the country and abroad by bringing the research to the level of other central banks in Central and Eastern Europe. As in other central banks, the main objectives of research activities were:

i. Conducting research relevant to the formulation of recommendations in the main functional areas of the NBU (monetary policy, financial stability, banking supervision, etc.)

ii. Disseminating new knowledge and communicating research results through NBU publications, as well as organizing and participating in research conferences and seminars

iii. Supporting the decision-making process in the NBU through development of modern analytical and modeling instruments

Coordination and organization of the research function was assigned to the *Research Division* created in the Monetary Policy and Economic Analysis Department. For more effective transformation of the NBU research function and its adaptation to the best international standards, the technical assistance of experts of the Bank of Canada was involved.

The most important research function of central banks in many countries is to disseminate research results among academics and experts. For this purpose, a *series of meetings and research seminars* was organized in cooperation with leading research institutions, such as Kyiv School of Economics. The best graduates of economic universities were invited to work at the National Bank.

d) Open market operations, available financial instruments and crisis-containment toolkit

During 2014, the difficult economic situation continued to put pressure on the money market that demanded the National Bank of Ukraine use adequate flexibility and efficiency in conducting monetary policy and instituting complex anti-crisis regulation measures.

It should be noted that we had to reconsider the approaches introduced by our predecessors in the central bank. Specifically, prior to my arrival, special mechanisms were in place to support the liquidity of banks that had a significant outflow of deposits. Since February 26, 2014, the National Bank had introduced loans to Ukrainian banks to maintain their liquidity, according to which banks that had a significant decrease in deposits of legal entities and individuals were granted loans for up to 360 days (upon my arrival, this option was cancelled). During the period of this provision, the National Bank provided loans to banks totaling UAH 23.0 billion. Further, a number of amendments were made to the provision of stabilization loans to banks, which extended the list of collateral under a stabilization loan. Thus, in just four months, from March to June 2014, the outstanding amount of refinancing loans grew by UAH 29 billion (or a quarter of the total amount of loans provided during all previous years).

As it turned out, when providing these loans, the National Bank did not conduct a thorough analysis of the bank's assets and quality of collateral, which indicate if the bank is able to repay the loans. Some of the banks that received these loans were withdrawn from the market throughout the year, and loans issued to them have never been returned to the central bank.

This required from us to introduce a **new crisis-containment toolkit**, which, on the one hand, toughened the requirements for providing refinancing to banks, while on the other hand, made refinancing facilities more transparent and relying on more understandable standard bank refinancing instruments. This would also prevent banks from manipulating the collateral on refinancing loans.

Thus, *we have improved the standard instruments and mechanisms of liquidity management.* The duration of refinancing loans through tenders was reduced, and the list of collateral for refinancing was optimized by excluding illiquid financial instruments. Unfortunately, our local capital market that time was overloaded not by junk bonds and illiquid equities but by real fraudulent instruments used for criminal activities and money laundering. Therefore, we introduced very strict rules starting in December 2014, that only government bonds, NBU certificates of deposit, five foreign currencies (USD, EUR, GBP, CHF, JPY), and bonds of international financial organizations could be accepted as collateral for refinance.

Since September 2014, banks' access to overnight and term loans has been amended by providing access to banks that do not have overdue debt on loans from the central bank. Starting in December of that year, the maximum term of the loan was set at 90 days instead of one year.

Emergency Liquidity Assistance was a new instrument introduced to support the liquidity of solvent banks. Taking into account the low-performing previous practice of supporting banks' liquidity, in December 2016, the NBU introduced a new liquidity support facility (ELA)[10]. The new facility is applied in emergencies, when viable financial institutions have exhausted other sources of liquidity; the NBU provides loans to them exclusively to cover *temporary liquidity shortfalls.* Banks must use these funds to fulfill their obligations to depositors and other creditors, except those related to the bank. The *eligible collateral for*

---

[10] NBU Resolution #411 dated 14.12.2016

ELA loans includes securities guaranteed by the government, liquid immovable property (except objects under construction), property rights under loan agreements to legal entities and sole proprietors that are backed by mortgage collateral or other assets, i.e., mixed collateral; and property rights under loans to individuals with liabilities backed by mortgage collateral.

This mechanism replaced the stabilization loans of the NBU. ELA contracts must be concluded by banks *in advance of any problems*, in order to have quick access to NBU loans in case of an outflow of deposits. This is essentially an insurance mechanism that allows banks to be protected in the event of external shocks that provoke the withdrawal of deposits by the general population and businesses.

In order to mitigate credit risks, the NBU **changed its approach to determining the value of collateral** for loans and credit transactions. Now, the value of collateral is determined on market principles through fair value. With the same purpose, the NBU also straightened out the use of adjustment coefficients (discounts) applied to a fair value of collateral, depending on the characteristics of the securities provided as collateral. This rule, requiring additional collateral from a bank if the fair value of pledged assets drops below the set limit, also contributes to risk mitigation.

As a result, the amount of outstanding refinance loans for the period of my tenure not only did not grow but actually decreased substantially due to repayment of loans and cleaning up our banking sector from insolvent banks (see Chapter 8) *Thus, only solvent banks experiencing liquidity problems could be eligible for refinancing from the NBU. And only banks with high quality collateral were allowed to apply for refinance.*

Exhibit 15. The stock of refinance loans for solvent banks

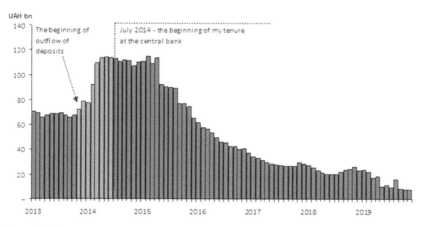

Source: NBU

The system of mandatory reserve requirements with the central bank's correspondent accounts has been changed. In the 1st half of 2014, with the aim of strengthening the flexibility of banks' liquidity management during the crisis period, the previous team at the National Bank reduced the reserve requirements for funds that banks must keep at the beginning of the operating day on the correspondent account with the National Bank of Ukraine on two occasions: on February 24th from 60% to 50% and on May 31, to 40% of the amount of mandatory reserves formed during the previous reporting period. Unfortunately, these measures only weakened the ability of the central bank to detect systemic liquidity problems in banks and respond promptly.

Therefore, to *unify procedures for the formation and maintenance of mandatory reserves* by banks, and adapt to the norms of European legislation, we introduced a new Regulation[11] on reserve requirements, which approved *new principles and approaches* for defining and forming mandatory reserves, namely:

- All banks have to keep mandatory reserves on their correspondent accounts with the National Bank of Ukraine

---

[11] NBU Resolution #806 dated 11.12.2014

- In order to alleviate a burden on banks when making mandatory payments to the budget at the beginning / end of the month and to make mandatory reserves requirements more predictable, the period that banks must maintain mandatory reserves was set from the 11th of each month to the 10th of the following month
- Reserve requirements were unified based on the duration of banks' liabilities: 6.5% for sight deposits and deposits payable on demand, and 3.0% for term deposits of individuals and legal entities in national and foreign currency
- In order to reduce the risk of non-compliance with these reserve requirements, banks were allowed to make allowance for funds kept in the Settlement Center (a bank institution entitled to provide services in securities settlement), in the amount of 100%, and to hold cash in the national currency at the amount of 50%.

Operations with Government bonds

Our active intervention to support the state budget, Naftogaz, and DGF via local QE, began to bear fruits. The structural surplus of liquidity on the interbank market was steadily increasing throughout 2014 and 2015 especially due to NBU support of the Deposit Guarantee Fund (which has to pay the guaranteed sum to the depositors of the banks withdrawn from the market) and increased motivation to use the domestic currency as a means to preserve value due to depreciation and inflation in early 2015.

Under these conditions, the NBU was affecting the interbank interest rates via liquidity withdrawal operations by placing NBU certificates of deposits. By the end of 2015, the outstanding value of CDs reached UAH 89.3 billion, representing a five-fold increase during a year. At the same time, the NBU withdrew liquidity by selling government bonds at the secondary market from its own portfolio. Since the government bond market held the lion's share of the entire securities market in Ukraine, it was also key to establishing and maintaining an efficient transmission of monetary policy.

Therefore, in July 2015, the national bank entered the secondary market with an offer of government bonds from its portfolio thereby contributing to building a yield curve up to 10 years. Sales of government bonds were held by public and anonymous trading on two stock exchanges, and all members of the exchange had access to these trades. In total, 119 contracts were concluded at 20 to 22.5% per year. Trading was active enough that the amount of t-bonds sold was substantial: by the end of 2015, government bonds of UAH 1.8 billion had been sold.

In December 2015, the NBU also started auctions of government bonds. Five auctions of government bonds were held that month, four of which were effective. The National Bank carried out the purchase and sale transactions of government bonds through the mechanism of bilateral quotations. In January 2016, the NBU stopped selling bonds from its portfolio as the Ministry of Finance went back to the market with a new line-up of t-bonds.

These developments in the monetary market contributed to meeting the quantitative efficiency criteria on net domestic assets and the indicative target of the monetary base at the end of 2015, established under the IMF Extended Fund Facility Program (EFF), with a considerable margin.

Corresponding link with a global custodian (Clearstream)

The well-known characteristic feature of many emerging markets (known in economic literature as *'original sin'*), is their inability to borrow abroad in local currency. High borrowing in FX currency carries a risk of financial and economic crises if external conditions deteriorate. In the case of Ukraine, exposure to currency risk was exacerbated by high internal dollarization, with 50% + nominated in foreign currency.

Therefore, we knew **extension of the local currency bond market was a logical step towards de-dollarization**, and began with the transition to a flexible exchange rate in 2015. One important decision was to establish *corresponding relations with the global securities depository*. This theoretically should have made it easier for foreign investors to access the domestic securities market, increasing its liquidity and lowering the cost of borrowing for the government.

Many foreign investors, however, did not attempt to invest in Ukrainian bonds, as investment was accompanied by significant bureaucratic red tape, the need to open an account with a local bank, and an account in securities at a local depository. Given the insignificant volumes of the Ukrainian securities market, the lion's share of which was transactions with government bonds, investors simply did not notice our market.

Thus, beginning in 2017, we started to work with the Ministry of Finance on establishing a so-called 'link' with an international custodian, which would allow non-residents to invest in Ukrainian securities in the local currency. The corresponding relations agreement for the further opening of a securities account at the NBU Depository between one of the two European international depositaries Clearstream, a member of the Deutsche Börse Group, and the National Bank was signed on March 13, 2019. The signing of the agreement was preceded by lengthy negotiations and due diligence from Clearstream.

Establishing a link with Clearstream simplified foreign investors' access to the Ukrainian securities market, specifically, government debt bonds in UAH. Transactions with t-bonds in UAH were now settled through the ICSD system, which reduces the transaction and time costs of international investors. In addition, if any non-resident buys Ukrainian bonds through Clearstream, these securities can be traded abroad for foreign currency.

At the same time, the signing of the agreement with Clearstream has increased the attractiveness and liquidity of the Ukrainian securities market. The Ukrainian Government has benefited from expanding the range of sources of long-term financing, reducing the cost of debt and improving the currency structure of public debt thanks to the extension of demand for securities denominated in UAH.

An indication of the attractiveness of Ukrainian local financial instruments was the **rapid increase in non-resident investment in**

government bonds, which was facilitated by opening a link between the depository of the NBU and the global depository, Clearstream. The growth of non-residents' investments in local currency government bonds allowed Ukraine's government to gradually increase the share of LCY-denominated debt, which will increase the sustainability of public finances. I hope that modernization of the stock exchange and clearing infrastructure in the near future will allow expanding the list of financial instruments available to both external and domestic investors, and will increase the depth of the local securities market.

e) FCY reserves management, FX SWAPS

A basic premise for the stability of the financial market in any country whose currency is not freely convertible is an adequate amount of international reserves. For Ukraine, which continued to experience difficulties in transitioning to a flexible exchange rate, this was especially true. The decrease in the absolute level of reserves, which took place against the backdrop of the 'triple' crisis in Ukraine in 2014-2015, only increased the acuteness of the quality of their management.

Analyzing the National Bank's processes for managing international reserves at the time of my arrival showed a number of shortcomings and the *lack of necessary controls*, which, as demonstrated by test calculations, led in some cases to a significant deviation of the actual terms of transactions from optimal market terms and, consequently, to implied losses from carrying out these transactions.

One such episode was our discovery in 2014 of a significant share in AUD-nominated assets in the structure of the central bank's FX reserves, while the share of USD-denominated assets was significantly below the adequate level. Regardless of the underlying reasons that led to the AUD presence in the NBU portfolio, from an investment point of view, it was unprofitable for the National Bank. Moreover, the presence of AUD was not substantiated either from the macroeconomic point of view (based on the structure of foreign currency settlements on current account operations and the structure of Ukraine's foreign debt) or from the point of view of international benchmarks of peer countries. We subsequently brought the NBU portfolio to the optimal structure, even though it led to a negative financial result for individual positions that underwent recalibration – another important lesson for the future.

This episode forced us to reconsider our approaches to formation of the NBU assets portfolio, as well as to substantially change the procedure for risk assessment and decision-making in this area.

With the aim of eliminating all possibilities for both abuse and for the negligent management of international reserves of the central bank, we introduced a **new independent inspection process to compare price terms of transactions with international reserves** to ensure they are adequate to market conditions. We also created a new framework of controls over the reserve management process, including verification of risk-to-return on investment positions.

The market conformity check was launched to verify that each transaction was carried out at fair value reflecting objective market conditions at the time of the transaction. Accordingly, the price of the transaction was compared with market prices, benchmarks or estimated price (fair value). The general rule was to prohibit operations on terms that did not match the market, though exceptions were possible in individual cases where there were objective reasons, duly documented, for deviating from market conditions.

For management of FX reserves, the inspection was conducted in cases of:

- money market operations (deposits, repo)
- securities transactions (bonds)
- spot currency transactions
- operations with valuable metals (gold)
- derivative transactions (interest rate futures, currency swaps, currency forward)

However, exceptions were granted for:

- Portfolio operations under external control (e.g., RAMP)
- operations with SDR
- transactions with central banks and governments of other countries, if executed in accordance with bilateral agreements (e.g. currency swaps)
- operations with the IMF
- operations in which the NBU is a market maker

According to the updated **International Reserves Management Strategy**, we introduced risk appetite categories and minimum yield requirements for individual categories of foreign exchange reserves, and improved our system for managing the credit risk of international reserves through:

- introducing a system of credit limits
- changing the methodology for calculating credit limits
- changing the method of utilization of credit limits
- streamlining the process of opening, reviewing (including redistribution) and closing credit limits;
- streamlining the control of credit limits

Within the updated process, the Risk Management Department became a "second pair of eyes" to monitor the compliance of the trading desk with the above-set limits, agree on revisions, as well as to monitor the integral indicator of market risks and indicators of the weighted average modified duration of the bond portfolio under NBU management.

This allowed us to build a credit limit monitoring system, with the first level of control being the Open Market Operations Department, which exercised control before and during the transaction; with the second level of control being the Risk Management Department (providing control after the transaction); and with the third level being the Internal Audit Department, which conducted periodic evaluation of the effectiveness of the control process.

The function of strategic management of the credit limit system was assigned to the asset and liabilities management committee.

Although this worked for Ukraine, *management of the reserves of the central bank could have been outsourced* to such organizations as World Bank or BIS with similar success. NBU partially used the Reserves Advisory & Management Partnership (RAMP), a program developed by the World Bank Treasury for central bank reserves management. For small open economies, I believe it is a good solution to outsource the management of the long-term leg of FCY reserves. I do not believe that it is possible to get the same high-quality expertise and efficiency at the local level. But via access to World Bank experts and their ability to solve advanced problems, we were able to achieve more efficient management of public assets. Due to the development of technology and management techniques, the convergence of profitability levels for various financial instruments, as well as the conservative investment strategy of central banks, this may well be appropriate for many developing countries.

FX SWAPS

Emerging economies all over the world continue to be highly sensitive to both regional and global shocks. Due to the acceleration of anti-globalization movements, uncertainty in global financial world grew even more. Therefore, small open economies need to pay close attention to global and regional economic developments in their policy planning, and deploy a diverse set of available tools in managing risks to financial stability.

Since FX reserves serve as a buffer for the economy, it is important to have sufficient amount of FX readily available to restore market balance. During Ukraine's crisis, we extensively used **bilateral swap agreements** to do so.

As governor, I made one of the biggest swap agreements in history in early 2015. It was a deal with Public Bank of China in Yuan for the equivalent of USD 2.6 billion (CNY 15 billion). The funds received under the agreement could be used to finance trade and direct investment between the two countries.

In September 2015, our biggest friends from Riksbank also concluded a swap agreement with the Ukrainian central bank, for the equivalent of EUR 500 million.

I also thank Marek Belka, then Governor of the NBP, for his support in arranging a swap deal in December 2015 between the Polish Central Bank and the National Bank of Ukraine in PLZ for the equivalent of EUR 1 billion.

In my view, a swap is a highly efficient mechanism allowing central banks to bilaterally support each other. Currency swap arrangements help to reduce the pressure on the exchange rate and stabilize the domestic FX market as well as limit the risk of shocks, which can have a negative impact on the economic situation of the entire region. In the case of Ukraine, we also used swap agreements for trade-finance acceleration.

f) Market communications

Timely and proper communication is the key to resolving many challenges of central banks. Current global trends associated with increased political pressure on independent financial regulators are vivid evidence that the *"never explain, never excuse" policy no longer works*, and in fact, can even work against central banks.

Central banks should become easier to understand. Their target audience should not be limited solely to financiers and industry experts. Central bank decisions must also be well explained to the end-consumer of financial services. Otherwise, if banks do not explain their decisions themselves, someone else will, and probably not always in the bank's favor.

The role of communications is important even under conditions of "business as usual", but amidst a full-scale crisis, the importance of good communications increases exponentially. The strongest pressure on the National Bank was observed in 2014–2015, when half of all banks in the country were withdrawn from the market, many of which kept citizens 'savings and business' accounts. The transition to a flexible exchange rate also led to tectonic shifts in the mindset of the population and business, who had been used to a fixed rate policy for two decades.

If we did not explain the reasons why we were taking certain actions, we could have easily bumped into a wall of confrontation that would have halted further progress in reform. In the case of Ukraine, this was especially true in light of the fact that the ownership of all major TV channels in the country belonged to local tycoons who were the beneficial owners of banks that went bankrupt. Thus, fake news about the central bank and its leadership gained significant dissemination, growing in the fertile soil of mass misunderstanding of what was going on.

During the tenure of our team at the National Bank, both internal and external communications were tuned up. As a result, every employee of the National Bank became an ambassador of the institution outside its walls, while in external communications, our task was to fill gaps in external stakeholders' understanding of the central bank policy objectives and its decisions.

It is no exaggeration to say we put a strategic value on our communications, which we made client-oriented, meaning that we used the most convenient and accessible channels to deliver our messages to different target audiences. We expanded the circle of the target audience, as well as the list of communication channels including: a new website, round tables with experts and journalists, Facebook, Twitter, Instagram, as well as maximum disclosure of data on banks, monetary and foreign exchange markets.

Moreover, eventually we came to the conclusion that even basic *financial literacy* needs to be improved not only amongst the general population, but also among many 'recognized' financial experts. Perhaps too many developed countries this may sound incredible, but we had to explain such basic concepts as why banks must have a transparent ownership structure, comply with global AML rules, and have a positive value of capital, as well as what foreign exchange risks are and why diversification and hedging are needed.

For many years, even decades, nobody was doing this in Ukraine. Thus, an illusion of stability was created, periodically interrupted by crises, in which banking "dummies" were functioning mousy, hovering money from the population and crediting the business of the bank's owner, with the National Bank assigned the role of a 'shadow' arbiter who, if necessary, supported non-viable banks with refinancing loans, without bothering about subsequent return of the loans.

For us, it was obvious from the beginning that *openness and dialogue with partners were the only ways to strengthen confidence, overcome populism and preserve the Bank's independence* in the face of the economic and financial crisis, the reform of the banking sector, and the radical internal transformation of the institution. To that end, we sought to find a common language not only with narrow expert and professional audiences, but also with the general public. After all, the targeting of communication is an important prerequisite for its effectiveness. To do this, we studied the needs of all our target audiences and constructed a specific dialogue with each target audience in a language understandable to it and on topics of its interest.

I am convinced that transparency, honesty, and personal and institutional integrity were our most important ammunition in the war against fake news. Once data are disclosed and publicly available, everyone can be independent in own judgments when deciding what is right or wrong, true or false.

I am proud that during the tenure of our team, the National Bank became transparent and understandable to society. The results of our efforts have been noted at the international level. The 2016 Annual

Report of the National Bank of Ukraine received the bronze award in a worldwide annual report competition, the ARC Awards.

Further, the **National Bank of Ukraine was recognized as the most transparent bank in the world in 2018 Central Banking Awards**. In previous years, the Central Banking Transparency Award has been awarded to central banks of countries such as Sweden, the Czech Republic, Israel, and Ireland.

Ukraine's National Bank began publishing a forecast of the key interest rate under the quarterly macroeconomic forecast in 2019. Publication of the key interest rate forecast was part of the evolutionary process of increasing the transparency of monetary policy for inflation targeting central banks. This enhances the clarity and predictability of monetary policy for market participants, and, therefore, makes it more effective.

…

Since 2017 Ukraine's acute phase of crisis has passed. The dynamics of the main macroeconomic indicators, as well as the key indicators of Program 2020, clearly show that the Ukrainian economy has come out of its 2014-2016 dive. **Macroeconomic stabilization was facilitated by the reorientation of monetary policy to inflation targeting, and by transition to a floating exchange rate regime**, as well as a prudent fiscal policy, which led to a significant reduction of the public and quasi-public deficit, a gradual reduction of public debt level and the implementation of medium-term budget planning.

Due to the macro-financial stabilization, the country's economic recovery was restored: GDP is now steadily growing with inflation following the sustainable disinflationary trend. Finally, in 2019, inflation slowed to 4.1%, thereby reaching the medium-term inflation target of 5% ± 1 pp declared by the NBU in 2015. Lowering inflation to the target was the result of a consistent monetary policy by the National Bank aimed at achieving price stability in combination with the sound fiscal policy of the Government.

Ukraine's successful disinflation was also the result of **two major reforms**: a *flexible exchange rate* that allowed the local currency to appreciate thus contributing to lower import prices, and *FX liberalization* that stimulated an inflow of foreign investment into the country. This means the exchange rate in Ukraine is no longer susceptible to seasonality based on behavioural patterns of economic agents as was the case in previous years.

Due to the favourable situation on the foreign exchange market and the steady inflow of foreign capital, primarily into the government debt, Ukraine's international reserves increased to US$26.3 billion as of February 2020, a seven-year high with net international reserves (net of borrowing from the IMF) reaching USD 16.8 billion.

Exhibit 16. The dynamics of international reserves, 2004-2020

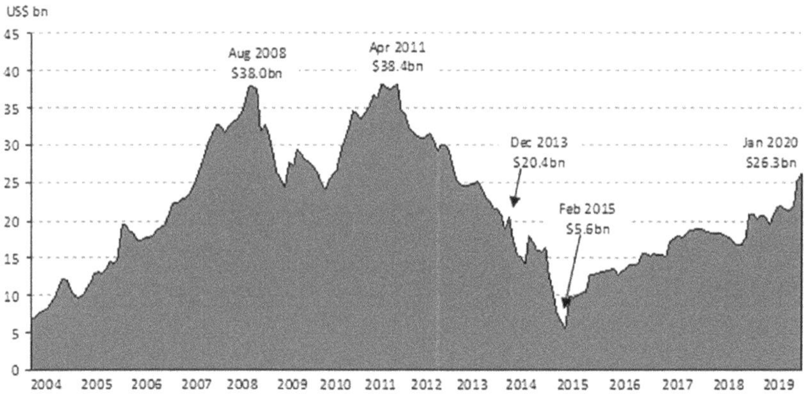

Source: NBU

Our current level of international reserves is $ 6 billion, or 29% higher than the pre-crisis level of late 2013. Given the rocky road of reforms and recalling the exhausted war chest of reserves at the beginning of my tenure at the central bank, this is a huge symbolic indicator. Adequacy of international reserves provided by a functioning economy, a stable inflow of export proceeds, and a return of foreign currency to banks are all important elements in renewing confidence in the country by both external and internal investors.

Of course a long way is still ahead in order to ensure sustainable price stability in Ukraine within the inflation targeting framework, including actions aimed at boosting public support with regard to achieving price stability, enhancing the role of the inflation target as a nominal anchor, further upgrading the monetary policy toolkit, strengthening of analytical support for monetary policy decision-making, increasing the transparency of monetary policy and improving communications with the general public in order to effectively manage economic agents' expectations. However, it is already clear that strong efforts at the beginning of the transformation process have produced tangible results for the society, which makes me confident that the reforms we launched in 2014 have been successfully brought to completion.

CHAPTER 7

FX liberalization and BEPS implementation

U NSURPRISINGLY SINCE MY team and I came to the National Bank from the private sector, we initially had a liberal and pro-market agenda of reforms in the banking and monetary sector. But, unfortunately, macroeconomic risks, and most of all, the war in 2014-2015, not only deterred us from starting an immediate FX liberalization, but also forced the central bank to introduce unpopular administrative restrictions (as described in the last chapter). Given the unreformed banking system, the inability of the central bank to exercise controlling functions, and the lack of anti-money laundering controls, we had to stop panic and unproductive outflow of capital through fictitious FX transactions. It could not be done with means other than drastic administrative restrictions.

Meanwhile, *currency liberalization was one of the most eagerly awaited reforms in Ukraine since its independence.* The 1993 Decree on FX Regulation forced Ukraine's FX market into the shape of a narrow-necked bottle for 25 years. There were practically no restrictions for inflows (if bureaucratic aspects were not taken into account), but any outflow of capital from the country was significantly complicated. At the stage of transformation from planned to market economy in early 1990s, this approach might have been justified. However, foreign investments were essential for further development of the economy, and to attract them, the two-way flow of capital was essential.

In the 10 years before I came to the central bank, a number of attempts were made to ease FX regulation, but they were unsuccessful both due to legislative restrictions (for example, the central bank was obliged by law to provide a license for each FX transaction and to register every loan from non-residents) and also to the lack of political will. For 25 years, the central bank pretended to control capital flows, while business and citizens pretended to comply with the requirements of the regulator. However, the pretence did not mask the reality that there were 1000+1 ways to get around the restrictions, including through the transfer pricing mechanism, which has been successfully used by high net wealth individuals and large corporates.

After stabilizing macroeconomic conditions, the need for tough administrative restrictions on FX transactions had mitigated, and after almost two years of maintaining anti-crisis measures, 2016 was the year of the long-awaited gradual liberalization of currency regulation. In particular, we eased the requirement for mandatory sale of foreign exchange earnings, extended the deadline for payments on export and import of goods, exempted foreign investments in Ukraine from the mandatory sale of FX, and allowed repatriation of dividends accrued to foreign investors for 2014 through 2015.

The speed of our FX liberalization depended, first of all, on the presence of *favourable market preconditions and maintaining macro stability*. We could not let our actions provoke pressure on the hryvnia.

I believe that **diligence, consistency, and flexibility are extremely important in the process of currency liberalization.** Despite a number of positive effects, haste in implementation can lead to macroeconomic complications associated with potential capital inflows and outflows. Thus, during a spike of FX inflows, the national economy may not be able to absorb significant volumes of foreign currency, which may lead to overheating of the economy with asset price "bubbles", and to an appreciation of the national currency (with the corresponding worsening of the current account balance). Indeed, such a situation took place in pre-crisis Ukraine (in 2008) with consequences that we are still trying to resolve today (taking into account the legacy of NPLs in the balance sheets of banks). On the other hand, an outflow of capital and the resulting excessive demand for foreign currency may contain significant risks to price and financial stability.

At the same time, **it is necessary to minimize the risks of reverse**. Thus, decisions towards the alleviation of foreign exchange restrictions should be clearly verified and based on the availability of favourable macro-financial conditions. False or premature mitigation, which might cause unexpected results that could lead to a return to previous (or even tougher) constraints, is unacceptable, since it will cast doubt on the central bank's credibility. And without confidence in the policy of the central bank, there is no way to stabilize the market.

We understood perfectly well that, as in the case of a fixed exchange rate, the regular use of (or the availability of) capital controls would lead to a regulator's dependence on these instruments, and a delay in the development of market instruments and capital flow management tools. That is why *restrictive measures should be short-term* (usually no more than a year), rather than serving as an element of long-term stability in the financial market.

The speed of FX liberalization should be deliberate. International experience has shown that excessively rapid liberalization does not contribute to the rapid recovery of macroeconomic equilibrium, but rather exacerbates already existing structural weaknesses, thus leading to a crisis (e.g., Iceland 2008, Thailand 1997-1998, and Mexico 1994-1997). Eastern European countries – the Czech Republic, Poland, and Estonia – also encountered a number of difficulties in the process of liberalization. However, they benefited from having a clear path to joining the European Union and the corresponding macro-financial support from the EU, which Ukraine could not count on.

The central bank should also take into account the risks of excessively rapid liberalization, which are associated with a higher probability of financial shocks, including speculative attacks due to the maintenance of a significant interest rate differential on assets in local and foreign currencies on top of high investment risks in an emerging economy like Ukraine.

a) Conceptual issues of FX Liberalization in Ukraine

Thus in 2016, the National Bank presented the concept of a **new liberal model of currency regulation**, taking into account relevant international experience.

According to the concept, the central bank followed the **gradual path of FX liberalization in several sequential stages**:

- At the initial stage, restrictions were eased on export-import operations and foreign direct investment aimed at increasing the export potential of the country
- In the second stage, portfolio investments and debt capital flows were liberalized
- At the last stage, all remaining restrictions and capital control for private individuals were eliminated

This approach was based on understanding that the liberalization of FX regulation must not lead to a breakdown of the still-fragile stability of the financial system. Accordingly, the speed of liberalization was **not time-based, but condition-based**.

The prerequisites for further easing steps, in particular, include:

- An increase of international reserves to a specified level
- Deceleration of inflation according to the forecast
- Equilibrium in the FX market
- A stable banking sector, confirmed by regular monitoring and stress tests

Given this flexible logic, restrictions were gradually lifted, including on the withdrawal of FX cash from bank accounts, payment of dividends to foreign investors, mandatory sale of FX earnings and FX purchase by banks, the repatriation of FX earnings and advance payments under import contracts, etc. As well, we simplified the procedures for purchasing foreign currency in the interbank market and for obtaining licenses for investment abroad.

Specifically, at the request of the National Council for Reforms, the National Bank introduced a **simplified procedure for licensing individuals' transactions** for depositing or investing abroad. Starting in February 2017, transfer of funds abroad provided through an individual license were no longer subject to licensing and could be carried out without restrictions (unlike other FX transactions with sources of origin outside Ukraine, in particular, wages, pensions, dividends received or inheritance). Moreover, to simplify the process of obtaining FX licenses, in July 2017, we introduced electronic licenses for individual investments abroad (in the amount of up to USD 50k in equivalent per person during one calendar year). This made it possible to automatically obtain a license from the central bank on the day of the operation without the need for prior submission of documents for approval. At the same time, banks were responsible for checking documents and complying with AML and KYC rules.

It is interesting to note that with regard to lifting restrictions, we were in many ways more resolute and liberal than the IMF experts working with our country. Under the IMF program, all actions to remove temporary restrictions were agreed with the Fund. For each measure, we provided our calculations on the projected effect of the liberalization on certain operations. In most cases, the Fund agreed with our proposed measures. Nevertheless, in some instances, we found ourselves in cognitive dissonance, explaining to the Fund, which always stood for free movement of capital, about the timeliness of certain relaxation in currency regulation.

Finally, **a new model of currency regulation was implemented via a new Currency Act**, which was developed by the National Bank with the participation of experts from the European Commission and was adopted by the Parliament in mid-2018. The new Law replaced the 1993 Decree of the Cabinet of Ministers of Ukraine "On the system of currency regulation and currency control", and also numerous regulatory acts of the central bank. It provided a single framework that determined the basic principles of currency regulation in the country. At the same time, specific norms were brought to the level of bylaws.

As a result, **currency regulation in Ukraine became transparent, simple, and understandable for the population, for businesses and for banks.** The new legislation, which was in line with legislation of the European Union, allowed the National Bank to respond more quickly and efficiently to changes in the balance-of-payments and to market conditions, and to focus on transparent financial monitoring.

The NBU switched from total currency control over each operation to currency supervision, built on the principle of "more risks - more attention; less risk - less attention." This involved a more flexible and transparent procedure for determining the impact of violations of FX regulations detected by National Bank inspections.

However, the new Currency Act allowed us to maintain a number of capital controls, which were gradually lifted later on, but which provided that the duration of new safeguard measures cannot exceed six months, and their entry into force will take place only after being approved by the Financial Stability Board.

To date, the central bank has removed all limits on repatriation of dividends; abolished the deadlines for payments for a number of export-import transactions; simplified the procedure for obtaining foreign currency licenses for individual market participants; allowed banks to provide short-term hryvnia financing for non-residents to purchase Ukrainian government bonds; and abolished the mandatory sale of foreign exchange earnings by businesses.

Currency liberalization will continue, with all currency restrictions gradually lifted in accordance with the pace of improvement of macroeconomic conditions in Ukraine, and with implementation of new tax legislation aimed at counteracting tax evasion and profit shifting, as elaborated in the next section.

b) BEPS Action Plan implementation

As I have repeatedly noted, while the Ukrainian economy had unique characteristics, at the same time, Ukraine is quite characteristic of many developing and even developed countries. The point is that **many cross-border transactions are performed via low-tax jurisdictions**. This issue is regulated by effective control over the transfer pricing rules in most developed countries, but in the case of many developing countries, such as Ukraine, transfer pricing controls are not sufficiently developed, allowing capital to uncontrollably flow out of the country, exposing fiscal and macroeconomic weaknesses.

With the introduction of FX restrictions to prevent an outflow of capital, we faced a rather interesting situation. At the time, we were scrutinizing all import contracts to ensure they were not fictitious. Then, in February 2015, we introduced mandatory letters of credit for import transactions and gathered leading oil traders and bankers at the National Bank in order to explain how to use them. Concurrently, we found that the operations of most of the largest oil traders that had a transparent retail distribution fell into the filter of suspicious financial monitoring transactions, since they were purchasing fuel oils through offshore companies with accounts in Baltic banks. Our meeting with the traders and bankers contributed to improving our understanding of the specifics of the local fuel market and allowed us to restore business activity.

A more generalizable example of the problem comes from balance-of-payments data on transactions of residents of Ukraine with non-residents. For example, in 2018, only three countries, with preferential tax regimes for foreign companies -- Cyprus, the British Virgin Islands and the Netherlands-- represented almost *two thirds of all non-guaranteed long-term investments and almost half of all foreign direct investment in Ukraine.* Fully *80% of dividends* ($2.6 out of $3.4 billion) were transferred from Ukraine to non-resident investors in Cyprus and the Netherlands in 2018.

Exhibit 17. Total amount of non-guaranteed long-term loans of non-financial sector, US$bn, as of 01/04/2019

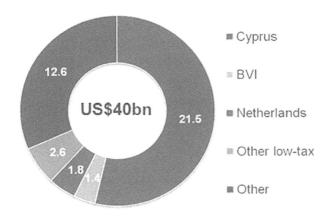

Source: NBU

Exhibit 18. Dividends paid to non-residents in 2018, US$bn (Outer circle – direct investments; inner circle – portfolio investments)

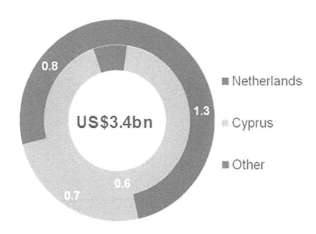

Source: NBU

No less startling was data on current operations: for 2018, the value of goods shipped from Ukraine to countries on the list of low-tax jurisdictions specified by the Cabinet of Ministers of Ukraine, as well as the Netherlands and Switzerland, which had preferential taxation for companies not active in the territory of these countries was USD

5.3 billion (11.2% of total exports). However, export revenues that came to Ukraine from these countries amounted to almost USD 25 billion (52.6% of total exports). The difference was almost USD 20 billion! A similar situation occurred in import operations -- the difference between the volume of physical imports and import payments to low-tax jurisdictions amounted to more than USD 10 billion in 2018. Since the vast majority of transactions with these countries presumably was carried out with related (affiliated) parties, they should have been subject to transfer pricing rules, which had to be improved.

Exhibit 19. Volumes of export-import transactions of Ukraine in 2018, US$bn

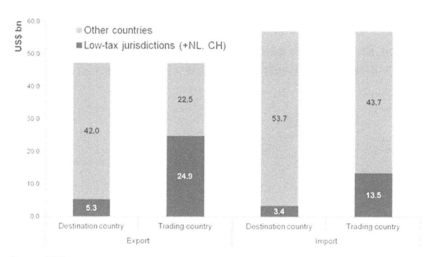

Source: NBU

The rules developed by the National Bank for *assessing the riskiness and veracity of operations with non-residents by banks* essentially assigned banks to control transfer pricing rules, which inevitably caused dissatisfaction on the part of banks and their customers. But given the inability of public institutions in charge of tax control to fulfil their duties, the independent central bank was forced to assume this *extrinsic role*. But the question remained: what should we do if a transaction was legal from an AML perception, but its real purpose was to reduce the taxable base?

Recalling our experience in the 2014-2015 crisis, when we had to check all foreign trade contracts for compliance with market conditions before allowing any company to buy FX, I note that we would not have done so if effective transfer pricing rules and controls were in place. Our financial monitoring unit stopped hundreds of contracts for the purchase of foreign currency related to transactions with fake securities and clear signs of fictitious risky reinsurance schemes with non-residents. In 2018, Ukraine's Stock Exchange Commission stated that in the previous three years, Ukraine had stopped the circulation of fake securities of UAH 1 trillion (circa USD 40 billion). These fake securities were being used to withdraw money from banks, including transferring them abroad, under various schemes, that in the essence followed the same pattern: banks bought junk securities in exchange for liquid assets and after the bank became insolvent, all that remained of the assets of such banks to compensate its creditors and savers were fake securities, not worth a single cent!

That is why one of the key prerequisites for a full-fledged transition to a liberal model of currency regulation should have been an effective tax regulation.

The new Law on Currency on one hand paved the way to simplify FX regulation but for deeper FX liberalization, implementation of specific actions under the OECD's *Anti-BEPS Plan and Ukraine joining the OECD's Common Reporting Standard (CRS)* regarding automatic exchange of financial information were required.

Exhibit 20. Implementation of OECD's Base Erosion and Profit-Shifting Action Plan as the necessary prerequisite for further easing of FX restrictions in Ukraine

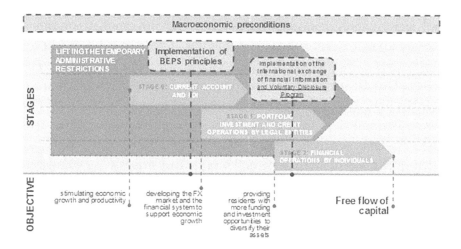

We proposed introducing **eight of the most critical and urgent actions** out of the 15 actions recommended by the Organization for Economic Co-operation and Development to counteract the erosion of tax base and shifting profits abroad (the so-called BEPS Action Plan). In 2016, the concept of the BEPS Action Plan implementation in Ukraine was presented to the National Council for Reforms, and the draft law needed for its implementation was prepared by a joint working group of the National Bank and the Ministry of Finance with the involvement of the best tax consultants from the Big 4 companies in Ukraine.

The *main actions* to counter BEPS activity envisaged by the draft law were:

- **Action 3: Implementing taxation of Controlled Foreign Companies.** Residents of Ukraine (individuals) will pay in Ukraine a tax on retained earnings of foreign companies that they own or control. Introduction of mandatory disclosure of participation (control) in CFCs.

- **Action 4: Limiting the accounting for expenses related to financial transactions with related parties** (thin capitalization rules).
- **Action 6: Preventing abuses in the application of double taxation treaties.**
- **Action 7: Preventing the artificial avoidance of permanent establishment status.**
- **Actions 8-10: Strengthening of transfer pricing rules.**
- **Action 13: Introducing country-by-country reporting by multinational companies.** For Ukrainian holdings, the minimum threshold for submitting documentation was lowered to EUR 50 million of annual turnover (from EUR 750 million under the OECD model framework).

The draft law also introduced general **anti-abuse rules for non-residents** (General Anti-Abuse Rules or GAAR) in connection with the application of double taxation treaties, and detailed the rules for handling cases under the **Mutual Agreement Procedures** (MAP).

The draft law on BEPS underwent review and was supported by the OECD, the World Bank, and the IMF.

The high-level legislation allowing *implementation of Common Reporting Standard (CRS) for automatic exchange of financial information* was coupled within one law with requirements for implementation of *FATCA*. Its implementation would allow Ukraine to join the international community of over 100 countries that are already sharing financial information with each other.

Last but not least, we drafted language to be included in the package of FX liberalization regarding *voluntary disclosure of individuals' assets*. This law was aimed at creating a legal basis for taxpayers to file a one-time declaration for all categories of assets (in Ukraine and abroad), from which no taxes had been previously paid. Under the voluntary disclosure program, taxpayers would be guaranteed exemption from criminal and administrative liability for violation of tax laws; though such a release did not extend to assets obtained in a criminal way or with the commission of corrupt acts. The standard tax rate would be applied to the declared assets. The effectiveness of voluntary disclosure was supported by the introduction of indirect methods for controlling tax obligations, and access of the tax authority to banking information and joining an international tax information exchange.

It is worth noting that in January 2017, Ukraine joined the *Inclusive Framework on BEPS*, confirming its commitment to implement the BEPS Minimum Action Plan (Actions 5, 6, 13, 14). *The Multilateral Convention* to Implement Tax-Treaty Related Measures to Prevent BEPS (MLI), which allowed us to implement actions 6 and 14 of the minimum package was signed by the Minister of Finance in July 2018, and ratified by Parliament in February 2019. It became effective in December 2019 and allowed Ukraine to amend most of international double taxation treaties in order to avoid transfer of Ukrainian capital to low-tax jurisdictions.

Given the global competition between countries involving competition between governments for stimulating local economic activity by lowering tax rates and limited fiscal space in most emerging economies, *the only way for us to remain competitive and successful was to expand the tax base by introducing the best world standards in the field of taxation.*

The laws on implementation of FATCA and Common Reporting Standard were adopted by the Ukrainian Parliament in December 2019 and a law on BEPS in January 2020. Further implementation of the package on the BEPS Action Plan in Ukraine will contribute to a true currency and tax revolution in our country, and will allow not only to move to a new, more liberal, stage of development of the financial system, but also to ensure the creation of equal and fair rules of the game for all market participants.

CHAPTER 8

The second priority: Cleaning up the banking sector

MASSIVE LENDING TO related parties. Opaque ownership structures with the real owners hiding behind a line-up of nominal directors. Window-dressing of financial reports. Fake correspondent accounts at foreign banks. Politically motivated lending by state-owned banks, resulting in large losses and a subsequent massive injection of public funds. Money laundering as a bank's business model. Shareholders and management walking away from failed banks with clients' money, escaping charges for driving clients to bankruptcy...

Sounds like a horror movie? Impossible in real life?

Wrong. It was a common way of doing financial business in Ukraine before 2014. We called it 'the oligarchic banking model': most of the banks (except foreign- and state-owned ones) belonged to local oligarchic groups, which used them primarily as vehicles to finance their activities, effectively through the banks' retail deposits, against a background of reckless regulatory forbearance.

Before going further, it is useful to recall that our reform of the banking system was divided into three stages: cleaning, reloading and sustainable development. But the paradox of the situation is that essentially there was no cleaning of the banks, because the institutions we withdrew from the market were essentially not banks. They had no real assets, no capital, no normal credit procedures, no risk management. There was nothing there! We used to call them "laundries", "zombies" and "hoovers".

For example, one of the largest banks had 100% of its corporate credit portfolio invested in the businesses of shareholders without any collateral; another two banks that belonged to one beneficiary had 64% and 96% of insider loans with no plan for repayment. This is how inflated business empires were built in Ukraine. The rest of these so-called "banks" had nothing but fictitious bonds and equities in their portfolios.

Those banks extensively used the practice of ever-greening loans provided to "zombie" firms, many of which were affiliated with the banks' owners, thereby crowding out funding for more productive companies and distorting the monetary transmission mechanism.

I always wondered when pseudo-experts, who knew nothing about banking, lament that liquidated banks should have been bailed out by the state (i.e., with taxpayers' money) knew that such banks had neither assets nor capital, and were used by their owners to siphon billions of dollars to their offshore accounts.

The burden of the past

From 2014 to 2015, Ukraine's economy and banking sector experienced the deepest crisis since the country's independence in 1991. The crisis was caused by structural imbalances that had been building up over decades, a lack of adequate regulation and efficient supervision, as well as the military conflict and loss of territorial integrity.

Looking back to mid-2014, the challenges were enormous and required a comprehensive approach. Our team had to start the task with the thankless process of banking sector clean-up. Many institutions did not perform as classic financial intermediaries. Some were identified as being involved in illegal operations or serving as funding vehicles for shareholders' businesses. Our position was firm: Those banks that did not address properly the NBU's requirements would be withdrawn from the market.

During 2014 to 2017, 90 banks (approximately one half of the total, representing about one-third of the sector's assets) were sent into receivership due to insolvency, involvement in money-laundering activities, or non-transparent ownership structures. In terms of market impact, our experience is unique and unprecedented in the history of global banking supervision. While imperative, the clean-up triggered a temporary loss of confidence in the banking system. Nevertheless, the painful process has reshaped the Ukrainian banking system. Only **solvent, fully transparent banks now have a place in our market.**

The 90 banks that were withdrawn from the market from 2014 through 1Q2017, comprised:

- 16 due to the opaque structure and unsatisfactory business reputation of the owners
- 3 by self-liquidation on the decision of the owners
- 4 due to annexation of Crimea and military conflict on the East
- 10 due to violation of legislation in the field of financial monitoring
- 57 due to violation of prudential norms, including capital requirements, poor financial conditions, low quality of assets, etc.

Exhibit 21. Number of banks withdrawn from the market in 2014-1Q2017

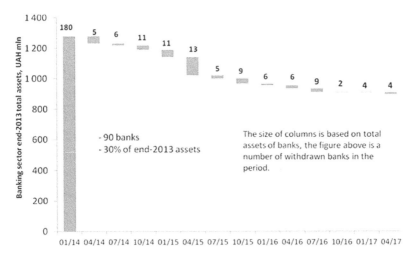

Source: NBU

Based on the law adopted in early 2015 regarding the responsibility of bank owners and related parties, thousands of cases were forwarded to law enforcement agencies by the NBU and the DGF from 2015 to2019. Unfortunately, in zero cases were the owners of insolvent banks convicted.

Improving the operation of the Deposit Guarantee Fund was yet another major challenge related to the clean-up process. We managed to improve legislation and strengthen the institutional framework in order to streamline bank insolvency and liquidation procedures, and to facilitate repayment of retail deposits.

Initially, our focus was priorities included in the IMF Stand-by Agreement:

- Continuing to provide liquidity to solvent banks in need (including introduction of the new mechanism of supporting liquidity)
- Assessing bank resilience through an independent asset quality review (AQR) for 35 banks (82 % of the system's assets) and stress-tests for the 60 largest banks (98% of the system's assets)
- Addressing bank solvency, with NBU requiring banks to submit business plans to demonstrate their solvency
- Upgrading the regulatory and supervisory framework to international standards
- Improving banks' capacity to resolve NPLs

In order to increase transparency and financial sustainability of the banking businesses, the National Bank prepared a list of amendments to existing laws, in particular relating to stronger protection of creditor rights, higher responsibility of bank owners for insider lending and manipulations with reporting, establishment of a central credit register, restructuring of foreign exchange loans, etc. In addition, to increase banking business effectiveness and make it more attractive for investors, the NBU drafted an array of anti-crisis laws that would, in particular, streamline M&A processes, and change taxation rules with the aim to clean up banks' balance sheets.

The shift in supervision paradigm

After the global crisis of 2008, it was clear even to outsiders that some banks were not in a good position, but they were still supported by the central bank. That is why one of our fundamental decisions was to quit the practice of artificially keeping banks with negative capital "afloat". This was a fundamental change from earlier periods when banks were able to obtain refinance, thus masking existing "holes" in their capital.

Our actions triggered a storm of indignation both from failed bankers, accustomed to having unrestricted access to the credit "feeder", as well as from ordinary citizens, who held their savings in failed banks.

Our policy was to abandon "window-dressing" and closing our eyes to banks' capital shortage. In this respect, we introduced the new categories of "**problem bank**" and "**curatorship**" in the central bank's regulations during the crisis. This allowed us to enter a bank that violated prudential requirements with our curator, who carried out daily control over the operations of the bank. Being onsite in the bank, the curator (a representative of NBU) exercised control over the bank's activities by conducting an analysis of financial, statistical reporting and other information on the activities of the bank. During 2015, we introduced curatorship in 51 banks (both banks that had arrears in loans provided by the NBU, and banks that were categorized as problematic). According to the information received from the curator and offsite supervision unit, the Board thus had an opportunity to react urgently to changes in the bank's condition if the situation did not improve.

A bank's problem status was not publicly communicated to avoid risking intensification of a bank run, and required shareholders and management of the bank to prepare an action plan to get out of problem status. Typically, these measures were aimed at finding additional sources for replenishing the bank's capital, including the conversion of its obligations to shareholders and related parties into bank's capital.

The National Bank of Ukraine intensified its supervision over the activities of banks provided with refinancing, in particular regarding implementation of their financial recovery measures in accordance with the developed programs of financial rehabilitation.

I have been accused of providing an excessive amount of refinance to banks. Opponents from various political circles often blamed us, citing the huge volumes of refinance provided to banks, but neglecting to mention that most of those loans were overnight refinancing, which was paid back to the central bank on the same day.

As for long-term loans, some of which were aimed at supporting liquidity and stabilizing the activity of solvent banks, the balance between loans issued and repaid in my tenure was negative. At the time of my arrival at the National Bank, the balance of refinancing loans amounted to almost UAH 112 billion; in May 2017 when I left the bank, the balance was less than UAH 60 billion, of which more than 45 billion was loans to bank provided before my team arrived, which were subsequently declared insolvent. The remaining UAH 15 billion were refinancing loans provided to state banks. **That is why we were able to report for every hryvnia of refinancing loans provided during our tenure at the central bank.**

At the same time, despite the fact that ¾ of the refinancing loans were attributed to banks that had been declared insolvent, each of them had owners — well-known local oligarchs and businessmen. I firmly believe that the bankruptcy of banks does not mean the freedom of their owners from the debts of their institutions. Numerous offenses related to the non-repayment of refinancing of insolvent banks to the National Bank continue to be investigated by law enforcement agencies and are under consideration by the courts. Money must be returned to the state and investors!

The rule to provide liquidity only to those banks that were solvent was fundamental for us. **The central bank provides liquidity, not capital.** It would be a good thing if many politicians and pseudo-experts learned this rule.

a) Efficient bank diagnostic-AQR and ST: Sweet Lie or Bitter Truth?

There is no doubt that a stable banking system, trusted by consumers and investors, is the foundation for the long-term development of the economy. Consequently, our first priority was to verify the financial soundness of banks.

It should be noted that the apparent "stability" of the banking system, pre-2014, had no reasonable justification. Until 2014, the central bank's banking supervision was of a formal nature, based on official reporting of banks, in which everything could be veiled: starting from an underestimation of the credit risk of related-party loans, to "washed up" capital from schemes with foreign jurisdictions involved.

Therefore, with the technical assistance of the IMF, in 2014 we initiated an assessment of the quality of banks' assets (**Asset Quality Review or AQR**), and launched **regular stress testing** of banks for assessing the vulnerability of their balance sheets under negative scenarios. The study, comprising an asset quality review and stress test of Ukraine's 60 largest banks revealed a pressing need for additional capital. The stress-test methodology was carefully designed to allow in-depth analysis of every single large-credit exposure.

In addition to the standard practice of stress testing homogeneous portfolios of bank assets, we also conducted individual stress testing of the largest borrowers who had debts in different banks. In particular, such borrowers were the largest agricultural holdings of the country, as well as the largest state enterprises in energy sector and infrastructure.

Our staff looked into the finances of thousands of corporations to assess their solvency and estimated impact on banks' capital. The NBU and supervisors in other countries had never undergone this *unique experience* before. Capital losses were huge even in sound foreign banks against the backdrop of economic collapse in the occupied eastern territories and massive hryvnia depreciation. For a while, we allowed institutions to operate with negative capital as capital was completely wiped out at most banks following adverse external shocks. Of course, a bank's capital is a buffer against unexpected losses and all the evils related to infringement of the country's sovereignty had happened to us in 2014.

Stress-testing in 2014

In 2014, within the framework of cooperation with the IMF and the World Bank, the NBU conducted a diagnostic study of the 34 largest banks, which in total accounted for almost 80% of the system's assets. *The diagnostic study included two stages*: (1) the review of the quality of the banks' assets, and (2) stress-testing of capital adequacy in the forecast periods 2014-2016. To implement the diagnostics, the NBU involved independent consultants with strong experience in external auditing of commercial banks in Ukraine.

The first stage of diagnostics was largely aimed at checking for compliance with Ukrainian legislation and regulatory acts of the NBU as of year-end 2013. The results of the first stage determined the correction of financial results with corresponding changes in the statement of financial position, and the main adjustments were related to provisions for impairment of the banks' assets.

During the second stage of the diagnostics, we used a balance model for forecasting the financial condition of the bank in accordance with basic and stressful macroeconomic scenarios for 2014-2016. The principles and basic assumptions of the balance model the consultants used were set by the regulator.

According to the results of the review, we estimated a capitalization gap in 17 banks in the total amount of UAH 57.9 billion (USD 2.3 billion or 31.5% of authorized capital as of January 2014). Due to a number of factors, including the deterioration of the macroeconomic situation, the results of diagnostics in 2014 were not fully verified by actual practice, and after the diagnosis, 10 of the 34 largest banks became insolvent. The insolvency of 6 banks was accompanied by substantial budget expenditures for repayment of guaranteed deposits.

In sum, our first exercise demonstrated all the drawbacks of our methodology. Lessons were learned and together with the IMF, we developed a new comprehensive methodology for improved AQR and new stress-testing.

According to the diagnostic analysis of the largest banks in 2014, several areas were identified for further improvement:

- Introduction of credit risk analysis for large borrowers on an individual basis
- Introduction of a single cashflow template
- Enhanced collateral analysis, in particular "soft" types of collateral (property rights, goods for sale)
- Strengthening of risk analysis of related party transactions

Stress-testing in 2015-2016

During 2014, stress testing was carried out for 34 of the largest banks, and in 2015-2016 for the 60 largest banks. Whereas the 2014 stress testing was performed with the involvement of external consultants, in 2015-2016, it was conducted exclusively by the National Bank. The methodology for stress testing was based on international experience and was improved according to the findings and lessons learned in 2014. The key changes were:

- Implementation of stress testing of large borrowers and issuers on an individual basis
- Introduction of a single template for calculating needs for additional capital
- In-depth analysis of the quality of collateral
- In-depth analysis of the credit risks of related party loans

Diagnostics on the largest 60 banks in 2015 were implemented under the new IMF Agreement under the EFF Program. The diagnostics were developed taking into account international practice and were reinforced by additional requirements. The capital adequacy was estimated as of April 2015, and the prediction horizon for the stress test included 2015-2017.

Additional diagnostic requirements were developed based on the 2014 diagnostic experience and IMF recommendations. The most important additional requirements were:

- Both stages of diagnostics were performed by the NBU
- Individual stress testing of large borrowers
- Simultaneous diagnostics of operations with related parties

Given the significant deterioration of the macroeconomic indicators of Ukraine during the period from 2014 to 1Q2015, the macroeconomic scenario for stress testing in the second stage of diagnostics (2015-2016) was developed according to a baseline scenario of economic development.

The implementation of diagnostics in 2015-2016 was performed by two departments of the NBU: The Inspection Department performed an Asset Quality Review (Phase I), and the Financial Stability Department conducted stress-testing of capital adequacy (Phase II).

Interconnection was provided by using results from the first stage as input for the second stage. Thus, the calculation model for stress-testing large borrowers was based on the register and characteristics of large borrowers (amount of debt, currency, risk indicator, borrower's financial class, quality of debt service, structure and valuation of collateral, reserves, etc.).

A balance model for stress-testing of capital adequacy was based on the financial statements of the bank at the date of diagnostics, and accounted for adjusted results of the asset quality review.

Table 1. Stress-testing (2014 and 2015-2016 compared)

	ST 2014	ST 2015-2016
Performed by	9 audit companies	NBU
Sample	34 largest banks; 79% of banking system assets	60 largest banks; 98% of banking system assets
Date of diagnostics	01.01.2014	01.04.2015
Macroeconomic scenarios	Baseline, pessimistic	Baseline
Asset quality review	Yes	Yes
Large exposures individual stress-testing	No	Yes
Credit portfolio stress-testing	Yes	Yes

Stress-testing exercises in 2014 and in 2015-2016 revealed systemic risks for the banking sector and weaknesses of the banks' internal risk management.

In assessing credit risks, banks tended to provide largely formal compliance with the rules and therefore often concealed the *substance* of the operations and the true size of their credit risk. In my view, the advantage of having detailed rules was that the role of the regulator's subjectivity was diminished, though this often led to ignoring essential information and underestimating risks of the borrower. Examples of such a negative practice were widespread lending to borrowers in poor financial condition, acceptance of risky types of collateral, and transactions with related parties. In order to increase the effectiveness of prudential supervision, the NBU to a large extent had to rely on its *professional judgment* to ensure the principle of *substance over the form*.

Further, during verification of asset quality revealed practices of certain banks to inaccurately present information in the accounting system in terms of characteristics of borrowers and their debts. In terms of provisions of reserves, the most obvious examples of this practice were cases of incorrect reflection in the books of a loan's number of days in arrears. This was mainly due to an intent to artificially comply with the standards.

Stress testing of large borrowers determined the low level of credit standards and the quality of credit analysis of individual banks. The most significant signs of unsatisfactory practices were:

- high exposure to large borrowers, and borrowers from specific industries, regions, lending in foreign currencies
- small share of large borrowers with financial statements, confirmed by an external audit
- small share of large borrowers, whose credit risk was assessed by the bank at the group level using consolidated financial statements
- non-use or limited use of a cash flow statement of borrowers in the credit analysis
- acceptance of risky types of collateral (goods for sale, property rights)
- providing loans to companies in poor financial condition

Since 2015, the NBU has conducted stress testing on a regular basis as a standard tool for analyzing the financial sustainability of individual banks and the banking system as a whole. Based on the conclusions made during stress-testing, the NBU has introduced methodology changes for credit risk assessment and improved banking supervision.

b) Transparent ownership structure of banks

The NBU put pressure on banks to reveal their **real ownership structures**, previously disguised behind numerous special purpose vehicles and asset management companies. Ukraine's banking sector is now fully transparent, and that would have been inconceivable in 2014. The key consequence of this reform is that the ultimate beneficial owners of banks can now be held legally accountable for driving the banks into insolvency.

Back in 2014, *about half of the banking system in Ukraine was transparent.* We were aware that the actual owners of some banks were hiding behind so-called *"football teams"* of 11 nominal owners and "National

Olympics" of 51 nominal owners. However, in many cases we did not even know who the main shareholder of a bank was. Therefore, we started with amendments to the law imposing unlimited liability on owners and major shareholders to force them to act more responsibly and prevent them from "simply handing in the keys if the bank fails". *In countries where ownership is opaque, it's important to clarify ultimate ownership and the lines of management reporting and control.* We also amended the law imposing unlimited liability on owners and major shareholders to force them to act more responsibly.

After receiving a letter of non-transparency from the regulator, banks were given 180 days to become compliant. In the event of non-compliance with the requirements, the bank was recognized as a problem bank and could be withdrawn from the market according to the regulations. As I explained earlier, 16 banks starting in 2014 were d to the DGF due to opaque ownership structure. Eventually by the end of 2016, the banking system's level of transparency was 100%.

After adoption of the law in 2015 regarding liability of bank owners and increased responsibility of banks' owners for acquisition of qualifying holding without NBU approval, we immediately amended the central bank's regulations regarding the ownership structure of banks. Namely, the concept of "**qualifying holding**" was clarified, which meant not only the formal ownership of the bank, but also the potential to influence management decisions or activity of the bank, independent of formal ownership[12].

The new regulation provided for the disclosure of **ownership structure by the beneficial owner, that is** an individual who owns a qualifying holding of the bank. With that, the National Bank obtained the right to determine if a person is able to exercise a significant influence on the management or activities of a bank, and therefore could determine whether a person holds a significant share in the bank. In addition, we increased **requirements for business reputation of banks' managers**

---

[12] NBU Resolution #328 dated 21.05.2015 (updated)

and owners as well as the financial position of qualifying holding owners.

The National Bank introduced a new category in local banking terminology - "**the key participant**", defined as any individual who owns corporate rights of a legal entity, or a legal entity that owns 2 or more percent of corporate rights.) The key participants were the 20 individuals who owned the largest shares of the bank. These measures were intended to promote the transparency of each bank separately, and the banking sector as a whole.

We started disclosing publicly detailed information regarding the acquisition of qualifying holding in banks. This information, available on the website of the central bank and updated bi-annually, contains the name of the bank and any applicant who has submitted documents for acquiring substantial participation in the bank, information about the size of their share in the bank, what the applicant intends to acquire, and our decision on the application.

In addition, we introduced the disclosure of information on the *composition of banking groups.* The National Bank of Ukraine had the right to establish requirements for a banking group on a consolidated and sub-consolidated basis regarding corporate governance, risk management, regulatory capital adequacy, economic standards, etc. These requirements have helped to reduce the risks of banking groups, and to ensure the stable functioning of the banking system.

c) Minimal capital requirements for banks

In early July 2014, Ukraine's Parliament adopted the Law "On Amendments to Certain Legislative Acts of Ukraine to Prevent Negative Impact on the Stability of the Banking System", developed on the initiative of the National Bank of Ukraine and the Deposit Guarantee Fund. Among other things, this law increased the **minimum amount of authorized capital of banks to UAH 500 million** (circa USD 20 million).

This decision was taken in order to increase the stability of the banking sector and to further promote its consolidation, though unsurprisingly, the new legislation was met with varied reactions by the banking community: from neutral by banks whose capital already exceeded the new minimum threshold, to hostile by small banks that then had to increase their authorized capital to ensure compliance. To alleviate burden on small banks, our regulation approved a *schedule* for bringing the authorized capital of operating banks in line with the requirements of the Law *over 10 years* (by 11 July 2024). For newly established banks, the minimum amount of authorized capital (H1) has been increased as well from UAH 120 million to UAH 500 million.

In my communications on this decision, I repeatedly demonstrated that we were not fighting with small banks. We were fighting for the bank to have capital that is real and not "fake". It had to be formed with cash and not with worthless assets, and had to be compliant with international standards on quality and transparency.

d) Recapitalization plans and unwinding of excessive related-parties' exposure

In order to restore banks' capitalization, *banks committed to develop their* **recapitalization programs** in conjunction with the regulator. We understood that the situation was complicated, and we were making every possible effort to alleviate the burden on the banks amid tighter requirements for credit risk assessment and increased capital requirements. Therefore, the conditions of the recapitalization program were a fair compromise: banks were given **four years to restore their capitalization and five years to unwind loans to related parties.** Based on the results of diagnostic studies, each bank had to submit a credible and binding recapitalization plan to the NBU.

Our plan with the IMF had never been implemented by any country before. The capital of the top 20 **Ukrainian banks were allowed to reach zero adequacy as of the 1ˢᵗ of April 2016,** and to increase gradually afterwards. By the autumn 2016, the adequacy rate was expected to reach 5%, and during the next three years, to enter the normal level of 10%.

According to the results of diagnostics, 21 banks out of 60 did not require additional capital. Nine banks completed a four-year recapitalization plan ahead of schedule. Four banks failed to execute their program, were declared insolvent and withdrawn from the market, and the biggest bank was declared insolvent and nationalised. Almost all banks have fulfilled their prescribed capitalisation programmes well ahead of schedule. Overall, during 2016, banks increased their total capital by UAH 108 billion (circa USD 4.2 billion). This was a significant step towards financial sustainability for the future, and hence restoration of confidence in banks.

In addition, we initiated legislative changes that allowed us to avoid classifying some banks as insolvent even in the event of a significant reduction in the regulatory capital, or as problem banks even if their volume of non-performing loans exceeded 40% or more of the total assets of the bank. However, this waiver could be applied only to banks that agreed to have their recapitalization plan approved by the NBU. This was done in order not to let the entire banking system go "under the knife" of the regulator.

I should also mention that since 2014 we have developed law on *promoting capitalization and restructuring of banks*. Among other things, this law introduced **simplified procedures for capitalization and reorganization of banks**, as well as specified the process for capitalization of banks with the participation of the state. The option of simplifying and accelerating the process of recapitalization could be used by banks, if results of the diagnostic study showed the need for additional capital. Specifically, the regulator would decide whether to provide a banking license, a general license for FX currency transactions for the bank created in M&A, within two weeks from the day the bank submitted its package of documents, instead of the previous turnaround of two months. In addition, the NBU simplified the conditions for recapitalization of banks by foreign investors. Authorized banks were allowed to make foreign exchange purchases from foreign investors in order to increase the capital of banks in the interbank foreign exchange market.

Besides the diagnostic studies, we also invested huge resources and efforts in **identifying banks' transactions with related parties**. Prior to 2014, underwriting loans to banks' related parties at favourable terms was a common practice and a long-term blight on the banking sector. Typically, related businesses were non-operating companies or enterprises with weak financials and **most never had any intention of repaying their loans**. In the past, the legislation, and the way it was applied, did not allow related-party lending to be properly identified and restricted, so it occurred on a large-scale and was covert. However, the crisis quickly made related-party debts non-performing, which became a powerful driver for instability in the financial sector and caused significant losses to the state, regular bank customers, and the economy as a whole.

For me, it was surprising that for decades, the regulator had not cast doubt on but was satisfied with many banks' compliance to imperfect, formal criteria, and banks' assertions that their level of lending to related parties complied with requirements. This meant that loans were in fact issued to related parties and were not duly reported as such by the banks. As a result, as of mid-2015, the total volume of related-party loans declared by all banks was just UAH 1.5 billion or a mere 0.2 % of the total portfolio.

In times of economic growth, related-party lending was not an obvious problem. Although such loans were usually made on non-market terms, in most cases, related businesses artificially serviced their debts via issuance of new and bigger loans, and the banks formally complied with norms and requirements.

But in some cases, related parties serviced their debt from business activities. However, related-party lending entailed huge hidden risks that manifested themselves later. It limited financial resources for unrelated businesses that could have used those resources much more effectively by paying banks' market interest rates and properly servicing their debt, and thereby making the economy more stable and dynamic. The related-party loans were often allocated to inefficient, risky, and eventually unprofitable investments, which created high risks for banks and the economy as a whole. All these risks fully materialized during the economic crisis of 2014 to 2016. The financial condition of the major business groups deteriorated, and their ability to properly service their debts decreased sharply. When legislation and the NBU's regulations were amended in 2015, obliging financial institutions to issue loans to related-parties on market terms and gradually wind them down, many bank owners decided that it made more sense to let the banks fail rather than repay loans or refinance their businesses at other banks on much less advantageous terms. This led to large problems in the banking sector, including an excessive load on the Deposit Guarantee Fund, and caused losses to the budget and to clients of financial institutions. If related-party lending had not been occurring on such a large-scale, the number of banks withdrawn from the market would have been much less.

Banks generally declared loans issued to related individuals correctly – that is, loans to owners, managers, and employees – but they substantially understated the debts owed by businesses related to the banks' shareholders. Thus, comprehensive diagnostics of bank operations with related parties, which were carried out by the NBU in 2015 and 2016 using a **radically new related-party identification methodology**[13] that expanded the list of indirect attributes of relatedness, **shocked a large number of banks**. The actual related parties lending (RP) volumes were much higher than those reported by banks earlier. By the end of the diagnostics, such loans totaled UAH 32 billion for operating banks (excluding Privatbank, whose UAH 200 billion, or circa USD 8 billion, loan portfolio was entirely provided to related businesses and whose

---

[13] NBU Board Resolution No. 315 On Approval of the Regulation on a Bank's Related Party Identification (updated) dated 12 May 2015; NBU Board Resolution No. 314 On Measures on Bringing Banks' Exposures to Related Parties in Compliance with Requirements dated 12 May 2015.

loans issued by banks failed before the diagnostics were completed). We estimated that the total amount of related-party loans with banks that were closed during the crisis was more than UAH 80 billion. As of March 2018, the direct expenses of the DGF on reimbursements to depositors of those banks exceeded UAH 38 billion[14]. The highest concentration of related-party loans was found in private Ukrainian banks. The diagnostics showed that the share of RP debt drastically exceeded 25% of the corporate loan portfolios of these banks. And the biggest related-parties nonperforming loan portfolio was in nationalised Privatbank – UAH 213 billion (including accrued interest) and direct expenses to the state for recapitalization of UAH 155 billion (see detailed case study on Privatbank below). Most of these losses could have been avoided if the owners of RP companies had serviced their debts.

Credit analysis within stress testing identified and confirmed the high risks associated with related-party lending. An analysis of banks' borrowers with a view to their interconnectedness identified a number of cases of lending to related parties on non-market conditions (low interest rates, insufficient collateral coverage) and unreasonable credit decisions (granting loans to insolvent companies). The high concentration of loans to related parties led to the bankruptcy of a number of commercial banks in these years.

An assessment of related-party lending was carried out by the central bank in stages with the first 20 banks going through RPL analysis in May to June 2015 and the remaining banks starting in August 2015. In the 1H2016, all banks had to have their plans for decreasing RPL to levels set by the central bank. Each bank was obliged to prepare an action plan to unwind related-party exposures above that limit within 3 years.

These unwinding plans included: (i) credible quarterly schedule; (ii) minimum first payments or related exposure reductions of no less than 5 percent of excess loans to insiders; (iii) proper loan collateralization;

---

[14] Financial Stability Report, June 2018

(iv) securing non-revocable written guarantees issued by qualified shareholders controlling more than 10 percent of votes pertaining to related loans.

These guarantees were to remain in place until the bank became fully compliant with the legal and regulatory related lending framework.

In total, 99 banks were inspected in 2015 and 2016. The review revealed a high concentration of related-party loans in the portfolios of banks with Ukrainian capital: 44 banks violated the H9 ratio, which caps exposures to RP. Several large banks with a high concentration of related- party loans in their portfolios went bankrupt. Eight banks that were in violation of the respective regulation brought the value of this ratio into compliance with requirements ahead of schedule by winding down related-party loans, or by increasing their regulatory capital. The 23 remaining banks developed action plans to wind down related-party debts and had their plans validated by the NBU.

After the diagnostics, the NBU introduced **constant monitoring of related-party transactions**, in line with the Concept for Transaction Monitoring and Identifying Potential Attributes of Relatedness, which the NBU adopted in 2016. By obliging banks to reveal the true story and bring related-lending volumes in line with prudential ratios, the National Bank significantly strengthened the banking system's resilience to shocks. Moreover, the prohibition of excessive lending to related parties allowed compliant banks to release financial resources for lending to more efficient enterprises on market terms.

Case Study: Privatbank

The resolution of Ukraine's largest bank, PrivatBank, at the end of 2016 deserves to be described in an entire book, and would be a true bestseller among banking professionals --not only in Ukraine, but across the globe. However, as the issue is not finally resolved at this writing, it merits at least a dedicated case study within this manual.

After all, the National Bank carried out an unprecedented "operation" to rescue the country's largest private lender. The accounts of the million-strong army of its clients were not blocked, and the infrastructure supporting billions of its transactions continued to operate smoothly.

No one guaranteed us a positive result, because there was no similar case in the world's financial history. However, our team carefully took steps after checking all the risks. Our calculations and actions were coordinated with the Government, the President, and the Parliament and allowed the state to nationalise Privatbank in a non-disruptive way. We refused to be disturbed by the violent pressure from various political forces who were not interested in the resolution of the country's largest lender.

At the end of December 2016, Privatbank became a state-owned bank. This saved the deposits of more than 20 million clients and minimized the risks to the nation's financial stability, which would have been triggered by a significant shortage of capital in such a systemically important bank.

Inside an enigma

As a market participant, I already knew PrivatBank had major problems. One didn't have to be a chartered financial analyst to conclude that the major share of Privatbank's loans went to the related parties. Even for an outsider it was obvious, having attracted one-third of all deposits of the banking system, that Privatbank did not have any loan to a large company not affiliated with the owners as its client. It was thus clear to everybody in the market, but not for Privatbank's external auditors, who continued to sign auditor's reports showing 5% related-party lending along with financial statements saying that more than one-third of all bank loans went to ferroalloy and petroleum refining businesses, which were officially known to be owned by the bank's shareholders.

Still, when I learned the full picture as governor of the central bank, I was truly shocked by the blatant schemes of the bank. It was a pure Ponzi scheme. The entire Privatbank corporate portfolio of loans was issued to related parties that were not normal businesses, but rather empty shells that had neither collateral nor any cashflow. According to the NBU regulation on identification of related parties, the financial flows between borrowing companies were an important signal of the relationship between the bank and the borrower. Thus, we analyzed all corporate borrowers of Privatbank. It turned out that many of them were serviced by, and borrowed exclusively from, Privatbank. Moreover, they were connected with other companies in the Privat Group or its owners, both financially and commercially.

A "black hole" of capital

As related above, back in 2015, the NBU launched the most comprehensive diagnostic studies in the history of the banking sector, comprising an asset quality review and an assessment of capital needs facing banks. Inspections and stress tests carried out by the NBU according to the methodology developed with the IMF revealed that Privatbank had incredible capital shortages: in fact, not even capital shortage but a drastic lack of real assets in its balance sheet. As of April 2016, the bank had capital shortages amounting to UAH 113 billion (41% of its assets), which, apart from crisis-related factors, were caused by imprudent lending policies pursued by the bank. **In November 2015, related-party loans had accounted for 97% of the bank's corporate loan portfolio.** After nationalisation, the new management of the state-owned Privatbank said the NBU was wrong – the corporate loan portfolio was not 97% related parties loans but 100%! Even three years after nationalisation, all these related parties did not repay one penny of their loans and the outstanding amount of that portfolio in 2019 reached UAH 240 billon.

The principles of recapitalization were equal for all Ukrainian banks. PrivatBank, like any other other financial institution where capital shortages were revealed based on the results of stress tests, was requested to address these capital shortages. All banks were given four years to comply, and in the first year, had to reach a capital adequacy ratio (CAR) of 0% by April 2016 before gradually building up their CAR to 10%, the mandatory minimum. At the same time, they had to reduce the amount of related party lending and deleverage. Over five years, they were required to repay all related-party loans and eliminate further lending to related parties.

Privatbank's management team designed a recapitalization program and a program to unwind its related-party lending. The bank's shareholders also provided guarantees as proof of their commitment to implement the recapitalization program agreed upon with the NBU. The owners agreed to the obligation and signed guarantee letters. The main shareholder of the bank personally provided a guarantee to fulfil these obligations, not just to pay off UAH 113 billion for the recapitalisation.

The agreed-upon recapitalization program was quite compromising from the beginning, and looked more like a financial settlement than a requirement for a direct cash injection from shareholders. It was thus quite a challenging task to convince the IMF to approve this approach. But having enormous problems in the Ukrainian banking sector, we succeeded with that task.

In the **first stage of the recapitalisation,** the owners were supposed to put UAH 31billion of shareholders' real assets on the bank's balance sheet at fair value. We were aware that these assets were non-liquid assets, but they could still generate real cash flows and had been already pledged to the NBU under refinance loans issued as assets of third parties linked to shareholders. Due to the fact that banks are not an asset-management company, the recapitalisation program provided for the gradual sale of these assets from the bank's balance sheet and relocation to liquid financial instruments. The first stage of recapitalisation was supposed to be completed before April 1, 2016, but unfortunately, Privatbank chose to put not valuable assets, but trash, on their balance sheet.

Finally, at the end of August 2016, under pressure from the central bank and after thorough verification of the fair value of assets by the NBU, the owners of Privatbank put in the UAH 31 billion assets to their balance sheet. However, when we checked the register five days later, 5.5 of the UAH 31 billion had already been withdrawn. This meant that shareholders didn't meet even the first of their obligations to recapitalise the bank. It was again a fraud. After that, we had no doubt that neither management nor shareholders had any intention to fulfil their obligations.

Nevertheless, we gave them another chance to return assets to the balance sheet and complete the second stage of recapitalisation program. In the **second stage,** they were obliged to put in UAH 74 billion via transformation of their corporate loan portfolio by transferring all loans from shell companies to real operational businesses with real assets, with real cash flows into the bank replacing shell companies. They would then fulfil their obligations and repay these loans over the next 5 to7 years. They could do so having a number of assets in the US, in the UK, and in other countries, as well as many liquid assets in Ukraine.

The NBU offered to allow Privatbank's owners to transfer the loans to those companies that were engaged in economic activity and had real cash flows. Another option was to unite various business areas in holdings, where some companies would only produce and others only trade, with cash flows between them visible. This would have helped increase the quality of borrowers and could have partially closed the gap in the balance sheet. The next step involved pledging real collateral for loans, e.g., property, equipment, vehicles etc., and then covering the rest with capital. However, in mid-October 2016, we saw management and shareholders start another fraudulent activity, and begin the transformation of the portfolio to new fake companies.

Clearly, neither the bank nor its shareholders had any intention of implementing the program. The NBU management and I personally, held over 30 meetings with the shareholders and managers of the financial institution. Given that PrivatBank was a systemically important financial institution, the NBU took a more flexible approach, extending deadlines for fulfilling the recapitalization program on many occasions.

As I mentioned before, the shareholders pretended to start the second stage. However, what they actually wanted was to take up time and attack us through the media they controlled and through direct threats to the management of the NBU. We saw that they clearly would not be meeting their obligations.

During all my public speeches and monthly press conferences in 2015 and 2016, I always reassured the market that we were working with Privatbank shareholders on a recapitalisation plan but that if they did not deliver on their promises, PrivatBank -- the biggest, most systemically important bank in the country -- would be nationalised.

In the end, nationalisation was unavoidable. After numerous meetings, shareholders sent us a letter asking about nationalisation, and sent a second, similar letter to the Prime Minister a few days before the nationalisation. Today, these shareholders have initiated 600 lawsuits against the NBU, Ministry of Finance, DGF and the state-owned Privatbank, challenging the nationalisation of the bank.

Before nationalisation, the NBU insisted that Privatbank have an audit. At the end of November 2016, Ernst&Young (E&Y) confirmed our suspicions, and documented the amount of the bank's capital shortfall. Later in 2017, a post-audit after nationalisation found an even larger shortage of capital, proving fraud at the last nights of the bank.

As of 1 December 2016, the capital shortage faced by PrivatBank was UAH 146 billion and its liquidity deteriorated significantly. The bank had not complied with reserve requirements for a year. The bank's problems were not only confirmed, but were shown to be even larger than our estimates. The related-party corporate loan portfolio was not 97% but 100%. This meant that the need for additional capitalization was even greater, and the state would have to invest even more money in order to compensate the losses caused by management of the bank and by the so-called oligarchy team. On their last night in operation, they carried out fraudulent operations totalling more than UAH 16 billion.

When we finally nationalised Privatbank at the end of 2016, its capital shortage was UAH 146 billion ($5.6 billion). It would have been even larger if, during the nationalization of Privatbank and in line with Ukrainian law, the financial obligations of persons affiliated with the bank (worth UAH 29.4 billion) were not converted by the DGF into the bank's capital and later acquired by the state. The list of persons related to Privatbank was approved by the NBU Commission in accordance with regulations equally applied to all other banks under the diagnostic study of operations of banks with related parties held in 2015 and 2016. The bail-out included all eurobonds of Privatbank.

Moreover, the post-audit of the bank, conducted by E&Y, showed the need for additional capitalization in the amount of UAH 38.6 billion (ca. USD 1.5 billion). The past-due debt owed to the NBU for stabilization loans amounted to UAH 14 billion. Altogether, **the direct fiscal expenditures for the privatization of Privatbank reached UAH 155 billion or 7% of Ukraine's GDP!**

Thus, the transfer of the bank to the control of the state was the only correct decision in light of the situation we faced. When I tell my colleagues from other central banks about the case, my counterparts from large countries do not fully understand what USD 6 billion meant for us. But when I say it was 50% of the country's monetary base and a third of the stock of individual deposits, they are shocked.

Roadmap for nationalisation

Being aware of all the problems faced by Privatbank and the risks it posed to the health of the financial sector and the economy as a whole, **we could not wait any longer.**

Therefore, we sent a letter to the Ministry of Finance saying it was time to consider nationalisation. Also, being aware of their inability to fulfil the recapitalization program, the shareholders filed a letter with the Cabinet of Ministers of Ukraine requesting State equity participation in the bank. The shareholders undertook commitments to restructure loans issued by the bank to corporate clients by 1 July

2017 (the above-mentioned transformation required by NBU), taking into account the requirements set by the NBU.

We were delighted that the Cabinet of Ministers of Ukraine (CMU) has backed our proposal and approved a decision transferring the bank to 100 percent state ownership. The Cabinet of Ministers of Ukraine adopted the respective decision on December 18, 2016[15].

The timeline for nationalizing Privatbank was:

- o *December 16, 2016:* The shareholders sent a letter to the Cabinet of Ministers of Ukraine requesting the state enter the capital of Privatbank
- o **December 17, 2016: A** detailed road map of cooperation within all authorities was signed and sealed (NBU, Ministry of Finance, DGF, State Securities Commission, Financial Stability Board, Cabinet of *Ministers and the National Security and Defence Council of Ukraine).*
- o *December 18, 2016:* At 9.00, the NBU declared Privatbank insolvent, and at 21.00, the Cabinet of Ministers communicated the transfer of Privatbank into a state ownership.
- o *December 19, 2016:* The President of Ukraine signed Decree No. 560 / 2016 on the decision of the National Security and Defense Council of 18 December 2016 "On urgent measures to ensure the national security of Ukraine in the economic sphere and protect the interests of depositors." A joint statement of the Ministry of Finance of Ukraine and the National Bank of Ukraine was released regarding the decision of the state to entering to the capital of Privatbank. The Deposit Guarantee Fund announced the introduction of temporary administration of Privatbank.
- o *December 21, 2016:* The Ministry of Finance of Ukraine announced that the Deposit Guarantee Fund had signed an agreement for the sale of 100% of shares of Privatbank.

---

[15] CMU Resolution No. 961 dated 18/12/2016

o **December 23, 2016:** The plan for the resolution of Privatbank was implemented, and from December 22, the temporary administration o Privatbank was suspended.

A separate book would be needed to describe all the details of our preparations for the nationalisation. Undoubtedly, Privatbank will be a case study in universities as the biggest financial fraud in history, even if not in absolute figures then definitely if weighted by the size of the country's economy and its banking sector.

I must add that we started preparing for the possible nationalisation of the largest bank in the country with Ministry of Finance as early as 2015. That is why the whole process went smoothly and how financial stability in the country was preserved.

I stress that Privatbank was transferred into state ownership in accordance with Article 41.1 of the Law of Ukraine "On Households' Deposit Guarantee System", which set the rules governing the sale of an insolvent bank to the State. That Article was introduced by the NBU and voted by the Parliament in 2015 as part of our preparatory process for possible nationalisation of systemically important banks (SIBs).

By transferring the bank into state ownership, we protected over 20 million Ukrainian citizens who were using services provided by this bank and held their funds there. This includes 3.2 million pensioners, over 500,000 students, and 1.6 million socially vulnerable households. To ensure the maintenance of financial stability and prevent further social tensions, it was equally important that 500,000 sole proprietors did not lose their funds and were able to continue operating smoothly, as well as 600,000 SMEs. Over 3.6 million employees retained access to their payroll accounts, including 2.2 million public sector employees and 1.4 million private sector employees.

Before the decision was finally reached, we did our homework and developed a clear (though, not public) Action Plan to make the transfer of Privatbank into the hands of the State **as painless as possible, and at the same time, to reduce risks to the financial system's stability**. We were aware that the situation surrounding this bank raised concerns not only for its clients, but also for all Ukrainians. Would price growth accelerate? Would the hryvnia depreciate sharply?

By smoothing the process of nationalisation, we tried to avoid disruption of the country's payment network, as Privatbank's payment system, Privat24, handled more than 50% of Ukraine's transactional business. Thus, we had to tackle the "red button risk" that operationally stopping the bank could mean a blackout in the whole country.

Starting from the first business day after nationalization, the NBU was ready to provide liquidity support if the bank needed it to ensure the repayment of deposits. Since long-term deposits constituted the largest share of the portfolio, the NBU did not expect Privatbank to face significant deposit outflows and this move would have a limited impact on inflation and the FX market. In any case, the NBU had enough tools in its toolkit to mitigate excessive exchange rate volatility. Ukraine's international reserves amounted to USD 15.5 billion.

We wanted to provide reassurances that the situation was under control. As a result:

- Privatbank continued to operate and keep card transactions and payments going as usual.
- The provision of services to corporate clients was temporarily suspended for only one day (December 19) for technical reasons.
- Customers faced no other restrictions.
- Customers retained unrestricted access to their current and savings deposits, but they were not allowed to withdraw their long-term deposits before maturity.
- ATMs and POS terminals kept operating and settlement transactions continued to be carried out.

Too big to hide, or All secrets sooner or later become apparent

An investigation by Kroll was consistent with Ukraine's commitments to the IMF, as set out in the Memorandum, "to perform a forensic audit of Privatbank's operations to identify whether wrongdoing or bad banking practices took place prior to the bank's nationalisation".

The investigation identified that Privatbank was subjected to large scale and coordinated fraud over at least a ten-year period ending December 2016, resulting in a loss of at least USD 5.5 billion.

Key findings of the investigation included:

1. **Extraction of funds.** There were clear indications that loan proceeds were used to purchase assets and to finance business enterprises inside and outside of Ukraine for the benefit of former shareholders and their affiliates.

2. **Disguising the origins of funds.** The mechanisms used to disguise the origin and destination of loan funds demonstrated the characteristics of a large-scale money-laundering scheme. The volume and timing of the transactions within minutes of each other, and with no declared connection between the entity repaying the loan and the original borrower, and the extensive use of Special Purpose Vehicle (SPV) companies based in off-shore jurisdictions, demonstrated indications of a concerted attempt to disguise the true nature of the economic purpose from regulatory and other stakeholders for the benefit of the former shareholders and their affiliates.

3. **Bank within the bank.** Central to the coordinated manipulation of the loan book, and extraction of benefit was a shadow-banking structure within Privatbank. Once the loans were gone, the bank issued new loans to affiliates to mask their default and to avoid the provisions. Through new loans, the old debts and interest were repaid through cyclical lending. The secretive structure processed and facilitated the movement of the proceeds of hundreds of loans, worth billions of USD, to parties related to the former shareholders and their affiliates. More than 500 employees worked within the "shadow-banking structure" to

keep the scheme running. Their task was to conceal the origin of money and the real purpose of loans.

4.   **Structure and administration of the loans.** The shadow bank administered the related-party corporate loan portfolio. It issued new loans, typically used to repay principal and interest on existing related party loans (Recycling Scheme), and was the architect of fund-flow mechanisms to disguise the origin and destination of the loan funds, presenting a façade of an ordinary client-focused bank. Privatbank attracted funds from private and commercial depositors from Ukraine and other countries, which facilitated the Loan Recycling Scheme.

This long-term hiding of such a large exposure to related parties required Privatbank to make repeated false representations of its financial position. This misrepresentation could only have been achieved through multiple instances of banking fraud and false accounting by the former management of the bank.

5.   **Balance sheet.** Prior to nationalisation in December 2016, more than 95 percent of corporate lending was to parties related to former shareholders and their affiliates. Towards the end of 2016, 75% of the loan book was consolidated into loans to 36 borrowers related to the former shareholders and their affiliates. The majority of these loans remained overdue and unpaid, resulting in a loss to the Bank of at least USD 5.5 billion.

The results of the Kroll investigation confirmed the previous conclusions of the National Bank.

Since the nationalization, in order to hold the former owners of the bank accountable and to compensate for the loss of taxpayers, the central bank and Privatbank have launched litigation processes against its former shareholders in various countries all over the world.

In December 2018, Ukraine's central bank filed a claim in Switzerland against the former major shareholder of Privatbank, seeking compensation for loans made to the bank before its nationalisation and aiming to collect the ex-owner's debt as the guarantor to the NBU under private sureties issued in 2016 with respect to five agreements providing refinancing loans to the bank.

In May 2019, Privatbank filed a lawsuit in the Court of Chancery of the State of Delaware, which described how Ukrainian money had been laundered in the United States. According to the statement of claim, starting from January 2006 to December 2016, the total cash flow (loans) through accounts of beneficial owners of the bank in the Cyprus branch of Privatbank, which were used for money laundering, amounted to $ 470 billion, which was nearly twice as much as the GDP of Cyprus for the same period. If this amount is proven in court, it would be the largest case of money laundering committed by a group of individuals in history.

The lawsuit showed how the scheme worked. The ultimate beneficiaries "used Privatbank as their own pocket bank", ultimately stealing billions of dollars from Privatbank and using legal entities in the United States to launder hundreds of millions of dollars or misappropriating Privatbank loans in the United States to enrich themselves and their partners. The illegally appropriated funds, laundered in the United States, were eventually used to acquire various US businesses and commercial real estate in Cleveland, Ohio, Dallas, Texas and elsewhere.

In October 2019, state-owned Privatbank won an appeal in the Court of Appeal in London, which ruled that the bank could continue to pursue claims regarding alleged fraud on a massive scale against former owners and six companies registered in the UK and British Virgin Islands affiliated with them. The Court of Appeal confirmed that the bank could pursue the full loss amount that it claims was caused by this "fraud on an epic scale", which is $3 billion (including interest). The appellate decision also maintained the worldwide asset freeze on the former owners' fortunes while the case is open in the UK.

Another lawsuit by the state-owned Privatbank was filed in December 2019 against Tel Aviv-based Discount Bank accused of aiding

Privatbank's ex-owners in stealing at least $600 million by allowing an alleged shell company to receive fraudulent transfers from Cyprus. The claim contained allegations of "fraud, robbery, violation of the money laundering ban and a host of other wrongdoings and offenses, which caused huge financial damage… of unprecedented sums".

In April 2020, PrivatBank filed a new lawsuit in Cyprus claiming $5.5bn damage from the bank's former owners. According to the Privatbank, the lawsuit relates to two series of fraudulent transactions that were carried out from 2013 to 2016 via the scheme that allowed payments of $ 30 million almost daily during a four-month period in 2013 through fictitious credit agreements to the affiliated offshore companies that have not been repaid.

Is there life after nationalisation?

It is worth noting that *out of Privatbank's multi-billion dollar portfolio of corporate loans, not a single kopek has been repaid since December 2016*. This fact confirmed again that we were right in recognizing those loans as related-party loans and claiming that all this money was taken out by the shareholders of the bank.

Unfortunately, with regard to debt collection with the former owner, despite ironclad legal grounds, our powers were limited. The National Bank is a regulator. We are responsible for monetary policy and bank regulation. We can recognize a hole in a bank's capital and warn that the quality of the loan portfolio is low, that there is no collateral and that the borrowing companies are fake. However, if money was deliberately withdrawn from the bank, it is the mandate of judicial and enforcement agencies to pursue offenders. **All the materials relating to the Privatbank case were submitted to the public prosecutor's office and to Ukrainian anticorruption agencies.**

At the same time, **litigation between Privatbank, its former owners and the National Bank has already been underway for more than three years in Ukraine and in foreign jurisdictions**, including proceedings in the London High Court. In courts at various levels in Ukraine, there have been several hundred cases in which the ex-owners, and companies associated with them, dispute both the nationalisation of Privatbank and other related issues, from forced conversion of assets into the bank's capital to the protection of the confidentiality of personal data.

However, despite the significant costs of litigation, Privatbank today is operationally profitable and showed a record net profit of UAH 11.7 billion (USD 0.4 billion) in 2018 and UAH 32.6 billion (USD 1.3 billion) in 2019.

A new **development strategy for Privatbank was** elaborated by the **independent supervisory board,** in accordance with the Strategy for the Development of State Banks: the bank should be operationally efficient, and have a healthy portfolio of assets aimed at crediting of real business. In the medium term, the bank may be acquired by a strategic investor or undertake an IPO. The central bank's vision has been provided to the Ministry of Finance. The NBU continues working fruitfully with both the Ministry of Finance and the bank towards the implementation of this strategy.

The development of events around Privatbank is a litmus test for Ukrainian authorities. Judicial decisions over the last year cast doubt on the legality and expediency of the nationalisation of PrivatBank in December 2016. These decisions are being currently appealed. The NBU, together with the Ministry of Finance and the DGF, needs an action plan in case of any future adverse developments. The central bank and other authorities should be guided by considerations of how to maintain financial stability and protect the rights of the bank's depositors.

Are there any other options for now? If a Ukrainian court decides that the bank should be handed back to its former owners, it would lead to an immediate withdrawal of government bonds injected into bank's capital. Then, the bank would be immediately recognized as insolvent and nationalised once again. Any other option would be a financial disaster and an existential threat for Ukraine as it would immediately lead to the discontinuation of cooperation with international creditors and partners, who were unanimous in a **joint statement** on April 18, 2019 declaring that "*the decision to nationalize PrivatBank at the request of its former owners was the only effective method of protecting the depositors of the bank - the Ukrainian people and business - and the stability of the financial system*". The IMF, the World Bank, the EBRD, the US Embassy, and the Delegation of the European Union to Ukraine jointly stated that it is important that the government does not cease its efforts to recover damages from the former owners and related parties of the bankrupt banks. Ukraine's prosecutors and the judiciary should make full use of the findings of the Kroll Report commissioned by the NBU. Ukraine's international partners should also closely monitor developments in this area.

I believe that the resolution of Privatbank will be included in textbooks for years to come, because there have been no similar cases in the world. It was the last step in the "cleaning-up" stage of banking reform, and fundamentally changed the "portrait" of the banking system in Ukraine.

e) Long liquidity assistance from CB and proper instruments

Following the shift of the supervisory paradigm, when the national bank discontinued providing long-term stabilization loans to banks as the practice showed unsatisfactory results, the bulk of long-term loans became non-performing. That meant banks needed another facility for obtaining long-term liquidity, especially given the shaky position of Ukraine's banking sector amidst wartime and political turbulence.

Therefore, we expanded the list of instruments supporting long-term liquidity due to the significant gap between short-term and long-term liquidity of banks. Namely, **we added a refinancing facility for 1 to 5 years to the list of standard liquidity support instruments** (standard facilities of up to 14 days and emergency liquidity assistance up to 90 days).

This long-term liquidity assistance was designed without a further lending purpose of the bank and was to be issued via unscheduled tenders. The interest rate for the liquidity assistance was floating (NBU key rate + 2 pp) and would change in accordance with changes in the key rate. As collateral for a long-term refinance, the same assets as for refinancing loans of up to 14 and 90 days could be used, i.e., government bonds; NBU deposit certificates (for long-term refinancing exclusively as additional collateral); foreign currency (USD, EUR, GBP, CHF, JPY); or bonds issued by IFIs. The liquidity assistance was allowed to replace securities that would have matured with other securities.

The terms of the long-term liquidity assistance, its volumes and frequency of tenders, was determined by the NBU Board on a quarterly basis at Monetary Policy Committee meetings. Information on the schedule of tenders for the next quarter was posted on the NBU's website. Information about the results of each tender was published on the NBU's website on the day it was held.

Banks were allowed to form a *pool of assets* that could be provided as collateral for overnight loans and other liquidity assistance facilities. To form a pool of assets, the bank would sign a general loan agreement with the National Bank for a period of five years (with the possibility of extending the term for another five years). With that, banks were authorized to *change some assets in the pool for other eligible assets on a permanent basis*, thus allowing the bank to manage assets under the collateral.

The availability of reliable and up-to-date collateral contributed to a faster and simpler process in obtaining liquidity assistance from the central bank. This in turn laid the foundation for the revival of long-term lending to the real sector.

f) New instruments for bank capitalisation

In 2018, the National Bank introduced **new capital instrument with a conversion /write-down feature** within the framework of adapting the local banking system to European banking standards, based on the Basic Principles of Effective Banking Supervision of the Basel Committee on Banking Supervision, and in order to increase the efficiency and ensure the stable functioning of the Ukrainian banking system. The new instrument opened new possibilities for boosting the Ukrainian banking system capitalization, and was the first step towards reformed capital requirements that were introduced in 2020.

The key characteristic of this instrument is that it can absorb losses through a conversion or write-downs using the investors' money, and not at the cost of other creditors or the state. A bank will have to convert or write-down the instrument upon the occurrence of a trigger event when the capital adequacy ratio of the issuing bank (without accounting for the instrument) falls below 6.25%.

The instrument may be converted into common equity through common stock acquisition, thus allowing increase to the authorized capital of a bank. In case of a write-down, the issuing bank will receive income that will absorb its going-concern losses. The new instrument is a long-term asset (with maturity of not less than 50 years) that will be gradually depreciated over 15 years to the maturity date.

Currently, the instrument will be included in Tier 1 capital of a bank, and after the new requirements to the capital structure are in place, it will become a part of additional Tier 1 capital. A bank requires NBU approval to include this instrument in its capital.

Requirements to the instrument were developed in accordance with EU laws, in particular Regulation (EU) No. 575/2013 of 26 June 2013, "Additional Regulations and Directive 2013/36/EU based on Basel III Recommendations."

g) Focus on AML, proper financial monitoring, and fraud prevention

For a country like Ukraine, in which the shadow economy is about half of the GDP, the role of AML gains nationwide significance. Considering that many schematic transactions involve banks, it falls to the central banks to lead the process of bringing the financial sector, and eventually the country itself, into the light.

I should note that the former approach to the implementation of AML procedures in banks, in effect until 2014, led many of them to more resemble *money laundering machines* than financial institutions. I am convinced that those banks should have been subject to all available sanctions (FATF and others) over the last 10 years. But my team stopped the activities of banks that carried out such illegal operations, including illegal transfer of capital outside Ukraine. My message to those banks was simple: none of them would have any chance to do operations as they used to.

To provide some context, in 2014 we identified a number of *money laundering operations of local banks using correspondent accounts at several European banks*. Thus, at the beginning of my tenure, I gathered all the banks at the NBU and warned they had to stop all operations with banks involved in money laundering in European territory. Then in 2014, I met with the Governor of the Austrian Central Bank and the Governor of Latvian Central Bank to inform them about banks engaged in illegal activities in their territory. It was almost five years before the money-laundering scandals flared up at the global level!

One of those banks – *Meinl Bank* (Austria) – was stripped of its banking licence by the ECB in November 2019. An investigation by the Organized Crime and Corruption Reporting Project[16] and authorities in four countries confirmed fraudulent operations facilitated by Meinl Bank between 2011 and 2015, when hundreds of millions of dollars and euros from other banks flowed through Meinl accounts before disappearing into shadowy offshore companies.

The outstanding balances with those European banks in mid-2014 amounted to about USD 2 billion (or circa 50% of FCY correspondent accounts' balance in Ukrainian banks), with 17 Ukrainian banks involved in this activity. Some banks used this practice not only for *money laundering* but also to artificially *increase their fake capital*. The scheme was that Ukrainian banks, under the guise of lending to clients abroad,

---

[16] https://www.occrp.org/en/the-austrian-bank-job/the-vienna-bank-job

opened correspondent accounts in European banks, and then, through a number of related offshore companies with opaque ownership structure, put the same funds into their own capital as subordinated debt. The other scheme was used to siphon money out of the country by providing a bank guarantee of a Meinl loan to an offshore company related to the bank's owners. After the "borrower's" default, Meinl invoked the guarantee and recouped the money from the originating bank.

Therefore, we developed the program and provided banks with the **deadline of April 1, 2016 to terminate all correspondent accounts and interbank transactions** with these banks. With that, we updated our regulations and determined that Ukrainian banks with accounts in a foreign bank without an investment rating were obliged to form **100% of provisions** for the funds held on those accounts. By doing so, we discouraged banks from transferring funds abroad to lend to related parties. The National Bank also introduced a weekly monitoring of correspondent accounts of Ukrainian banks in foreign banks, and actively cooperated with central banks of European countries in order to exchange information on suspicious transactions.

Today, none of the operating banks in Ukraine has any relations or holds any accounts with these banks. In 2016, *we provided banks with a list of risky European banks including 8 banks in 5 jurisdictions*. Today, any bank that opens an account to do some sort of transaction with such a bank will fall under the 100% of reserve requirement. As you can imagine, nobody will ever do this.

In the crisis period of 2014-2015, the national bank also intensified *the role of financial monitoring due to the need to use its toolkit to counter the capital outflow from the country*. In particular, we identified schemes for withdrawing capital from Ukraine by depositing funds with foreign banks that served as collateral for the fulfilment of contractual obligations of persons associated with the bank.

In order to prevent the outflow of capital, during 2015, the National Bank introduced *a set of anti-crisis measures in order to prevent abusive*

FX currency transactions by authorized banks and their clients, in particular, while purchasing foreign currency by fictitious contracts aimed at the use of funds for illegal purposes. We processed more than 250,000 applications for the purchase of foreign currency / payment orders in foreign currency. During 2015, the National Bank exercised control over the import of banking metals and FX cash, the export of FX cash for replenishment of correspondent accounts abroad, and compliance with the requirements that individual licenses use FX cash as a means of payment in the territory of Ukraine.

In parallel with extinguishing the fire, we launched *the review of the whole AML regulatory system.* Specifically, since 2014, the National Bank of Ukraine was actively involved in the drafting of the Law of Ukraine on prevention and counteraction to money laundering and terrorist financing, as well as in the development of a nationwide strategy for the development of financial monitoring until 2020, which was adopted in December 2015.

In pursuance of the IMF Memorandum, the National Bank of Ukraine, with the support if the IMF technical assistance, implemented international standards for *risk-based off-site and on-site AML supervisory tools*, focusing on risks related to AML. This reform ensured that reporting entities would focus their reporting efforts on suspicious transactions, as defined by the Financial Action Task Force (FATF), rather than sending thousands of routine reports yearly, the large majority of which did not contain any useful information.

The risk-based approach implied an **ongoing analysis of customers' financial transactions** taking into account their financial position, business activity, and an economic sense of the transactions. Specifically, AML supervision was focused on cash and scheme transactions, fictitious entrepreneurship, politically exposed persons (PEPs), identification of ultimate beneficial owners, and terrorism financing.

Implementation of the risk-based approach was aimed at:

- optimizing the usage of banks' resources

- increasing the efficiency and effectiveness of the measures taken by banks
- rational setting of banks' AML procedures
- adjusting the intensity of preventive measures proportionally to identified risks

We have developed a new regulation on AML/CFT, adopted in 2015, which substituted the formal quarterly analysis of bank's clients' transactions with a *permanent analysis* of banks' activities using a risk-based approach. That means that each client transaction should be verified by the bank with a view to ensuring the consistency of the financial condition of the client, the nature of his business, and the presence of an economic purpose for the transaction. Banks thus became responsible for the proper and timely detection of suspicious and/or scheme financial transactions.

The main principle implemented in AML supervision processes was the principle of **professional judgment**, which allowed banks to check clients' operations based on *substance over form*. Each transaction passing through the bank was checked for compliance with economic substance, since many operations during that period were carried out with the aim of cash withdrawal and tax evasion.

Banks were required to comply with the requirements of Ukrainian legislation to identify PEPs and related persons, existing clients or their representatives with high risk within three months after the regulation came into force; and with respect to other clients or their representatives, within six months.

The National Bank developed and provided banks with a *list of indicators of risky activity* of banks and their clients[17]. In particular, the signs of riskiness were:

- a lack of documentary evidence of the economic sense of a bank's or client's transactions and a lack of information as to

---

[17] NBU Resolution #369 dated 15.08.2016 (updated)

whether the client has sufficient funds to carry out certain financial transactions

- participation of the bank in financial transactions that may be related to cashing-out activities and/or implementation of fictitious business
- the use of non-purported accounts, the execution by the bank or its clients of financial transactions using stolen or invalid documents
- repeated prepayments for foreign contracts that the counterparty systemically violates or does not perform at all, based on information from public sources or from other financial institutions.

Under the risk-based approach, banks were allowed to define their own relevant indicators of risky activity and a list of clients to which additional AML monitoring should be applied. Banks did not apply enhanced AML measures to low-risk clients who do not conduct transactions in large amounts and are not suspect, including those who have accounts exclusively for receiving salaries, pension and other social payments, and have financial transactions that are not risky,.

In cases of establishing a customer's relationship to an entity that has signs of being fictitious, we recommended that banks assign an unacceptably high risk to such a client and use their legal right to withhold business relations with that client (including through termination of business relations).

To facilitate banks' risk assessment of customer transactions, the National Bank and the Independent Association of Ukrainian Banks introduced a joint project on financial monitoring "Best Practices in Financial Monitoring." We also provided banks with illustrations of the most common schemes for money laundering.

The success of the implementation of a risk-based approach to building an anti-money laundering system in banking institutions in Ukraine was acknowledged by the Committee of Experts on the Evaluation of Anti-Money Laundering Measures and the Financing of Terrorism (MONEYVAL). In their 2017 report on the evaluation of the effectiveness of our AML function,

MONEYVAL said that "*NBU resources appear to be directed at the areas of greatest risk in relation to banks and the quality of its supervision is highly regarded*". The report confirmed that Ukraine is a reliable jurisdiction in regard to counteraction of money laundering, financing terrorism, and financing proliferation of weapons of mass destruction, and does not require special controls by MONEYVAL and FATF.

Case: Veles Bank

About a dozen banks were withdrawn from the market solely due to violations of financial monitoring and fraud. At the same time, the actual number of banks involved in money laundering and fraud operations was substantially larger, though many of them also had significant problems with capital.

Noteworthy is the case of Veles, one of the small banks that was withdrawn from the market and liquidated due to violation of the AML legislation. Despite clear signs of the bank's risk-taking activities and the systematic violation of AML legislation, Veles actively used judicial tools to return its banking license. At the same time, Veles' affiliation with a sponsor of a political party -- the national bank's ardent opponent-- was also given a political flavour, as we were accused of political reprisals, although Veles bank was involved in an obvious criminal activity.

The decision to revoke Veles' banking license was taken in December 2015 due to systematic violation of the legislation in the area of AML, and its failure to comply with the regulations of the central bank.

Shortly before the liquidation, in September 2015, the National Bank prevented an attempt to transfer abroad about USD 460 million using fictitious documentation. After stopping the transaction, we initiated an onsite inspection of the bank on financial monitoring issues.

During the inspection, we were astonished to find that 90% of all transactions carried out by the bank were fraud and money-laundering. Most transactions were carried out using false documents. Bank accounts were opened to fake individuals including homeless individuals or even fake passports.

But the most interesting thing happened later when representatives of the Deposit Guarantee Fund came to Veles Bank to urgently withdraw the license and begin the liquidation procedure, but could not find it! The chairman of the bank came to the DGF representatives and said that only the day before (!), the bank had terminated its tenancy agreement and moved out of its office with all its equipment and servers to an unknown direction. According to documentation in 2015, only 3 people worked at Veles, and they disappeared with the bank.

The liquidation of this bank had no effect on financial stability, since there were never assets in this bank (the estimated market value of the securities **in the bank's portfolio** was 100 times (!) lower than their book value), as there were no obligations, since this bank was solely engaged in money laundering and illegal transfer of foreign currency abroad, and the number of clients was about 150 individuals.

Despite the protracted legal process, in which the courts took the opposite decisions, the central bank strictly stood its ground -- "zombie banks" should not be present in the market. And even in the face of unlawful court decisions, the central bank used its legal right to prevent such financial institutions and their owners from returning to the banking business.

h) Market communication of diagnostic results and recapitalization plans as «an art of the impossible» during crises

As the IMF recently said in a paper on communications, "Building understanding of policy is fundamental to its effectiveness. Better communications can help in the success of a country's reform efforts[18]."

---

[18] Frontiers of Economic Policy Communications. Departmental Paper No.19/08, IMF 2019.
https://www.imf.org/en/Publications/Departmental-Papers-Policy-Papers/Issues/2019/05/20/Frontiers-of-Economic-Policy-Communications-46816

My experience with banking sector reform showed that communications are extremely important. Although we tried to communicate during the crisis as comprehensively as possible, it turned out that communications were not enough, especially when we were forced to be responsible not only for the results of our work, but for all the mistakes made in previous decades.

Could we have done more with communications? Perhaps, but it remains a real dilemma.

The devaluation of the hryvnia in 2014-2015 was painful. But in the Ukrainian people's memory, this was not the first episode associated with depreciation of the national currency. Similar crises had already taken place in 1998 and 2008. Yet it was precisely the cleaning of the banking system that was associated with the greatest wave of outrage in society, since the withdrawal of banks from the market led to the direct losses of enterprises' assets and some households were not covered by the deposit insurance.

This led to an inevitable decline in trust of the central bank. The mass media also added fuel to the fire. I called the media the "heavy artillery", which was directed against us: all the key media in the country were in the hands of those with whom we fought for three years to clear the banking sector.

We had to respond to this barrage.

If we could use existing best practices with regard to monetary policy communications, then with regard to communicating issues related to financial stability, we had to be more cautious, by experimentally testing the acceptable degree of transparency in order to avoid destabilization of the financial markets and society.

Even today, communications in the area of financial stability are less explored and trickier than those on monetary policy issues. The truth is that communications about monetary policy are directed at a general audience to let them know how the central bank assesses the current economic stance and its prospects. That can be shared without any immediate change in the behaviour of economic agents. However, *in communicating issues related to financial stability, especially the results of diagnostics study and stress-tests, we had to be very careful not to trigger a bank run.*

Therefore, by communicating the results of the first AQR and stress tests, we avoided mentioning individual banks, instead focusing on informing the professional community and the general public about approaches we used to assess the quality of banks' assets, how we stress tested scenarios, and the overall results (specifying groups of banks, such as state-owned banks or Russian-owned banks).

In our communications, we emphasized that the need for banks' capital should be covered by implementation of a mandatory capitalization plan within a certain time frame. For example, the findings of the diagnostic studies of 2015 were communicated as a need for banks to take measures aimed at ensuring that regulatory capital adequacy requirements were met. At the same time, when we announced the recapitalization framework for all Ukrainian banks indicating their obligation to reach a 0-capital adequacy ratio on April 1, 2016, I worried a lot. For the professional community, it was clear – if banks had negative capital, according to the Basel principle, they were bankrupt.

It is thus a real dilemma between transparency of central banks' communications and possible negative market perceptions. That is why I have called it the "art" of CB communication. Yet, we succeeded and our public communications properly calmed market participants and the population at large.

First of all, we effectively pointed out the reasons why banks were declared insolvent. During 2014-2015, 5 of the 18 banks that failed to withstand deterioration in the economic conditions and ran out of liquidity were later declared insolvent.

The remaining 13 banks successfully executed business plans based on diagnostic study results and in line with commitments undertaken by banks to take corrective measures within a set timeframe. In particular, banks were able to increase their authorized capital, using subordinated debt to increase Tier 1 capital, by receiving irrevocable financial assistance or by reducing the portfolio of assets.

We stressed that *the results of stress testing, especially in the negative scenario, did not mean instantaneous insolvency of the bank*, but only reflected the potential need for additional capital. That is, *the results of the assessment in the baseline and pessimistic scenarios were not predictions of financial indicators*, but were intended to reveal the impact of the main risks on the bank's current financial condition.

We insisted that the results of stress testing should be interpreted carefully and exclusively in the context of the underlying model's key assumptions.

Similar information was translated at roundtables with experts and journalists, and via publication of individual reports and presentations. The results of the assessment of the financial stability of banks and information on trends of the banking sector development were published in periodic publications of the NBU including the Financial Stability Report, Banking Sector Review, and bank surveys on lending activity and systemic risks.

In addition to occasional communications for each bank that was withdrawn from the market, we created a *special landing page on the NBU main site* (http://badbanks.bank.gov.ua/), where we provided information about all causes and results of the major cleaning up of the banking system. It described the factors that led to the need for the regulator to take tough decisions regarding banks, and provided examples of violations by banks of sectoral, and even criminal, legislation.

As the situation stabilized, we launched an assessment of the financial soundness of banks and the banking system, and published *the results of stress testing of individual banks annually.*

Starting in 3Q2017, the National Bank began publishing monthly bank balance sheets, which until then had been availably only quarterly. In our opinion, more frequent publication of the balance sheets enabled external users, clients, and bank analysts, to track the dynamics of key bank indicators.

According to VoxUkraine, *the National Bank of Ukraine in 2015 ranked second among ministries and other authorities in terms of public awareness about reforms in different areas.*

Therefore, my strong recommendation is to communicate, communicate, and communicate more. Even if communication does not increase the degree of confidence in the regulator overnight, it will at least help improve public sentiment towards reforms when you explain to society the causes of the crisis and the actions taken by the regulator to resolve them.

CHAPTER 9

Introduction of systemic macroprudential policy

THE GLOBAL CRISIS of 2008-2009, as well as the debt crisis in the EU, also changed the perception of the main objectives of central banks' economic policy. Before the crisis, conventional wisdom was that the central bank should focus on ensuring price stability and contributing to sustainable economic growth. This approach made regulators blind to when the financial sector has accumulated systemic imbalances and related risks, since neither price stability, nor conventional banking supervision ensures that the systemic financial sector risks are prevented. In particular, successful implementation of basic rules on capital and liquidity doesn't ensure the absence of systemic financial sector risks.

As Paul Volcker noted as far back as 1984 when he was Chairman of US Fed: "A basic continuing responsibility of any central bank -- and the principal reason for the founding of the Federal Reserve – is to assure stable and smoothly functioning financial and payment systems.... Historically, in fact, the "monetary" functions were largely grafted onto the "supervisory" functions, not the reverse"[19].

In Ukraine, both crises led to a consensus for the need for even more emphasis on *macroprudential supervision* based on analysis of systemic risks and aimed at preventing financial crises. Today, macroprudential policy is valued as close to, or sometimes even equal to, the price stability goal of modern central banks.

---

[19] Volcker, Paul A., 1984, "The Federal Reserve Position on Restructuring of Financial Regulation Responsibilities," Federal Reserve Bulletin, Vol. 70 (July)

This means that a modern central bank has not a dual, but a *triple, mandate*: price stability, financial stability and economic stability. However, there is still no clear answer how all the three components can and should coexist within the mandate of a modern central bank.

Looking back, I concede that the crises of 2008-2009 and 2014-2015 in Ukraine were vivid reminders of the absence of a reliable and effective system of maintaining of financial stability. Both crises demonstrated the inappropriateness of delegating excessive responsibility to financial institutions for managing risks and market behavior without developing proper regulatory algorithms, reducing incentives for unfettered growth of loans to the private sector, and thorough implementation of a supervisory system that includes reforms of financial reporting and transparency. The threats to macro financial stability, emanating both from external (e. g., the volatility of international capital flows) and internal (weak corporate governance and risk-management) factors have shown that maintaining financial stability is no less important than ensuring prices stability as the goal of central bank policy. It also became evident that development of a toolkit for modern financial stability policy in Ukraine had lagged behind the pace of development of a monetary policy toolkit.

Maintaining financial stability was an acute issue for Ukraine. The country was among the top-3 globally in terms of the frequency of crises: over the last 20 years, Ukraine has experienced three deep crises, the last in 2014-2016. The direct fiscal costs of resolving that crisis amounted to almost 16% of GDP in those years, which is moderate relative to other countries. However, the indirect costs to the economy overall were much higher, at 38% of GDP. The consequences of Ukraine's systemic crisis continue to limiting bank lending and economic growth in the years since the crisis.

Exhibit 22. Fiscal costs of banking crisis resolution, % GDP

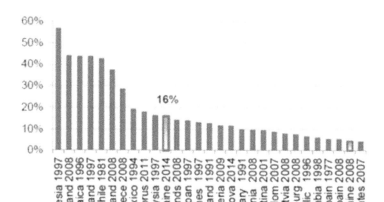

* Fiscal costs are defined as the percent of gross fiscal outlays related to the restructuring of the financial sector. They include fiscal costs associated with bank recapitalizations but exclude asset purchases and direct liquidity assistance from the Treasury.
Source: IMF, Ukraine 2014 – NBU calculations

The depth and frequency of the systemic crises in Ukraine was a function of multiple *fundamental problems*. These included the absence of effective banking regulation at the micro-level or a financial stability framework for measures to mitigate the emergence and build-up of systemic risks. In other words, the banking sector was not prepared for the crises. The NBU thus had to intervene in the midst of the crisis with strong measures, such as limits on deposit withdrawals, that were quite unpopular with bank clients.

Compared with the 2008-2009 crisis, which was provoked by cyclical factors including a rapid credit expansion, the 2014-2016 crisis was *structural in nature*:

- The dollarization of the economy and banking sector
- Banks had accumulated considerable loans to related parties prior to the crisis. For example, 100% of corporate loans at

Privatbank, the largest Ukrainian bank, were issued to companies related to its shareholders

- State-owned banks lent excessively (almost two-thirds of their credit portfolios) to companies belonging to politically exposed persons
- Many captive banks did not provide financial intermediation, but instead served the interests of business groups or specialized in withdrawing capital abroad or money laundering
- The banking sector had low liquidity and substantial maturity mismatches
- Weak banks were highly interconnected in specific segments including in interbank lending. That caused a domino effect once a single weak institution failed.

Most of those problems emerged prior to the crises of 2014-2015 or even 2008-2009. Nevertheless, they were not properly assessed and the regulator reacted to them insufficiently, both prior to and after the crisis. The two crises show the high cost ineffective financial regulation at the level of individual financial institutions as well as at the systemic level[20].

I must concede that *until 2014, the National Bank, in principle, had no systemic macroprudential policy.* The bank had carried out micro-prudential supervision, formally assessing the status of banks' assets. At the same time, an assessment of the current state of the economy and the forecast had not been taken into account when assessing the sufficiency of capital, which is extremely important for creating the necessary capital buffers to ensure the stability of the financial system under stressful scenarios.

Being responsible for the regulation and supervision of banks that constituted over 85% of the total assets of Ukraine's financial institutions, as well as conducting an oversight of payment systems, the NBU was

---

[20] NBU Macroprudential Policy Strategy, December 2018

de-facto carrying out the responsibility for financial stability in the country even though it lacked proper instruments for fulfilling this mandate.

Thus, given a bank-oriented financial system in Ukraine as well as widespread international practice, *we initiated amendments to the Law "On the National bank"* (approved by the Parliament in June 2015) giving the National Bank powers to ensure financial stability, including the stability of the banking system. This was the result of our belief that the function of ensuring financial stability was not limited to banks, but included responsibility for non-bank financial institutions, as well as the need to coordinate the work of other state institutions whose policies affected the maintenance of financial stability.

There was no public discussion of whether to entrust the National bank with a macroprudential mandate since a dominant trend across the globe at the time was to delegate the macroprudential mandate to the authority that already had a mandate for supervision and regulation of the financial sector.

In practice, the abovementioned Law provided the NBU with a mandate to design and implement macroprudential policy. This met EU standards in the recommendations of the European Commission and the European Systemic Risk Board. In promoting financial stability, the NBU was guided by the recommendations of the Basel Committee on Banking Supervision, the ESRB, and EU Directives CRR/CRD IV.

We defined several *streams of activities and areas of responsibility* to support financial stability:

- Macroprudential analysis, and macro stress-testing to detect systemic risks
- Development and implementation of macroprudential policy instruments to prevent crises
- Drafting legislation to regulate banking
- Serving as lender of last resort for the banking sector

- Control over financial soundness of individual banks, especially systemically important banks, *inter alia* through stress-testing
- Oversight over payment and settlement systems
- Cooperation with other authorities that contribute to financial stability

Moreover, the National Bank undertook certain obligations in the area of restoration of stability and confidence in the financial sector under an IMF-sponsored program.

Apart from the mandate for promotion of financial stability, the National Bank had at its disposal instruments for banking system regulation, access to financial sector microdata, analytical and forecasting models – everything for an efficient response to the crisis. Therefore, the National Bank was the appropriate authority for micro- and macroprudential regulation.

The internal **Financial Stability Committee (FS Committee)** was established to coordinate macroprudential policy within the NBU's mandate. This strategic policy-making committee was chaired by the Governor of the NBU, and met at least once a quarter, more frequently if needed.

The key tasks of the FS Committee were to identify systemic risks and ways to mitigate them, make recommendations on the use of macroprudential tools, and coordinate actions that promote financial stability at the NBU level. The FS Committee made recommendations to the NBU Board, which made decisions on macroprudential interventions. If a risk that the FS Committee has identified was beyond the NBU's mandate, then the FS Committee could recommend that the interagency Financial Stability Council step in.

a) Macroprudential Policy Strategy

Following best practices of numerous central banks and aligned with recommendations from the European Systemic Risk Board, the National

Bank of Ukraine published a **Macroprudential Policy Strategy**. In the Strategy, the NBU outlined objectives and principles of macroprudential regulation as well as a possible toolkit that for attaining the objectives.

According to the Macroprudential Policy Strategy, a **macroprudential policy cycle** was set up with **four main stages**:

Stage 1. Identification of Systemic Risks. The NBU analyzed the conditions of major markets based on open data and information from NBU departments (banking supervision, monetary policy, payment system oversight, open market operations, etc.), as well as information from other financial sector regulators. To identify risks, the NBU looked at quantitative indicators and expert judgments, *inter alia*, including but not limited to:

- Macroeconomic, monetary, and banking statistics, and indicators in the financial and real sectors
- The real estate market
- Solvency indicators for financial and industrial groups, which were the largest borrowers from Ukrainian banks, as well as for households
- Surveys of banks and other financial market players

Stage 2. Selection and Calibration of Tools. The NBU chose a macroprudential instrument based on the best fit for its identified systemic risk. To choose a macroprudential instrument, the NBU considered the following factors: scale of the systemic risk (affecting the entire system or only partially), its source (on the borrower or lender side), impact of the instrument on the bank's balance sheet or its market behavior, its impact on the financial cycle (limiting expansion or limiting downturn), and possible unintended consequences.

Then, the NBU made the instrument consistent with its other policies and calibrated it to the scale and potential contagion area of the risk, and to the conditions of and prospects for financial sector development. Instruments were pre-selected and pre-calibrated for eventual activation.

The NBU based its selection for an appropriate instrument on the basic list of instruments recommended by the ESRB. However, the NBU also deployed other macroprudential tools as appropriate, especially to mitigate risks specific to Ukraine's banking sector.

Stage 3. Macroprudential Intervention. The NBU reacted to systemic risks using risk warnings and macroprudential instruments. The NBU communicated risks to financial stability to financial market participants, other regulators, authorities, and the public. This was a mandatory stage of macroprudential policy. If stricter macroprudential measures were premature, unsuitable, or impossible, the NBU would have limited its intervention to communications alone.

If communication related to a risk was deemed insufficient, the NBU introduced the macroprudential instrument that had been selected based on prior analysis of its pros and cons. The FS Committee would recommend and the Board would approve decisions on the use of macroprudential instruments and their characteristics. If the NBU could not mitigate identified risks with those instruments, the NBU could initiate a discussion at the FS Council and invite other authorities to work on the solution. The NBU would inform market participants in advance of using most macroprudential instruments.

Stage 4. Assessment of the Impact of Macroprudential Policy. The NBU collected and analyzed data on the impact of the macroprudential instrument to understand all its effects. The regulator estimated the instrument's impact on the financial system based on an analysis of individual bank reports, key indicators for the banking system and for markets, and from changes in market sentiment. This helped the NBU understand whether the risk had been correctly identified, whether intermediate objectives were achieved, and whether the instrument was effective. Individual instrument evaluations sum up to an assessment of overall macroprudential policy.

The NBU was also able to study transmission mechanisms for instruments, ex ante and ex post, to better understand them and to improve their calibration. The regulator assessed the efficacy of an instrument based on the output of models and feedback from market participants. In order to understand the whole picture of the financial market stance, the NBU monitored a set of indicators.

Based on results of analysis of financial system and economy as a whole, a **Financial Stability Report** would be published twice a year. The aim of the Report was to identify risks to financial stability in Ukraine, analyze their impact on national economy and financial system and offer recommendations on enhancing financial stability. The focus of the Report is risks and recommendations.

Other important *regular publications* included the Banking Sector Review, the Systemic Risk Survey, and the Bank Lending Survey. Annually, the NBU published the results of stress tests and the FSC produced reports on its activities. The NBU also issued occasional communications, conducted research on specific events/topics, and held seminars and lectures, including at universities. Communications were mainly disseminated through the Financial Stability section of the NBU's official website.

Given the *structural weaknesses of Ukraine's economy*, we considered *tailored macroprudential solutions* in the Macroprudential Policy Strategy. Regular monitoring of numerous systemic risks, which can vary depending on different stages of the financial and economic cycle, and can also depend on external conditions, allowed the central bank to intervene accordingly.

Using that logic, the national Bank introduced a LCR requirement (from December 2018) and NSFR (in 2020), and tighter requirements on internal liquidity management at banks to tackle the short maturity of bank funding. As over 70% of bank hryvnia liabilities had a residual maturity of less than one month, the NBU encouraged banks to keep more assets in high quality liquid components and to extend the maturity of funding, for example by attracting longer-term deposits.

Introduction of Basel III Requirements

Preparatory work for the introduction of Basel III requirements started in 2015 with a roadmap for LCR[21] and NSFR[22] implementation.

Prior to our implementation of Basel principles of banking regulation, regulation was based on local operating standards, including bank liquidity and sustainability ratios, which were not consistent with EU and Basel requirements. The old coefficients for liquidity were obsolete, static and developed for banks operating in regular conditions. But they were useless in times of distress when the market situation could change so rapidly that those coefficients were inadequate due to their rigidity. Instead of Basel coefficients based on stress-scenarios, the old coefficients were backward-looking.

The roadmap for Basel III implementation was thus based on a gradual approach defined by modeling of different scenarios on real bank data. The idea was to secure a smooth transition to the new requirements and not to hurt the regular activity of banks. The timeframe for the introduction of LCR and NSFR was set in stages and revised later as estimates became more precise about their effects and in consultations with banks.

---

[21] **LCR** – liquidity cover ratio. Purpose: to ensure a higher ability of banks to absorb short-term liquidity shocks within one month. Calculation: the ratio of the volume of highly liquid assets to the total net cash outflow within 30 days ≥ 100%, calculated on the basis of the relevant stress scenario.

[22] **NSFR** - net stable funding ratio. Purpose: to provide banks with a higher ability to absorb liquidity shocks within one year and to stimulate banks to finance their activities at the expense of reliable long-term sources. Calculation: the ratio of the available amount of stable funding to the required amount of stable funding for one year ≥100% calculated on the basis of the relevant stress scenario.

Table 2. The timeline of introduction of Basel III coefficients

Instrument	2015	2016	2017	2018	As of 01.01.2019
LCR	60%	70%	80%	90%	100%
NSFR	To be introduced in 2021				

First stage (second half 2015-2016): concentration on the liquidity ratio

- Studying international experience and establishing a working group with banks on LCR
- Calibrating the coefficient components, determining input parameters and their differentiation according to their sensitivity to shocks
- Determining an acceptable set of stress tests (also setting the "severity level" of the stress scenario)
- Assessing the impact of new requirements on the banking sector and the determining the optimal minimum regulatory value, as well as the timing of its phased implementation.

Second stage (2017-2018): determining the strategy for applying liquidity ratios and introducing a net stable funding ratio

- Drafting legislation on LCR with World Bank experts and obtaining approval of the legal act
- Introducing a net stable funding ratio that provides for implementation of measures similar to the liquidity ratio
- Development of the strategy and tactics for using liquidity prudential instruments (norms)

Third stage (2018 forward):

- Starting calculation of LCR in test mode (simultaneously with the transition to IFRS 9), and conducting quantitative impact analysis

- Monitoring and gradually increasing the minimum normative value of liquidity ratios up to the 100% recommended by Basel III
- Discussing the concept of NSFR within the working group, and developing draft legislation on NSFR.

By the beginning of 2019, the LCR became mandatory for banks. Its introduction went painlessly given the preliminary preparatory work and a structural surplus of liquidity in the banking system.

The NSFR will become mandatory at the beginning of 2021. For some time, the current short-term liquidity ratio (H6) will be applied concurrently with the NSFR, and eventually it will be repealed. Banks will be required to comply with the NSFR across all currencies, as well as ensure that NSFR is constantly calculated and monitored separate in national and foreign currencies.

Introduction of capital buffers and a leverage ratio

Aside from minimum capital requirements, we have introduced **capital buffers** compliant with Basel III and CRR / CRD IV. Capital buffers were aimed at creating a "safety cushion" to absorb losses incurred if the risks to stability of the financial sector materialize. The introduction of capital buffers implied increased requirements for Tier 1 capital. In 2015, the NBU introduced *three buffers of capital* -- conservation, counter-cyclical, and systemic importance. These buffers would be activated *no earlier than 2020.*

The *capital provision (conservation) buffer* is accumulated by banks during the period of economic growth to offset potential losses arising in a general economic recession. Buffer size will increase annually from 2020 to 2023 by 0.625 p.p. (from 0.625% to 2.5%, as defined by the Basel Committee on Banking Supervision).

The countercyclical capital buffer is intended to protect the banking sector from accumulation of risks in times of credit expansion. Depending on the phase of the economic cycle, the buffer size will range from 0% to 2.5%. The introduction of a specified the countercyclical capital buffer will take place only after careful calculations and under conditions of sustainable economic growth in the country.

The National Bank of Ukraine also established certain requirements for systemically important banks because of their importance to the stability of the entire banking system and the economy in general. For systemic banks, the *buffer of systemic importance* was activated starting on January 1, 2020. Its size will depend on the category of a bank's systemic importance, with a range from 1% to 2%.

In accordance with the recommendations of Basel III and the CRR / CRD IV package, the minimum capital requirements will be in line with the requirements for a *leverage ratio, or the* ratio of capital of Tier 1 to total assets (both on and off-balance) without risk weights. This tool allows limiting the growth of active bank operations through the use of borrowed funds. The NBU introduced a leverage ratio in 2020.

Role of Stress Testing

Stress testing plays a major role in the identification of systemic risks. Stress test scenarios build on assumptions of deteriorating macroeconomic, sectoral, and specific financial indicators. The stress test helps evaluate the impact of economic shocks on banks and assess the related costs for the banking system. Even if the shock never materializes, the stress test yields valuable information. That information underpins actions that can be taken regarding a bank and recommendations for individual financial institutions or on the use of macroprudential instruments.

The NBU holds stress tests at the micro and macro level. The testing cycle for individual banks and the entire banking system comprises one year.

Micro Stress Tests

The NBU normally holds an asset quality review at banks before conducting micro stress tests. The tests model the operations of individual financial institutions in detail. These are top-down stress tests. This means that the NBU bases its calculations on the information reported by banks. The NBU applies additional requirements on banks based on the results of the test, including additional capital buffers or restructuring of assets or business processes. Compliance with those requirements should enhance a bank's resilience in the event of a crisis.

The NBU annually stress tests banks that account for 90% of banking sector assets. The tests are not be conducted at small banks, as any loss of capital at a small bank does not pose a systemic risk.

Macro Stress Tests

Macro stress tests are held for the total sector and mostly do not look deep into the operations of individual financial institutions. The macro stress tests are based on aggregated data. If a test identifies systemic risks that apply to many banks, the NBU may deploy macroprudential instruments. A macro stress test can also be based on assessments of individual banks. The test would then model feedback loops between financial institutions.

Macroeconomic Scenarios for Stress Testing

Stress tests are conducted based on two macroeconomic scenarios: baseline and adverse. The key risk factors feed into the model of the adverse scenario that helps the NBU measure the resilience of banks to crises. The baseline scenario provides the background for a comparison and helps to detect weaknesses in banks' current business models. The NBU develops scenarios on three-year horizons, which allows the model to capture all potential stages of a crisis, from the outbreak to the initial recovery.

The baseline scenario is generally in line with the NBU's macroeconomic forecast. The adverse scenario models a severe-but-plausible scenario. It does not necessarily reflect the experiences of past crises and does not constitute an alternative macroeconomic scenario of the NBU.

Scenario modelling builds on *four key groups of indicators*:

- **GDP and output volumes.** The scenario assumes that GDP and output will plummet, with varying impacts across different sectors
- **Exchange rate.** The scenario projects a substantial depreciation of the hryvnia
- **Inflation.** The scenario assumes the pace of price growth will accelerate during a crisis, in particular because of currency depreciation
- **Interest rates.** The model includes a sharp hike in the NBU's key interest rate that would squeeze the interest spreads and margins of banks

The NBU adjusts the list of risk factors in the adverse scenario based on the development path of the banking sector and the economy. The NBU also conducts reverse stress tests; this test first defines the amount of losses banks must be able to absorb, and then models the projected change in key macroeconomic indicators that generate such losses.

The aim of modelling indicators for individual banks or the entire banking system is not to forecast their precise change. This is impossible because of the assumption of static balance sheets. However, baseline and adverse scenarios show how existing imbalances could materialize, and their potential impact on bank profits and capital.

The NBU annually communicates macroeconomic scenarios for stress tests to banks and to the public explaining the rationale for their design.

Along with stress-testing, the NBU uses other macroprudential instruments. In the coming years, the bank plans to introduce more instruments. Over time, the NBU will adapt them to suit Ukrainian conditions, collect the necessary data, and revise the models to assess the impact from the instruments' use.

b) New prudential regulation and new credit
risk assessment; IFRS implementation

The results of stress-testing in 2015 also outlined the direction for improving the NBU's supervisory role in the future. In particular, the need to move from compliance to risk-based supervision was confirmed. The main benefit of supervision based on risk assessment is the mandatory presence of a predictive element during risk assessment and active use of professional judgment.

The main actions of the regulator were aimed at transitioning compliance-based supervision of banks to risk-based supervision, and to principles of continuous proactive monitoring. In particular, the NBU:

- Introduced identification of risk activities
- Modernized the Early Warning System
- Implemented a system of complex assessment of banks' risk activities

Identification of banks' risk activities

Empowered by amendments to existing legislation, the NBU identified indicators of banks' risky behaviour, including actions that may contradict with anti-money laundering requirements. Based on those indicators, the regulator obtained the rights to enforce compliance with the rules, and to impose penalties on banks.

We were able to conclude whether the bank was carrying out risky activities based on results from an analysis of the bank's reporting, banking supervision, and verification of compliance with the requirements of FX legislation or legislation on financial monitoring. Among other things, risk indicators may be triggered if a bank's operations (direct or indirect) have no obvious economic sense, or if the bank:

- is carrying out indirect lending of related parties
- does not include in its list of related parties' entities that have signs of affiliation with the bank

- is conducting transactions with fictitious securities
- uses financial instruments to artificially improve the financial results of the bank or to distort its reporting
- allows early repayment of term deposits to persons associated with the bank
- systematically violates requirements for cash transactions

Early Warning System – EWS

We created an Early Warning System to detect signs of deterioration in a bank's financial position in the preceding three to six months. The EWS was aimed not only at detection of risks based on current state of bank, but also at timely identification of trends in the bank's activity that might indicate how likely the bank's financial position was to deteriorate in the future. The EWS covered areas of risk assessment such as capital, assets quality, liquidity, and earnings.

The EWS was based on analysis of statistical and financial reporting both of the individual bank, and through comparative analysis of peer banks. For each system indicator, thresholds were set so that violations would signal in advance potential problems in the bank. Deterioration of EWS indicators and/or violations of thresholds would activate appropriate supervisory procedures with regard to the analysis of causes of deterioration and/or violations, assessments of possible consequences from deterioration of the bank's financial position in the future, and, if necessary, preparation for further supervisory actions or mitigation measures.

Thus, the EWS was proactive in nature and served as a support tool under the full supervision cycle, starting from estimation of indicators, through regular monitoring of the financial position of the bank, and up to application of appropriate supervisory actions.

Comprehensive risk assessment system (CRA)

The comprehensive risk assessment system (CRA) was created to provide a general assessment of a bank's riskiness, under which a bank supervision regime is established. It combines both quantitative and qualitative indicators. When assessing overall risk, the NBU takes into account the transparency of the ownership structure, the level of support of bank capital by shareholders, the sustainability of the business model, and other indicators.

Application of the CRA system enables:

- identification of the most important bank operations for supervisory analysis
- adherence to the supervisory principle of proportionality, which underlines that the intensity of supervision should be proportional to the risk level of the bank and its possible impact on the stability of the banking system
- optimization of the burden on supervisors and curators
- coordination of the activities of various NBU divisions including supervisory departments, financial monitoring, FX control, etc.

Thus, CRA results are used not only to determine a regime of on-site banking supervision, but also for the purpose of off-site banking supervision.

Assessment of banks' business models

An important component of the CRA system is an assessment of a bank's business model.

The business model is the aggregation of the means and methods used by the bank to perform its main activities, obtain profit, and further develop. A business model is a combination of multiple interrelated components (ownership structure, organizational structure, sales channels, customer base, product series, main business areas, income structure, expenses, etc.). For the purposes of banking supervision, the business model is an important instrument that ensures understanding inherent risks as well as enabling evaluation of the bank's contribution of individual risk to systemic risk, in order to define necessary supervisory actions and/or mitigation measures.

From the regulator's view, universal business models targeted on a broader range of customers (sectors of the economy), as well as business models based on servicing the bank's related parties were ineffective and could pose a systemic risk to financial stability; therefore, banking supervision proactively introduces measures aimed at curbing excessive risks connected with inefficient business models.

Thus, a new supervisory paradigm was set up to regularly identify and revise business models, monitor changes, and assess the level of compliance of the models with changes in the business environment, which also allowed the NBU to transition its perspective to a strategy of proactive supervision, oriented towards early detection of problems in a bank's activities and timely responses.

Exhibit 23. Early Warning System and Comprehensive Risk Assessment System in the system of supervisory decision-making

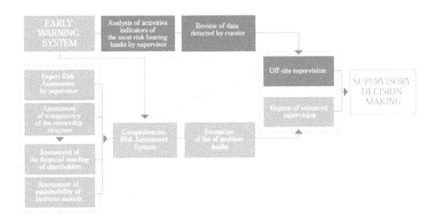

Source: NBU

New credit risk assessment

The early AQR revealed defective lending practices in a number of banks, especially those with local capital and state-owned banks. These banks were reluctant to act as a market intermediary and focused instead on the interests of their shareholders' business by lending to "friendly" borrowers, mostly with low financial condition.

Regulatory guidance on credit risks was not generally used nor taken into account in management decisions. The calculations of risk were usually done by back offices that used quite arbitrary interpretations of regulatory compliance requirements when assessing the value of property rights and corporate securities used as collateral for bank loans. *In some cases, there was a ten-fold difference between the bank's and the regulator's estimation of the value of collateral.*

The previous approach to assessing credit risk by banks had allowed assessment of a loan's quality based on the financial condition of the borrower, and the regularity and timeliness of the loan servicing. Such rules allowed artificial overestimation of the quality of the category through servicing old loans via financial assistance or attracting new loans. With regard to securities, a number of banks actively used the practice of ensuring artificial quotations on the stock exchanges, which allowed them not to create reserves on securities, even if the issuer's financial condition was unsatisfactory.

Given the high share of non-performing loans and incorrect presentations of assets, quality in banks' financial statements was a crucial challenge. The diagnostic study helped to uncover loopholes in banking regulation and identify window-dressing practices and overstatements of the quality of banks' credit portfolio. All this led to hidden capital shortfalls, which the NBU reviews revealed. The incapacity of the existing regulatory framework to evaluate credit risks enabled numerous abuses by banks in carrying out this assessment in order to conceal the real amount of their credit risk (which created fewer provisions for credit operations), meaning that we had to completely reloaded the credit risk assessment system for banks.

To rule out risky practices in the future, the NBU introduced **new credit risk assessment rules** for local banks. In June 2016, we adopted a completely new provision for the estimation of banks' credit risks, which complied with the basic principles of effective banking supervision of the Basel Committee, in particular with regard to the need to assign the amount of uncovered credit risk (the difference between risk under the

IFRS and aggregate reserves to cover losses from asset-side transactions) to reduce banks' regulatory capital[23].

In compliance with Basel principles of banking supervision, the new rules required credit risk estimation based on the *'expected loss' concept*. Prudential credit risk assessment methodology provided a basis for accounting provisions. If the estimated credit risk was higher than IFRS-based provisions, the excess was directly deductible from the regulatory capital. These new rules led to full and timely recognition of credit losses, and gave banks a strong incentive to improve their internal risk management practices.

This regulation was developed over a year in close cooperation with the banking community and experts from the IMF, the World Bank, Oliver Wyman, and USAID. An important feature of the new approach was the combination of clear, detailed rules and general principles for assessing credit risk, which indicated the need for well-grounded professional judgment both by the bank and the regulator. As a result, banks were no longer able to avoid recognition of low quality of assets, referring to formal rules. To calculate the expected loss level, the provisions relied on the formula recommended by the Basel Committee on Banking Supervision, which uses *three components*: PD -- probability of default, LGD -- loss given default, and EAD -- exposure at default.

The provisions also included:

- application of *standardized approaches to assessing the financial condition of the bank's debtors* (an econometric scoring model for legal entities, and a list of qualitative and quantitative indicators for other debtors)
- an option to assess the borrower's credit risk based on the *characteristics of the group of companies* with which the borrower is linked by the control relationship or joint economic risk.

---

[23] NBU Resolution #351 dated 30.06.2016 (updated)

(The financial condition of the group of companies could both improve or worsen the credit risk assessment of the borrower.)

- other factors for identifying the level of credit risk (in particular, meeting debt obligations in a timely manner). If high credit risk indicators were triggered, then the quality of the loan would fall even if the econometric scoring model determined a higher quality of the loan
- an expansion of *portfolio asset valuation* and definition of the main criteria for such an assessment. Loans to business entities and individuals in the amount of up to UAH 2 million were valued by banks on a portfolio basis
- improved requirements for collateral and its applicability. In particular, property rights (except for property rights to deposits) were excluded from the list of collaterals that can be taken into account by banks when determining the amount of credit risk

The provisions were applied in the test mode as of September 2016 and became mandatory in March 2017.

New standards of risk management in banks

The introduction of new standards for credit risk assessment in banks was associated with the new requirements for the organization of banks' risk management system.

The diagnostic studies of 2014 and 2015-2016 showed that the credit decision-making processes in banks were extremely inadequate, and that the "appetite for risk" was unjustifiably high, even in conditions of a stagnating economy. Lending to many companies and individuals was carried out without proper assessment of their financial situation, which had led to a significant deterioration in the quality of the loan portfolio in previous years. Banks were advised to adhere to conservative risk management standards, to carry out a comprehensive assessment of the financial position of potential borrowers, and to analyse the business reputation of management and shareholders of borrowing companies in detail.

Two years later, in order to standardize risk management in banks, a *regulation on the organization of a risk management system in banks and banking groups* was approved in June 2018[24]. The requirements were based on the principles provided by the Basel Committee on Banking Supervision and were considered international best practice.

This document was carried out in cooperation with the banking community and international experts, and strengthened the supervisory role of the bank's Board in creating a powerful risk management culture, monitoring compliance of the risk profile, and general monitoring of compliance with principles of risk management.

The document introduced requirements for a bank's organizational structure in the area of risk management, strengthened requirements for the competence and independence of the risk management and compliance units in banks, and ensured the sufficiency of financial and human resources to carry out their tasks. It also located reporting on risk management directly within the bank's Board.

The regulation also set requirements for ensuring proper risk management using ***three lines of protection***:

- First line: at the level of business and support units of the bank. These departments bear the responsibility for risks and report on the current management of those risks
- Second line: at the level of the risk management unit and the compliance control unit
- Third line: at the level of the internal audit unit, for verifying and assessing the effectiveness of the risk management system

The regulation required documentation of internal risk management, including risk-disclosure declarations, risk management strategies and policies, methods for identifying material risks, codes of conduct (ethics), and risk management procedures. It also enumerated a list of primary risks (credit risk, liquidity risk, bank book interest rate, market

---

[24] NBU Resolution #64 dated 11.06.2018

risk, operational risk and compliance risk), which the bank is obliged to identify, evaluate, monitor, and report.

In order to ensure that banks had effective models and risk assessment tools, stress tests were aimed at determining the bank's ability to withstand potential shocks and threats, and to create a reliable information system on risk management and reporting. Given the scale of work that banks had to accomplish in order to implement the requirements of the regulation, the National Bank of Ukraine provided for their implementation by April 2020.

To continue implementation of European legislation and the recommendations of the Basel Committee on Banking Supervision, the National Bank introduced **capital requirements to cover banks' operational risks** at the end of 2019. The banks' capital needs in order to cover operational risks will be determined in accordance with the new standardized approach of the Basel Committee on Banking Supervision (Basel III: Finalizing post-crisis reforms, December 7, 2017) taking into account specificities of the Ukrainian banking system.

New capital requirements will be introduced gradually. Test calculations of the volume of operational risk will begin in 2020 following publication of 2019 annual financial statements. Starting in January 2022, banks will be required to cover their operational risk.

Definition of systemically important banks

In 2014, the procedure for **identifying systemically important banks (SIBs)** was introduced at the legislative level. The high-level criteria for determining the systemic importance of banks were the bank's size, its degree of financial interconnection with other financial institutions, and its main area of activity.

Within the framework of the Law, the National Bank of Ukraine developed and approved the methodology for identifying SIBs that could rely on government support if their shareholders failed to solve problems with the banks' capital[25]. These banks would be subject to more strict regulatory requirements. The definition of SIBs was set to be carried out annually with the use of a multi-factor model, based on criteria of systemic importance.

The methodological principles for identifying SIBs were developed taking into account the recommendations of the Basel Committee on Banking Supervision on the principles of supervision of local SIBs, as well as the relevant provisions of EU legislation.

According to the methodology approved in December 2014, the indicators of systemic importance of the bank were calculated using the following weight coefficients.

Table 3. Indicators of systemic importance of banks

#	Indicator	Coefficient (W), %
1	Total assets	35
2	Deposits of individuals, business entities and non-bank financial institutions	35
3	Loans provided to legal entities by type of economic activity: agriculture, industry, construction	15
4	Funds borrowed from other banks	7.5
5	Funds deposited in other banks	7.5

According to the criteria in force as 2016, two major state-owned banks (Ukreximbank and Oschadbank) as well as a bank that was nationalized in December 2016 (Privatbank), were determined to be systemically important. They retained that status in 2017 and 2018.

For SIBs, the regulator can apply enhanced prudential requirements, in particular, increased liquidity and capital ratios. This is consistent with generally accepted world practice. Also, SIB status conveys a special mode of bank supervision.

---

[25] NBU Resolution #863 dated 25.12.2014

Introduction of a Credit Registry of the NBU

An important step towards better risk assessment was introduction of a **central credit registry** (CCR) of the National Bank. This was set in order to enhance information-sharing between banks regarding their borrowers. We were not pioneers on this path. According to the World Bank, public CCRs (in most cases within central banks) were already operating in 91 countries, including 16 EU countries. A number of other countries (the Netherlands, Luxembourg, Greece, Finland, Estonia and Cyprus) were planning to have CCRs in place as well.

The establishment of a CCR in Ukraine was extremely important since many borrowers had debts in different banks, while servicing their debt differently: paying to one bank, but not to another. As a result, the banking system had a *distorted risk profile of credit exposure* for certain borrowers: the banks in which the loan was serviced rated the borrower as reliable, without setting up provisions for the loan, despite the fact that in other banks, the loan could be recognized as in default.

Considering the systemic importance of this project in terms of improving the quality of banks' credit risk assessment and reducing the share of non-performing loans in the medium term, we developed a draft law for a central credit registry, which was included in the Memorandum with the IMF and the EU cooperation program.

I admit it was not an easy task. As expected, we faced a great deal of opposition from private credit bureaus who feared that introduction of the NBU credit register would destroy their business. Although we repeatedly explained that the NBU credit register was created for the purposes of prudential supervision and in order to improve the risk system in banks, various changes to the draft legislation slowed down the process for more than a year. In addition, during Parliament's consideration of the bill, more changes were made to it, setting the threshold value of the loan amount, below which information on it is not transferred to the credit register, at the level of 100 minimum wages (or equivalent in foreign currency).

The fully operational NBU Credit Register was preceded by a semi-annual period during which banks sent information to the National bank without receiving it back. During this period, we verified the quality of the data provided and established an IT interface for data exchange. Further, the Deposit Guarantee Fund, which was managing the assets of insolvent banks, was connected to the system.

The NBU credit registry became operational in September 2018. The NBU now uses the register to recalibrate the PD and LGD ratios used by banks to assess credit risks. The Credit Register helps promote effective monitoring of credit risk concentrations in the system.

c) IFRS 9 implementation after the crisis

The transition to IFRS was one of the first, and perhaps most important, steps that we made in 2015. For the first time, as regulators, we could obtain *reliable, complete, and unbiased information about the financial conditions of banks* and their operating activities. It is particularly important to understand that this transition occurred during a rigorous analysis of assets and stress-testing of banks -- a correct reflection of the financial condition of banks was key to making effective banking supervision decisions. We applied IFRS in the development of the stress testing methodology in the context of calculating the volume of provisions for the impairment of bank loans.

Specifically, we introduced conformity with IFRS with respect to:

- operations with securities and financial investments
- preferred shares and investments by associates
- transactions with shareholders of the bank, formation and use of provisions for credit risks
- accrual of interest income on assets for which impairment had been recognized

The transition to IFRS ensured the formation of a *single database for statistical, financial, and tax reporting.*

The National Bank also enabled the transition to IFRS by other economic entities. In an effort to solve the problem of high concentrations in the sector, we introduced new requirements for the calculation of credit risk, such as the inclusion of information on the aggregate lending volume of companies that are part of the groups under common control. Banks were required to take into account the risks of the group to which the borrower belonged and additionally to use consolidated financial statements of the parent company of the group in order to calculate the credit risk of the individual enterprise. As of 2018, all borrowers of banks with an outstanding loan amount above UAH 200 million (ca. USD 8 million) needed to have financial statements in accordance with IFRS standards, as verified by an auditor.

Thus, by 2018, the National Bank, together with Ukrainian banks, had switched to a new international financial reporting standard -- IFRS 9. The transition took place concurrent with the global international financial community.

IFRS 9 has met the need to streamline requirements for classification of financial instruments and credit risk assessment. Its main innovations were the introduction of a **new classification of financial assets** directly based on the bank's asset management models, economic characteristics of cash flows generated by the financial instrument in accordance with contractual terms, and the introduction of a **new model for assessing credit losses**. Unlike earlier local standards, which were concerned with losses that had already occurred, under IFRS 9 what matters is the expected loss assessed by applying potential risks. In addition, we were confident that reporting in accordance with IFRS 9 would generally increase the confidence of key stakeholders in the financial statements of the Ukrainian banking system.

I am proud to note that the Ukrainian *National Bank was one of the first central banks in the world to transition to IFRS 9*, given the importance of its impact on the development of the economy and financial markets, and its aid in promoting transparency of financial statements of banks and the central bank itself. Adopting IFRS 9 also allowed the National

Bank to have direct impact on public finances. Our positive experience transitioning to IFRS 9 enabled us to:

- ensure a smooth transition of the Ukrainian banking system to a new standard
- share our experience with other central banks, for example during an international round table in the fall of 2018

The banking sector switched to IFRS 9 gradually:

- In early 2018, banks were granted a **three-month transitional period**, during which no sanctions were applied for violations of the prudential requirements and reporting rules that occurred due to changes in the valuation of financial instruments in accordance with IFRS 9
- Later, we extended the transitional period until the end of June 2018 so that banks could gradually adopt to the new reporting

As a result, the transition to the new standard did not have a significant effect on the operational efficiency of the banking sector. In addition, despite the fear that the new reporting standard would lead to additional capitalization, **transition to IFRS 9 did not affect the capital adequacy of banks**.

Our preliminary estimates suggested that the transition to a new standard that assessed credit risk losses based on expected losses, not those already incurred by banks, could have had a *noticeable but one-off impact on the banks' capital*. The impact on regulatory capital was expected to be lower, as *banks already had to comply with the NBU's regulation on credit risk assessment*, which was based on estimation of expected losses on financial instruments. This means that Ukraine's rules for assessing credit risks contributed to the preparation of banks for the timely and full-fledged introduction of IFRS 9.

In December 2017, the NBU conducted its *first survey* to find out how the banks were assessing possible loan losses. The survey, which covered 30 banks, concerned expected loss parameters over a horizon of 12 months for retail loans that were at the first stage of assessment according to IFRS 9, i.e., those that had not seen significant growth in their credit risk. The survey found that that significant portion of banks were still at the stage of developing models, and their assessments had not been finalized. In addition, there were substantial discrepancies between the banks' assessments of similar loans, which showed there was a need for continued monitoring of the banks' provisioning approaches.

Then, in April 2018, the NBU held a *broader survey* of banks on their assessment of possible losses in the event of borrower default. This time, all banks were polled about both retail and corporate loans. Banks provided information on quantitative parameters of expected losses for loans at the first stage (according to IFRS 9), and about an algorithm for calculating the lifetime PD. In Q1, most banks had already finalized their models. An analysis of the survey showed that, on average, the banks' assessments of the parameters were not much different from the previous ones, while the range of assessments across banks remained wide.

Actual implementation of the new standard thus confirmed our preliminary assumptions: **the transition to IFRS 9 did not have a significant impact on banks' capital**.

The negative effect of transitioning the banking sector to IRFS 9 amounted to only UAH 10 billion (circa USD 400 million). These losses were driven by provisioning for expected loan losses that were assessed at stages 1 and 2 according to IFRS rules, and by increasing provisions for impaired loans (stage 3). However, this decrease was largely *offset by the sector's earnings in Q1 2018* of UAH 8.7 billion.

After banks transitioned to IFRS 9 and began applying the expected loss approach to provisioning, the NPL coverage ratio reached 87%. That coverage ratio approached the levels of credit risk (prudential provisions) as measured according to the NBU's requirements.

As a result of our transition experience, I conclude that the timely implementation of international best practice in credit risk assessment allowed a smooth transition to international financial reporting standards, which in turn contributed to an efficient supervision over the financial market and development of the country's information infrastructure.

In general, the application of IFRS 9 in Ukraine has been a positive step that will encourage the banking system to be more responsible and risk averse, and thus the whole banking system will be able to react more positively to potential threats to financial stability and to eliminate them in a timely manner.

Summary

I can confidently say that since 2017 the medieval horror in Ukraine's banking sector no longer exists. The new team, which came to the National Bank of Ukraine in 2014-15 managed to profoundly transform the country's banking system and turn it from an ugly duckling into a beautiful swan. Today, three years on, we are positive that the landscape of Ukraine's financial sector has been dramatically changed and that the foundations for a sounder and healthier banking system have been established. The banking system is currently showing evidence of recovery as deposits are flowing back into the system, banks are cautiously optimistic on new lending activity and capital adequacy, and financial ratios are improving.

The banking sector was able to demonstrate a gradual recovery: after more than three years of crisis, virtually all key performance indicators of banks now have positive dynamics. Due to high operating efficiency and a low cost of credit risk, today, Ukrainian banks are highly profitable: Their profit increased from UAH 21.7 billion ($820 million) in 2018 to UAH 59.6 billion ($2.3 billion) in 2019 -- an all-time high -- and the ROE indicator increased from 15% in 2018 to 34% in 2019. Today, Ukrainian banks are well-capitalized: Regulatory capital adequacy ratio has grown from 12.7% in 2018 to more than 19% by year end 2019. By contrast, back in 2016, for most banks, that figure was close to zero.

The share of assets and liabilities in FX decreased from their peak values of 2015; today, the share of FX deposits and loans is slightly more than 40% of the total volume. The NBU expects the de-dollarization trend will continue as a result of maintenance of financial stability and slowing down inflation. According to the NBU, the natural level of dollarization should be about 20% for economies similar to Ukraine.

Profitability risks are low now, but banks are aware that in the medium-term, profitability will normalize to average European levels. At the same time, most of banks' current profits will have to focus on the formation of capital stock, as future requirements for capital of banks will increase significantly. First, a buffer of capital conservation will be launched, followed later by other capital buffers. The structure of regulatory capital will change. The list of risks, which should be secured by capital, will be expanded. In order not to have difficulties with meeting the new capital requirements in the future, it is expedient for banks to build up capital now.

The Ukrainian banking system is now in the third stage, sustainable development. **A full-fledged revival of lending is a priority goal of the National Bank in the mid-term.** However, it is clear that in a country that has only recently gained macro-financial stability, loans cannot become cheap with the wave of a magic wand. However, thanks to comprehensive financial reform, all necessary prerequisites for the recovery of lending have already been created.

Firstly, the deliberate tightness of monetary policy of the central bank helped inflation decrease to the target range, slightly above 4% in 2019, while four years ago, at the beginning of Ukraine's transition to inflation targeting, it was 10 times higher! This has allowed the central bank to continue the easing cycle of the key rate, which is now close to a single-digit rate for the first time since the start of the war in the country.

Secondly, the banking sector is in very good shape, as evidenced by the level of capitalization, profitability, and liquidity. Across many comparable indicators, such as the provision rate for non-performing assets, the banking system of Ukraine is in better condition than the banking systems of peer-countries that haven't gone through an economic "clinical death" like we did.

Thirdly, Ukraine adopted necessary laws aimed at strengthening the rule of law in the country, including the protection of creditors' rights, improving bankruptcy procedures, etc. This allowed banks to increase their risk appetite by having a better system for exercising their creditor rights.

Of course, reforms should be carried out in related areas as well, such as judicial and legal enforcement reforms. The level of companies' transparency should be increased to increase their eligibility to apply for bank loans. However, even at the level of the banking sector, the work done is already beginning to bear fruit. Ukrainian banks have begun to lend -- not to their owners or other related parties, but to real businesses and households. During 2018-2019, consumer lending grew at a rate of 30% year-over-year, and lending to non-default companies grew by 15%–20% year-over-year. The return of public confidence in the banking sector of Ukraine has been confirmed as well by steady growth in the volume of household deposits in local currency.

Nevertheless, **the mission is not entirely accomplished.** More changes in prudential regulation and supervision practices are required to secure sustainable recovery of lending and to enhance banks' resilience and capacity to withstand shocks.

Huge opportunities for banks are opening up due to upcoming agricultural land reform in Ukraine. Bank loans will be needed to increase investment in improving productivity of agricultural production. At the same time, after the transfer to private ownership, land will be able to be pledged as collateral for loans, thus significantly expanding the credit capacity of the banking system.

Equally important is the development of mortgage lending. The reduction in mortgage rates in the national currency is capable of giving new breath to the construction industry while avoiding repeating mistakes of the past related to mortgage-lending in foreign currency.

CHAPTER 10

The third priority: Internal transformation of the central bank

WHILE REFORMING THE banking system, it was equally important to transform ourselves. The main goal of our internal transformation was to show by example the qualities we wanted to see in the country's banking sector: transparent, well-managed and efficient.

Internal transformation is a reform not always visible from the outside. But in terms of its systemic importance and magnitude, it was comparable to the other reforms we did in the banking sector and monetary policy. The primary objective of our internal transformation was to improve efficiency and strengthen the central bank's institutional capacity to implement its core monetary and financial policies.

At the time of the arrival of the new team in the National Bank in 2014, we found the National Bank to be a huge organization of 12,000 staff, 500 fleet vehicles, and 150,000 square meters of premises. For decades, the NBU had been expanding well beyond central bank functions and assets. The central bank owned a university and academy, a TV channel, hotels in resorts areas, hospitals and sports complexes. It seemed as though it could perform any function except quality central banking.

We immediately started our ***transformation project*** in order to increase the central bank's institutional capacity as a regulator. We planned a 30-month transformation, divided into *4 stages*: (i) preparatory, (ii) organizational transformation, (iii) process reengineering and (iv) realization of a new vision of the National Bank. The patron of the central bank's reform the *Interim Steering Committee* on the reorganization of the structure of the National Bank, which became the *Change Management Committee* in September 2015. In order to increase our efficiency, we adopted a project management approach with several key goals:

- simplification of the organizational structure and optimization of the number of personnel
- centralization of management and reengineering of all processes
- focus on key functions and increased efficiency of the decision-making system
- reduction of hierarchical levels in the central office and increased efficiency in the internal processes of interdivisional interactions
- optimization of support and other non-core functions
- optimization of regional branches

NBU Strategic sessions

Unity and a shared understanding of priorities and ongoing processes in the organization were crucial to implementation of our reforms. Therefore, we launched strategic sessions of the NBU, held during weekends twice a year (spring and autumn). At these sessions, the management of the central bank, including members of the Board and heads of departments, summed up the results to date and determined future tasks.

Guided by the Japanese proverb, *"Vision without action is a dream. Action without vision is a nightmare"*, at the 2015 strategic session we defined our *mission, vision, and values*. Five years on, they continue to serve the central bank as the main direction for future development.

- Our *mission* was to ensure price and financial stability that contributes to the sustainable development of Ukraine, according to the NBU law.
- Our future *vision* was to become a modern, open and independent central bank enjoying public trust and integrated into the European community of national central banks.
- Our *values* were the "5Ps" (based on the first letters of the respective words in Ukrainian): Patriotism, Professionalism, Transparency, Integrity and Partnership.

Exhibit 24. Mission, vision and values of the National Bank of Ukraine (defined in Strategic session in 2015)

OUR MISSION ◄

To ensure price and financial stability contributing to the sustainable economic development of Ukraine.

► OUR VISION

A modern, open, and independent central bank enjoying public trust and integrated into the European community of national central banks.

OUR VALUES

Patriotism   Professionalism   Transparency   Integrity   Partnership

Source: NBU

a) New modern structure

During the first (preparatory) stage, which lasted until November 2014, we carried out a deep analysis of the current structure, functions and processes in the National Bank, and held a number of consultations with international organizations, missions, leading international and local experts. We analyzed more than 100 organizational structure models of central banks used in different countries.

We approved the B-1 target organizational structure, a new concept of administrative and functional subordination; and subordinated the structural divisions of the regional offices according to the relevant structural units of the central office.

Transformational changes developed during the preparatory stage gained full momentum after adoption of legislation aimed at strengthening the

NBU's institutional capacity and effectiveness. The amendments, passed by Parliament in June 2015, transformed the Board into an Executive Committee composed of the Governor, the First Deputy, and each Deputy responsible for specific function within the central bank. The procedure for decision-making by the NBU Board was also set as a simple majority of votes with each board member having one vote. The amendments also strengthened the supervision mandate of the NBU Council as well as the personal autonomy of the Council members.

This model was fundamentally different from existing decision-making in the central bank, in which the size of the board was determined by the Governor (in certain periods, the Board had comprised up to 15 people), and decisions were made almost individually.

Upon my arrival, the "One man show" model was gone. Under the updated structure, each of the 6 members of the Board was responsible for a key functional group: prudential supervision, monetary policy, open market operations, payments and settlement, finance and administration. According to best practice, several general functions were subordinated directly to the Governor (Legal, Security, Internal Audit, etc).

Exhibit 25. New NBU organizational chart focused on 6 core functions

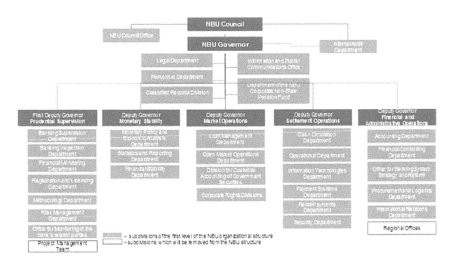

As a result of these organizational changes, the number of hierarchical levels in the National Bank was reduced by two, which, in turn, led to a 60% reduction in the number of management positions.

This new structure also made it possible to delegate sufficient authority for making operational decisions to the B-1 level, and to focus the work of the Board on truly strategic decisions and assessing the impact decisions had on various aspects of the Bank's activities.

Introduction of project management at the National Bank

In 2015, the NBU began the transition to integrated project management using the framework defined in the *Project Management Model Concept* approved by the NBU Board.

Eighty initiatives and projects based on this concept were implemented, 51 of which were related to the implementation of the Comprehensive Program for the Development of Ukraine's Financial Sector 2020, and 34 of which were related to the internal transformation of the NBU (including a pool of 15 projects for the removal/reorganization of non-core functions).

Project management consisted of the following *main elements*:

- the decomposition of strategic goals into the portfolio of projects
- introduction of uniform criteria for projects, allowing for separation of project activities from daily operations
- introduction of a unified approach to project management including uniform standards on the organizational structure and a role model for project management
- clear division of project management functions between a sponsor, project leader, and project manager
- creating a project management office to support projects at all stages of the life cycle
- building a project reporting system and synchronizing projects in the portfolio;

- establishing the Change Management Committee, a collegial body for centralized project management
- development of a project management culture by developing and implementing standard methodologies and project management tools; a system of continuous development of project managers' competences, including trainings and other modes of study; collection and analysis of project experience as a basis for improving methodology and project management

Centralized project management provided us with internal transformation at the desired pace, allowed saving project resources due to the introduction of standardized approaches, methodologies and project management tools and synchronization of projects according to the strategic vision for the development of the NBU and the Comprehensive Program for the Development of Ukraine's Financial Sector 2020.

b) Non-core assets elimination, new procurement procedures, and outsourcing

In the post-GFC period, the *global trend in both public and private sectors has been to gradually abandon non-key activities and focus on key businesses.* Central banks are no exception.

Under the next stage, implementation of organizational changes, optimization of the non-core and auxiliary functions of the central bank was completed. **Functions that were not related to the direct mandate of the National Bank of Ukraine were eliminated**, transferred to other public authorities, or outsourced.

As a result, the number of employees in regional offices and departments decreased more than two-fold, and the number of staff at the central office decreased by almost a quarter. Educational institutions of the National Bank of Ukraine were fully transferred to the Ministry of Education. A number of divisions that performed non-core functions of the central bank were withdrawn or reorganized such as the TV channel, medical, sport and recreational complexes, etc. At the same time, the National Bank of Ukraine as an employer adhered to all applicable laws and fulfilled all its obligations to employees.

An important driver for optimizing the costs of the National Bank was the centralization of the procurement process, and the introduction of the electronic trading system

Previously, there were no clear mechanisms for monitoring needs, initiation and procurement processes; no direct links between budgeting and procurement plans; no clear processes for procurement planning; and a lack of quality managerial reporting. The procurement process was also decentralized and involved a dispersed set of coordinating bodies (36 committees and 57 procurement points not including procurement procedures).

Four main elements were introduced to **reorganize the procurement process**:

- Planning and controlling the relevance of procurement needs with dynamic driver-based requirements, and integration of procurement planning with the budget process
- Centralization of regional procurement offices and structural units of the central office
- Introduction of new tools, including switching to purchases made through an electronic procurement system, and establishing a database of typical contracts
- Categorization of procurement needs for the purpose of market analysis, construction of procurement strategy, and definition of critical procurement

The National Bank of Ukraine took part in a pilot project with *ProZorro*, which was one of the most advanced electronic procurement platforms in the world. This system had significant advantages for the National Bank of Ukraine: public procurement through electronic trading ensured the transparency and simplification of procurement procedures, fair competition among suppliers, and savings of up to 20% of purchasing costs.

The *Competitive Bidding Committee* was established in accordance with requirements of the Law of Ukraine "On Public Procurement", with the following issues subject to consideration at Committee meetings:

- Planning the implementation of procurement procedures
- Drawing up and approving a public procurement annual plan, an annex to the public procurement annual plan, and amendments
- Selection of a procurement procedure

In total, during 2014 to 2016, the bank's **cost-effectiveness** from internal transformation amounted to UAH 7.3 billion.

c) Centralization of functions, closure of regional branches, drastic staff reductions

While focusing on basic central bank functions, we disposed of most non-core functions and assets. The National Bank evolved towards being a *branchless central bank* by closing regional offices (previously the 25 regional branches did not have much activity) and centralizing all key functions in the central office.

According to the target model, we reformed 24 regional offices (excluding the Crimean branch, which was occupied) through implementation of a *series of interrelated projects*:

i. centralization of all regional office functions into the central office, with the temporary presence of specific functions in several macro regions (cash operations, administrative, "Single Window" for documentation, IT support), and further centralization or outsourcing (e.g., project for implementation of delegated cash handling)

ii. centralization of the remaining regional offices into a single system for accounting, and transfer to a single code of the bank the liquidation of the respective regional offices as separate structures of the National Bank

iii. centralization of payroll accounting

iv. implementation of the "Single Window"

v. outsourcing of security function, etc.

Reforming the regional offices enabled us to:

- improve the regional efficiency of the National Bank's functions
- eliminate duplication of functions and optimize the Bank's expenses
- strengthen the regulator's main functions and simplify the Bank's organizational structure
- optimize the number of staff whose working places had been located in the regions

Today, only the cash-support function is carried out in the regions.

While most of central bank's functions were centralized by withdrawing them from the regional branches, some functions were centralized such as the ***depository function***.

The outcome of this project was that all depositary functions, which had been previously performed in different departments, were centralized at the NBU Depository Unit without duplication of functions. A single database of contractual agreements was introduced along with centralization of the budgeting processes, and control of income and expenses of depository activities.

Today, reporting on all types of depositary activities of the NBU is carried out within a single reporting and controlling framework.

Further, documentation of all market participants has been implemented centrally via the newly introduced **Customer Service**.

In turn, this has created the preconditions for further centralization of the depository system at the national level in accordance with the Comprehensive Program for the Financial Sector Development 2020.

Centralization of functions and closure of regional branches allowed a **massive optimization in the number of staff**. In 2014, we had approximately 12,000 employees, and at the end of 2015, this number **had been cut by 55%** to 5,300. We not only reduced staff, but also attracted 710 new professional employees during this period of internal transformation.

Of course, *no large-scale transformation can occur* **without pain**. There was opposition, but we were ready for this. As US President Woodrow Wilson once said, *"If you want to make enemies, try to change something."* Reducing the NBU staff by half naturally caused discontent among those who had worked at the central bank for decades. For context, in only a few years, 45 out of 48 B-1 managers were replaced.

Generally speaking, it is very important to **be consistent and principled** in this process so there is no feeling of a biased approach to the selection of key personnel or the distribution of functions. We chose the strategic direction of eliminating non-key functions and moving the Bank to a very flat organizational structure.

At the same time, it was very important to **communicate openly with staff**: people needed to understand why we are doing this. Open communications thus lessened internal resistance to change and attracted the maximum number of people to our plan.

To ensure continuity of business processes, it was important to have trained personnel that could replace key personnel in the event of their departure. To do this, we started a program with one of the leading business schools to train *successors* for key positions in the Bank, with 30 to 40 people annually taking part.

I should note that, unlike a private company, we were very *dependent on political factors*. This meant that sometimes trip-ups occurred when we did not expect them.

I recall one episode when, during the most active period of transformation, Parliament decided to limit the salaries of civil servants to UAH 10 thousand (equivalent to USD 400). Since at that time employees of the National Bank had the status of civil servants according to the Law, this restriction stayed in effect for half a year for all employees, including Board members. As we did not know how long this period would last, it significantly complicated our recruitment of new people, since wage levels at the Bank did not correspond to market levels. Accordingly, we initiated corrective legislative changes. Today, salaries in the National Bank correspond to the market, which allows us to attract highly professional staff.

d) Re-engineering of internal processes

Removal non-core functions from the central bank was probably the simplest task of the transformation, and at the same time generated excellent results. However, our task was not simply removal. Or, rather, not only removal. The task was to **reengineer processes** in the central bank itself, to actually make electronic document workflows, to establish an effective interaction of functions.

The key to high efficiency in managing internal processes is clear consistency at all levels of organization, delegation of powers, and implementation of horizontal communications. Our work on modeling processes facilitated employees gaining a deeper understanding of processes and information about the level of involvement and accountability of various units of the National Bank in one or another process.

Before I came to the National Bank, internal communication between departments was carried out mostly via paper letters, with each letter going through the structural hierarchy before being sent to the addressee, who might be behind a neighboring wall. A low level of horizontal communication existed between departments, as seen in the fact that more than *80% of internal documents passed through the heads of departments*, and more than *60% of the documents in the central office were on paper* (for example, in the first half of 2015, more than 175,000 documents were processed, of which, more than 60% (106,000) were on paper). The total workflow of the NBU for 2014 (including regional offices) amounted to almost 900,000 documents. You can only imagine the level of technical overload of managers, for who much of their working time was consumed by internal documentation!

External communications with banks were also done on paper and were practically one-way. I remember one case when I needed to consult with the chair of one of the banks, and I sent him an e-mail. From my previous experience, this was an absolutely ordinary action, but my correspondent was stunned. In response, he told me it was the first e-mail he had ever received, not only from the chair, but from any central bank employee.

Therefore, one of the highest priority projects in our internal transformation was a project to develop **electronic workflow**. Its goal was to simplify document workflow processes within the NBU, to strengthen horizontal links, to eliminate red tape in related processes, and to reduce costs.

The key areas of the project were:

- automation of processes using software
- introduction of a methodology
- synchronization with other processes

For each area, a separate action plan was developed and a responsible manager was assigned. At the beginning of the project's implementation, in the 2nd half of 2015, workflow at the B1 level of the central office was reduced by more than 20%. In fact, the share of internal paper workflow declined despite centralization and a 1.4 times increase in workflow.

After completion of the project, the internal workflow to the NBU was completely translated into electronic: correspondence between departments, including the preparation, issuing and signing of documents, is now carried out through special software. We approved regulation on the use of corporate e-mail as an official channel of communication and the exchange of information among NBU employees, including the possibility to send restricted-access information using electronic signatures.

Generally, we developed a **three-tier structure of processes** at the central bank, in which all processes were modeled using international management practices and process modeling. Each of the processes had an "owner" who became responsible for the continuity of the process and its continuous improvement.

In order to streamline assessing the effectiveness of the National Bank processes, we introduced a *quantitative and measurable approach* to process management. Implementation of the quantitative approach and development of key performance indicators and service level agreements were based on the core management principle of creating value for the client. One objective of the evaluation was a better process, and the end goal was value for the client.

One of the main products provided by the central bank to customers represented by commercial banks was regulation of their activities. Therefore, we launched a project to **transform the central bank's regulatory function**.

Until 2014, the regulatory and legal framework of the NBU contained a huge number of documents did not share logic in construction, and contained internal contradictions. At the time, the process of developing regulations and requirements was decentralized: there were about 20 different procedures for preparing regulations, and 34 units of the National Bank of Ukraine were involved. There were no uniform rules or standards for the preparation of documents.

Market impact analyses were carried out for only about 15% of cases, while in 90% of cases, alternative solutions were not even considered. Moreover, there were no effective communications at various stages of this process; and there was no proper analysis of the rationale for certain regulations, the right choice of mechanisms, or the prediction of consequences. For example, the foreign exchange market was regulated by 108 regulatory legal acts, containing over 1,000 cross references to other documents. The average age of legal acts was 15 years.

It was clear that any investor who first entered the Ukrainian market should have been immediately frightened by the confusing system of regulations, and the possible risks from violation of one or another. Accordingly, regulation suppressed investments to Ukraine and to the banking sector in particular.

Therefore, we changed the approach to implementation of the NBU's regulatory function. In particular, we built a *process of interacting with banks* to discuss drafts of regulatory legal acts prior to their adoption. Of course, the approach was not applied to decisions on the withdrawal of banks from the market, but for NBU regulations on banks' regular activities, requirements for credit risk assessment, corporate governance, information disclosure standards, we publicized regulations on the NBU website and discussed them with market participants. This allowed us to carry out a *Regulatory Impact Assessment* of planned regulations planned, thereby minimizing the risks that the market was unprepared for proposed changes.

Even after the adoption of regulations, the National Bank remained open to discussion. That is, after a certain period of the regulations being in effect, their shortcomings were discovered, the National Bank discussed them with the banks and made appropriate changes.

e) Implementation of new decision-making process via committees

In 2015, we introduced a new decision-making system based on committees. This allowed us to bring the central bank's management system in line with best practices of central banks throughout the world.

The establishment of a system of committees marked the *transition from the practice of making individual decisions to collegial decision making by bodies*. It also facilitated the exchange of information, as well as more effective workload distribution among Board members. This practice was already used by many central banks, including the European Central Bank, the Bank of England, and the Central Bank of Ireland.

The National Bank of Ukraine established **nine specialized committees** (at later stages, three additional committees were established). This system of committees covered all the main functional areas of the National Bank that required collective decisions and were divided into **three main groups**: policy development (strategic level), policy implementation (tactical level), and policy support.

Exhibit 26. Streamlined decision-making process via system of internal committees

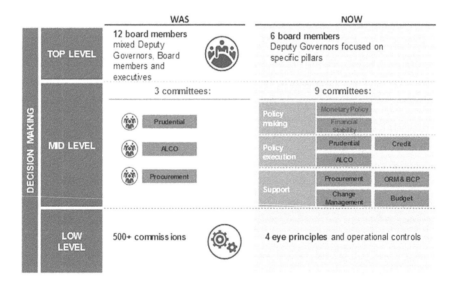

The two-strategic policy-making committees, namely the Monetary Policy Committee and the Financial Stability Committee, both were advisory and consultative collegial bodies, with the former allowing an exchange of information and opinions on monetary policy formulation and implementation, and the latter being responsible for drafting proposals and recommendations on the formulation of principles and implementation of macroprudential policy. (Both were discussed in more detail in previous chapters.)

The three-tactical level policy execution committees were the Credit Committee, the Assets and Liabilities Management Committee, and the (Prudential) Committee on Banking Supervision and Regulation, and Payment System Oversight. The *Credit Committee* was designed as an advisory and consultative collegial body, whose main objectives were to develop and submit to the NBU Board recommendations on granting loans to banks to support their liquidity, formation and use of provisions to cover the financial risks associated with impairment (depreciation) of NBU assets; activities related to the repayment of loans received from the NBU by banks classified as insolvent; and methodology for assessing credit risk (including the collateral appraisal). The *Assets and Liabilities Management Committee* was authorized with the powers delegated by the NBU Board under Article 17 of the Law of Ukraine "On the National Bank of Ukraine". The Committee made decisions on the management of assets and liabilities, including gold and foreign exchange (international) reserves of Ukraine, and ensuring the monitoring of risks and financial results of transactions with assets and liabilities of the NBU. Finally, the *Committee on Banking Supervision and Regulation, and Payment System Oversight* was a collegial body with powers delegated by the NBU Board for banking regulation and supervision, regulation and supervision in the financial monitoring area, for supervision (oversight) of payment systems, and for currency regulation and control.

The four policy supporting committees were the Change Management Committee, the Competitive Bidding Committee, the Budget Committee, and the Committee on Operational Risks and Business Continuity Management. *The Change Management Committee* was established as a collegial advisory body for the centralized management of project activities of the NBU. *The Competitive Bidding Committee* was established in accordance with requirements of the Law of Ukraine "On Public Procurement" and assigned responsibility for organizing and carrying out procurement procedures in accordance with the aforesaid Law of Ukraine. *The Budget Committee* was established to ensure professional discussion by heads of NBU departments on issues related to the budget processes of the NBU, the processes of cost management, and the acquisition and disposal of NBU property. *The Committee on Operational Risks and Business Continuity Management* was set as a standing collegial body of the NBU, whose main objective was coordination of issues related to operational risk management of the NBU and consideration of proposals for decision-making.

The Committee for the Audit of Ukrainian Banks held the special status of being an intergovernmental body established by the NBU, whose main functions were to control the compliance of banks and audit firms with the requirements of statutory and regulatory enactments of the NBU from external audits, monitor the quality of an audit of annual financial statements, and consolidate financial statements of banking groups and other information on financial and economic activity of banks conducted by the audit firms. The committee consisted of six representatives from the National Bank, one representative from the Audit Chamber of Ukraine, one representative from the National Commission for Securities and the Stock Market, and one representative of the National Commission for State Regulation of Financial Services Markets.

Decisions of most of the committees were not final, since according to the Law on the National Bank, such decisions should be taken by the Board. One example is the Committee on Monetary Policy, which was discussed in Chapter 6. Decisions taken by the Committee are recorded, but the final decision on the interest rate is made by the Board in accordance with relevant procedures.

There were a few exceptions, such as the *Committee on Banking Supervision and Payment Systems Oversight*, which was legally delegated with the authority to make decisions in the area of banking regulation and supervision, including the application of measures for banks and other entities (e.g., payment systems) supervised by the central bank (except for measures related to bank insolvency, as well as the withdrawal of a banking license, which remained the prerogative of the Board).

Another case was the *Assets and Liabilities Management Committee*, which was legally assigned to make decisions on the management of gold and foreign exchange reserves, risk monitoring and assessment of financial results for transactions of NBU assets and liabilities.

Each member of the Board was an optional member of the committees and had the right to be present at meetings, though Board members could be a full member of only two to five committees. It is noteworthy that, per the distribution of Committee responsibilities, as Chair of the Board, I was not even a member of the Banking Supervision Committee!

In summary, the new decision-making system at the National Bank had several advantages:

- an effective distribution of the workload between the Board and committees
- creation of conditions for cross-functional information exchange, analysis results and expert opinions
- involvement of middle managers in discussing issues during preparation before submissions to the Board
- significant strengthening of the National Bank's ability to plan and improve the efficiency of work

The new structure that the National Bank implemented, with the system of committees and control over decision-making, was not built to satisfy today's needs nor one person's wishes. The idea was to *create a system that can work effectively even without its creators.* Our success was confirmed when, after I left the National Bank, the system continued to work and develop effectively. The collective control system over decision-making processes, and the system of checks-and-balances allowed the central bank to withstand influence from political factors, whose pressure has intensified many times and throughout the world. Thus, no matter who chairs the National Bank of Ukraine today or tomorrow, it will be difficult for any person to destroy the system or use the central bank's tools for purposes for which they not intended.

f) Risk based supervision, and centralised special monitoring unit for related parties

Along with systemic changes in the banking sector, we reformed our own supervisory function. As part of transforming internal regulatory and supervision processes, we launched a *reorganization of the supervisory process* in accordance with recommendations of the European Banking Authority.

Starting in 2016, the National Bank categorized banks based on their systemic importance and evaluation of their business models. We also introduced key elements of a *Supervisory review and evaluation process* (SREP). To streamline SREP implementation, we reformed the *Prudential Supervision Department* by combining supervisors' and curators' functions into groups based on the similarity of bank characteristics under their supervision. The new organizational structure of the department corresponded to the principle of proportionality in the SREP guidelines. The frequency, depth, and intensity of supervision thus became dependent on the degree of systemic importance of the banks, their risk profile, and possible impact on the stability of the banking system.

Accordingly, the National Bank introduced a *set of new activities* for bank supervision:

- Testing use of SREP elements, such as bank categorization and bank pooling by business model
- Establishing a fundamentally new format for reporting based on the Uniform Bank Performance Report format (UBPR). A single report is an analytical tool created for banking supervision that allows better understanding of the bank's revenues, liquidity, capital, and the quality of its management of assets and liabilities
- Optimization of analytical and supervisory reporting, in particular by improving supervisory analytics, and introduction of new monthly and quarterly management reports

- Regular dialogue with banks to explain changes in prudential regulations
- Improvement in the rating system of bank assessments under the CAMELS inspection, by adding Operational Risk ("O"), and updating the assessment criteria

The additional benefits of the **new CAMELSO rating system** were detailed criteria for indicators of the components of CAMELSO, which provide a comprehensive assessment of the financial state of the bank, its corporate governance, internal and external audit, and internal control and risk management systems, per the recommendations of the Basel Committee and the International Standards on Internal Audit. The new rating system also reduced the risk of arbitrary decision-making in bank assessments.

Exhibit 27. Illustrative relationship between SREP and CAMELSO

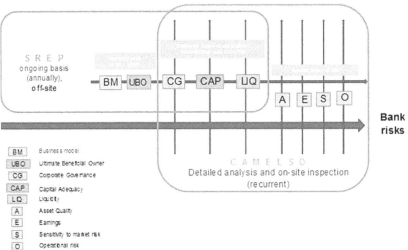

Source: NBU

We also resolved the issue of **banks' related parties**, an important problem we faced s we sought a more stable banking system. During any crisis, owners are more likely to protect their core business rather than the bank, which can lead to the bank's insolvency. Therefore, ensuring full transparency of the structure of bank owners became one of the obligations of the National Bank of Ukraine under its Extended Funding Facility with the IMF.

In the framework of an integrated approach to the identification and disclosure of beneficial owners or significant shareholders of banking institutions, the National Bank established in 2015 a special *Monitoring Unit for related parties* to identify all major economic groups as well as those related to banks, that would monitor their structure and credit exposure on a continuous basis. In 2016, we adopted the *Concept for monitoring of related-parties' transactions,* which facilitated further identification of persons associated with banks and monitoring of new counterparties of banks with signs of connectivity. The document also strengthened the requirements for statistical reporting of banks, which allowed the regulator to identify the chain of corporate rights of a related party, the nature of the relationship between this person and the owners of the bank, as well as to regularly monitor the types of bank operations with related parties.

In general, in 2015-2016, the National Bank of Ukraine complied with the requirements of the Memorandum with the IMF, and completed the diagnostic study of banks' operations with related parties. This process was the first stage in the development of a **comprehensive program for the identification and monitoring of transactions with related parties**, the implementation of which eliminated the risks of banks financing the businesses of their owners and other related persons in violation of the regulatory requirements of the central bank.

In total, 44 banks out of 99 institutions that went through diagnosed were identified as violating the requirements. Each of these banks was obliged to develop and submit to the National Bank a *program for the reduction of excessive amounts of loans to related parties,* and to submit monthly reports on program implementation. The program was aimed to bring banks into compliance with the requirements within three years. Looking at the experience of individual banks in implementing these plans, in 2017 the National Bank allowed banks to file requests for an extension of action plan implementation for up to two years.

Permission would be granted if the bank carried out all measures indicated in its plan in a sound manner, particularly, reducing the volume of excessive loans to related parties by 20% during the first year of plan implementation.

Going forward, the National Bank's next steps (like many other central banks of the world) should be to increase the efficiency of its supervisory process, introduce *regulatory and supervisory technologies*, and enable the use of *Big Data technologies*.

Replacing manual processes with an automated system will lead to improved supervision in terms of *data collection* (real-time monitoring / automated reporting / consolidation of data collection) and *data analytics*, in particular, monitoring of the operations of related parties, and identification of suspicious transactions for AML / CFT. Together, these steps will further optimize internal processes and increase the central bank's performance.

g) New risk management

Prudent risk management is essential in any financial institution. A central bank should be no exception. This is particularly true in a real financial crisis, when a lightning-fast response is required from the central bank when making decisions as lender of last resort.

It is no exaggeration to say that before my team came to the National Bank, there was no professional risk management at the NBU. The result was that the volume of overdue refinancing loans resulting from the withdrawal of insolvent banks from the market exceeded UAH 40 billion, or more than a third of all refinancing loans issued to the banking system. The workout of this portfolio has already taken more than three years and is still underway.

Our first step was to create a unit responsible for assessing risks related to active operations of the NBU and equip it with professional staff.

In 2015, in accordance with the recommendations of the IMF mission, we made a radical change in the integrated risk management system at the National Bank in order to strengthen safeguards and internal control.

We drastically revised the organizational structure of risk management and the whole system of identification, assessment, analysis and risk management, taking into account best international practice, with the following objectives:

- Achieve a quantum leap in the quality of risk management at the National Bank in accordance with modern international standards and best practices
- Ensure optimal distribution of risks in the National Bank, minimizing vulnerability and possible losses from the risk factors' influence on the activities of the National Bank
- Clearly separate the functions of the lender of last resort and bank supervision to eliminate conflict of interest
- Create a specialized committee to manage credit risk, including providing emergency liquidity to Ukrainian banks, and management of problem assets
- Implement a transparent and effective process for analysis and approval of credit decisions, as well as processes for monitoring and administration of banks' liquidity support facilities
- Strengthen internal controls built into the credit process

During 2015, we conducted the diagnostics and identified deficiencies of the existing risk management system. This stimulated us to implement measures and risk management tools in the following areas:

▶ Credit Risk Management

Within the framework of the project, the Reorganization Committee developed and approved the concepts of analysis and decision-making on providing refinance to banks, and of the monitoring process. The new credit process involved differentiating the supervisory and lending functions, an in-depth analysis of the need for liquidity and the bank's ability to repay the loan, a standardized monitoring process and regular reviews. In addition, in order to manage the credit risk of the National Bank, the Credit Committee was created as an advisory body within the decision-making process. An internal methodology for determining credit ratings of banks for disclosure of credit quality information in accordance with IFRS was introduced.

▶ Assessment and monitoring of collateral

In order to protect the rights of the National Bank as a creditor, the concept of cooperation with independent appraisers was revised; a special structural unit responsible for verification of the quality of valuation of property / property rights was set up; a unified methodology for valuation of property and property rights was introduced; monitoring of the physical condition and presence of collateral objects was strengthened; the methodology for determining the discount factors and the discounting period was developed, taking into account the type of collateral, and applying the value of collateral during calculation of bank provisions; and a database of the fair value of property pledged to the National Bank as collateral was established.

▶ Market Risk Management

To improve the efficiency of market risk management, we adopted a unified methodology and procedure for assessing the fair value of securities the National Bank held had taken as collateral, as well as a methodology for calculating diversified adjustment factors for securities that were accepted as collateral for the fulfillment of banks' obligations under refinancing loans and repo transactions. We also developed a methodology for zero-coupon yield curves for Ukrainian government bonds and began regular publication of these yield curves on the National Bank's official website; and we developed a new management concept for gold and foreign exchange reserves management (see Chapter 6). In order to manage the risks of derivative financial instruments, we also developed a methodology and procedure for calculating the fair value of currency swaps.

▶ Resolution of non-performing assets

In 2015, we developed and approved a concept and target process for working with non-performing assets on the central bank's books. The process required the central bank's mandatory approval of the initial price for the DGF to sell assets that the central bank took on its books for outstanding refinance loans.

With the support of the National Bank, starting in 2017, the DGF introduced the sale of assets pledged as collateral to the National Bank exclusively through the **electronic ProZorro. Sale system**. This provided a transparent and effective mechanism for the realization of non-performing assets. As a result, the amount of assets sold from the National Bank's books increased by 13% in 2017 compared to 2016.

Together with the DGF, we also introduced "Dutch auctions" for selling non-performing assets from the NBU portfolio in pools. We held a **joint pilot project** with the DGF, which involved organizing the sale of asset pools with leading foreign advisers; in particular, we attracted subsidiaries of The Debt Exchange and the First Financial Network. These foreign advisers provided a range of services, including due diligence on loans, preparation of marketing materials, attracting potential buyers, creating virtual "data rooms", and organizing open bidding.

▶ Operational Risk Management

Operational risk management in central bank was built from scratch. The impetus for the creation of this function came on one of the first days of my work. Accompanied by news of explosions in the war zone, I wondered where the server facilities that support the central bank's electronic payment system were located. It turned out the servers were located on the second floor of an office building outside the city center. At the same time, it was completely unprotected! The question immediately arose in my mind: What if someone tried to destroy this system? Is there spare capacity to maintain the continuity of financial market operations?

In response to these concerns, the National Bank introduced proactive operational risk management, linking processes and projects with the need to control operational risks, and shifting the emphasis to warning of such risks. We established a permanent collegial body -- the Committee on Operational Risk Management and the Business Continuity-- and launched a *Risk and Control Self-Assessment* (RCSA) exercise, as recommended by the Basel Committee on Banking Supervision, as part of our operational risk identification and measurement tools.

The National Bank also carried out *Business Continuity Planning* (BCP) to deal with unforeseen events in order to minimize their negative impact on the activities of the central bank and the banking system, as well as to accelerate return to normal operating mode.

h) Excessive daily and monthly reporting from banks to NBU and transformation of the statistics and reporting division

One of the first things I encountered in the central bank was a huge amount of reporting that had almost no added value as it was absolutely formal and did not contain any analytics. Moreover, all the reports were in paper form, and therefore at the end of the working day, my desk would have a tower of paper filled with data, which in most cases, duplicated and even contradicted one other.

The National Bank collected many times more information than other central banks of the world, but did not analyze it at all! It was physically impossible to process the amount of incoming information, and some banks used this systemic flaw to circumvent prudential requirements.

During my time at the central bank, I repeatedly heard biting remarks like, "Where was the National Bank until 2014 that a large number of banks had to be withdrawn from the market almost overnight?" In my opinion, the poor quality of analytical work with bank data played a considerable role in what happened to banks later.

One problem was that there was no single owner for reporting from the banks: the functional departments individually interacted with banks, while communication and reception technology was cumbersome and closed. As there was no unified methodology and aggregation of data, indicators were duplicated and incompatible with each other. The lack of functional departments' staff competencies led to the impossibility to fully use the functionality of special software. Management reporting was not coordinated, resulting in excessive reporting that led to a further deterioration in the quality of management decisions.

For commercial banks, excess reporting was also a problem and inefficient use of resources, which worsened their operational results and diverted from direct banking activities.

Once we implemented the **project to reengineer the processes of collection,** it became possible to introduce advanced technologies for collecting and disseminating statistical reporting data. Under the new system of statistical reporting, the central bank finally stopped paper-based reporting, and instead standardized the use of electronic signature, introduced a **XML format** for reporting through the National Bank's web portal, and switched to the use of open channels for collecting and disseminating data through **secured APIs.**

Technological solutions to the reporting format allowed flexible management of the reporting system and facilitated the transition to the international formats FINREP and COREP. According to the Comprehensive Program 2020 and under the European Union technical assistance, we started *implementation of IFRS and FINREPXBRL Taxonomy* in order to switch our reporting system from static forms to dynamic reporting of data.

In order to extend analysts' options for access to data, we opened a number of data sets in a **machine-readable format**. In particular, as part of the Project on introduction of common standards of reporting and information exchange, we opened 26 sets (more than 130,000 indicators) of data in computer readable format (XML, JSON), which became accessible through the API on the NBU's website.

In light of this achievement, the NBU was recognized as one of the top 3 state authorities in the Open Data Forum 2017 in the category of "Highest standards for the publication of open data by public authorities".

The process of data transfer was greatly facilitated since banks were allowed to use their own software. For the convenience of the reporting entities, the National Bank also developed a **public register of statistical reporting indicators** based on a data model and published detailed descriptions of control elements, calculation formulas and handbooks. Within this project, the National Bank also developed new rules for organizing statistical reporting.

Just as good forecasts are essential for prudent monetary policy decisions, so too are reliable bank data required for prudential decisions. Thus, we launched a far-reaching **transformation of the statistical function** towards centralization and unification of data-collecting processes, reports control, distribution, and introduction of up-to-date accounting standards. During 2015, we transferred the *function of collecting statistical reports submitted to the NBU to the central office.* During this centralization process, we ensured a smooth transition for collecting statistical reports submitted to the NBU, data quality control and analysis by unifying reporting control procedures, distribution of the reporting calendar, and regular consultations.

We introduced a **centralized approach to collecting and processing reporting and statistical information** with the Department of Statistics and Reporting. On the one hand, this made it possible to increase the quality and efficiency of compiling and publishing of statistical data, and on the other hand, it also promoted maximum satisfaction of information needs for both external and internal users.

Statistical function reforms covered all the processes of *reporting distribution within the NBU.* We transformed management reporting and data available to NBU experts by establishing and updating a unified reports portal. This greatly simplified the process of finding information and analysis through means of a modern data visualization system, thereby promoting quality improvements in decision-making processes.

In close cooperation with banks and bank associations, careful and massive work was done to improve statistical reporting submitted to the National Bank. In particular, in order to reduce the burden on suppliers of statistical reporting, we reviewed the list of forms, their structure, and the procedure for compiling and submitting information.

Notably, the National Bank not only improved the process banks' reporting to the regulator, but we also contributed to *improving the efficiency of the banking system* itself. For that to happen, the National Bank took an active part in the **Paperless project** initiated by the Association of Ukrainian Banks, which was part of the Comprehensive Program for the Development of the Financial Sector.

The project was launched after an independent study by McKinsey and Finalta in 2015. The study revealed the need to create conditions for increasing productivity in Ukraine's banking sector and recommended the introduction of paperless business processes.

The main goal of the project was to switch to electronic workflow in banks and simplify business procedures. Thus, the project concept envisaged the abolition of any need for a physical presence by bank clients; cancellation of exclusively using paper documents; and cancellation of handwritten signatures on documents.

In general, during the implementation of the Paperless project, amendments were made to 14 regulations of the National Bank, for which 8 separate working groups were created, in the areas of identification and verification, settlement and cash operations, currency transactions in the interbank market, documentary operations, credit and archiving operations, and others.

The banking community appreciated the results from this project, which opened up new opportunities for banks to further modernize business processes and improve banking service.

In 2017, with a view to adopting a unified approach to **electronic signature** use in the Ukrainian banking system, the NBU Board of Ukraine approved the Regulation on the Use of Electronic Signature in the Ukrainian Banking System[26]. This regulation established a regulatory framework governing the application of paperless technology while providing banking services. Its adoption represented a step toward the implementation of the Paperless project to move away from paper documents when servicing bank customers.

The regulation, inter alia, defined types of electronic signatures used in the Ukrainian banking system; set out requirements for the use of each type; and set out requirements for the creation and storage of electronic documents in the banking system.

The new regulation allowed banks to substantially decrease their non-productive losses and lower the cost of banking products. It also contributed to improved service quality, making services more user-friendly and speeding service delivery.

The National Bank's next step will be moving towards the introduction of modern technologies for processing *Big Data*. Full implementation of this project will not only enhance the quality of the statistical function, but also significantly improve the central bank's implementation of its mandate on price and financial stability.

Summary

The internal reform of the National Bank of Ukraine has been completed. Since 2014, the organizational structure of the National Bank of Ukraine has been radically changed. I am proud that today, due to our reforms, we have built a modern, open and independent

---

[26] NBU Resolution #78 dated 14.08.2017 (updated)

European central bank. To do so, we switched to a functionally oriented organizational structure, significantly reduced hierarchy, created a new central bank management system based on collegial decisions by committees, centralized and rethought functions of structural units, and got rid of non-core assets. The new system of collegial decision-making continues to perform smoothly. All internal processes have undergone re-engineering. This result was achieved only by long and hard work by a large team at the National Bank.

As the IMF's mission said in its January 2019 report: "*The modernization reforms undertaken by the NBU—for the financial system and for the institution—is impressive. The powerful change in focus, structure, and staffing since 2014 is … unprecedented in modern central banking, especially taking into account the challenging environment the NBU operates in*".

Today, the National Bank of Ukraine strives to best global practices in central banking even as they continually change and develop. Its targets are based not on an outdated image of the perfect central bank from the past, but – towards the point where central banks are moving for the future and where they see themselves in five to ten years.

I want to underscore once more that institutional transformation of a central bank will help for the future. It will definitely be a safeguard mechanism, not only to implement reforms but also to protect reforms and reformers down the road. Recent developments in Ukraine after the presidential election of 2019 fully demonstrated that vision, as all international institutions including the IMF, WB, EBRD, EU countries, and the G7 all strongly supported continued independence of the NBU.

CHAPTER 11

Unresolved problems hindering the proper growth and further development of banking system

a) Legacy of FCY mortgages

FCY MORTGAGES WERE the legacy of the buoyant growth of 2005-2008, when on the back of an economic upswing and inflow of investments into the banking sector from abroad, banks willingly lent FX mortgage loans to individuals who did not have FX earnings or any currency risk-hedging tools. In effect, banks were transferring the implied FX risk to the borrowers, which was perceived as negligible given a de-facto fixed rate of hryvnia to the US dollar at about 5 UAH / USD. In August 2008, before the 2008-2009 crisis, the share of loans granted to households in FX exceeded 60%, with almost 60% of those being mortgage loans. Indeed, 86% of total mortgage loans to households were issued for a term exceeding five years.

Some of the FX loans became non-performing during the first wave of the crisis in 2008-2009, when the hryvnia exchange rate was devalued by 40% (from 5 to 8 UAH / USD). After the transition to a flexible exchange rate and the 3-fold depreciation of hryvnia, mortgage FX loans almost completely ceased to be serviced. Moreover, taking into account the post-crisis drop in real estate prices, the cost of mortgaged apartments became lower than the residual of mortgage loans on banks' balance sheets.

I should note that since 2009, Ukraine had instituted a legislative ban on lending to individuals in foreign currency, but the legacy issue still had to be resolved.

There is no doubt that the ideal solution would have been to prevent the occurrence of such a problem. And the *timely transition to a flexible exchange rate could serve as a safeguard*, allowing borrowers to take into account the "price" of currency risk. But since the issue was already in place, it had to be solved quickly so as not to exacerbate the debt problem, and in negotiations with stakeholders.

Ukraine's case was not unique. In recent years, among Eastern European countries, Hungary, Poland, Croatia, Romania and Serbia also faced FX mortgage debt problems on loans provided in Swiss francs. However, only Hungary, in November 2014, introduced a massive conversion of FX loans into national currency. Hungary's measure, though was ineffective since in 2015 its share of non-performing loans to households in the total portfolio decreased insignificantly while Hungary's Central Bank sold 9 billion euros to banks to compensate the conversion of loans.

As a central bank, we were committed to supporting a ***voluntary negotiation process between borrowers and banks*** for the restructuring of foreign currency-denominated mortgage loans that were being serviced by struggling, but still performing, borrowers. We understood that an efficient mechanism was needed to support some categories of individuals, primarily low-income and socially disadvantaged groups. However, as a banking regulator we were also concerned about the banks, since even a mild compromise solution could lead to additional losses and the need for additional capital.

Under my leadership, in the second half of 2014, the central bank created a platform, sponsored by the First Deputy Governor, for negotiations between banks and FX borrowers. We sought a role to facilitate negotiations between banks and borrowers while not interfering in bilateral negotiations, and to ensure a fair process.

Negotiations were lengthy and complicated by the lack of a unified position by borrowers (among them there were some individuals who owned 3 or more mortgages and refused to sell them or to repay loans) and by bankers (some thought their debt collection model would allow them to work effectively with this category of debtors).

The situation was further complicated by the unhelpful position of social activists, including those who came to Parliament on the wave of the revolution. These individuals considered it their duty to protect negligent borrowers from greedy bankers, but in fact their behaviour merely prevented reaching consensus.

Nevertheless, in early 2015 the *Memorandum on the restructuring of mortgage loans in foreign currency* was signed. This document provided for the conversion of foreign currency debt into UAH at the official rate on the day of restructuring, and forgiveness of at least 25% of the restructured debt if the borrower fulfilled new obligations in a timely manner. For borrowers who purchased social housing (up to 60 square meters for apartments and up to 120 square meters for houses), the document provided for the forgiveness of 50% of restructured debts. Eleven banks with the largest exposure to FX borrowers signed the Memorandum, which was preceded by the NBU's adoption of amendments to the Tax Code and regulatory acts of the National Bank, regarding forgiveness (cancellation) of part of the debt.

The restructuring of mortgage loans implemented by the banks that signed the Memorandum contributed to a reduction of USD 3.6 billion of debt by January 2015, down to USD 2.4 billion as of August. The number of mortgage loans decreased accordingly from 73,500 to 55,700. However, these positive dynamics were lost due to the introduction of temporary administrations by some banks that were major mortgage lenders (which made it impossible to restructure FX loans), and by Parliament's adoption in early July of the populist Law, "On the Restructuring of Foreign Currency Loans", which provided for converting the balance of foreign currency debts of individual borrowers to hryvnia at the official rate as of the date the loan agreement was signed, and preserving an unchanged rate on the loan.

Ultimately, the initiative for the forced conversion of foreign currency loans into UAH contradicted the terms of Ukraine's cooperation with the IMF and created the risks for the country's financial stability. Therefore, the President vetoed it.

In place of a populist law, the banking community, with the support of the National Bank, prepared a socially equitable and balanced solution for the problem of FX borrowers. The draft law, "On Restructuring the Obligations of Ukrainian Citizens on Foreign Currency Loans Acquired for Single Housing (Mortgage Lending)", was developed taking into account Ukraine's international commitments and was supported by 19 banks, major mortgage lenders, including banks with foreign capital. According to the draft law, restructuring was possible on FX loans from banks as well as from factoring companies and other institutions. For borrowers who had received foreign currency loans for the purchase of single-dwelling housing, the draft law provided for the conversion of FX loans into hryvnia, and for partial forgiveness for individual borrowers. This bill was a compromise and reflected banks' voluntary willingness to restructure loans to those borrowers who faced financial difficulties due to job losses or declines in income. Expected losses to the banking sector from implementation of this law were estimated at about USD 370 million.

Unfortunately, instead of adopting the compromise law, Parliament supported a draft law introducing a moratorium on the foreclosure of mortgaged real property. As a result, the problem of currency borrowers has remained frozen for years.

The issue of FX mortgage settlement remains unresolved to this day. However, it is no longer of critical value, since banks have formed almost 100% provisions for such loans.

The moratorium was finally lifted in July 2018, when Parliament approved the Code of Bankruptcy Laws. By that same law, a new category of individual bankruptcy was introduced into Ukraine, which opened the prospect of a final resolution of the FX mortgage issue at some point in the future.

b) NPL problems

The problem of non-performing loans (NPL) in the banking system of Ukraine has a long history, although it had a low profile for a long time. The previous management of the central bank preferred simply not to notice it, as well as many other problematic aspects of the banks, such as lending to related parties, pervasiveness of money-laundering schemes, etc.

One paradoxical episode occurred on the eve of the 2008 crisis: On an order from the central bank, the level of NPL in Ukraine "dropped" immediately! Since such large-scale change in the quality of banks' assets at one time were simply not possible, clearly a fundamental change in the methodology for calculating NPL was in order.

Exhibit 28. Non-performing bank loans, % of total loans

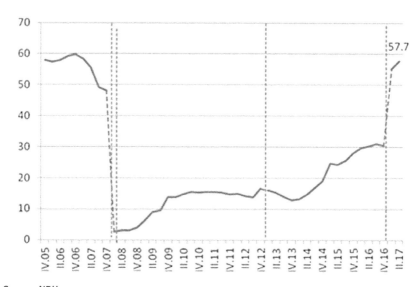

Source: NBU

Before 2008, last four of the five main categories of loan quality (standard, under control, substandard, doubtful, and loss) were used to identify non-performing loans; at the beginning of 2008, only the last two were used for this purpose. In international practice, NPLs were usually defined as the sum of substandard plus doubtful and loss. Alternative calculations carried out by the IMF and international experts showed the deficiency of this approach since the local methodology indicated 15% NPL in the banking system of Ukraine during 2010-2013 whereas the IMF and rating agencies calculation showed 40% for the same period.

The point is that the **central bank must have the courage to face the truth**, and not replace international standards for assessing asset quality with the invention of a "local bicycle".

My team at the National Bank called things by their proper names and forced banks to reveal the true amount of bad assets in their portfolios and to make adequate provisions.

The implementation of international standards in credit risk assessment in 2014-2016 was not unnoticed in the banking system. With the completion of the transition to IFRS, and introduction of a new regulation on credit risk and risk-oriented banking supervision, the overall regime for bank supervision improved significantly. This action, along with the National Bank's diagnostic and stress testing of the banks, positively affected banks' balance sheets of banks, since it reflected the real quality of a bank's loan portfolio.

Following the changes to the definition of NPL in 2017, and the transition to the international practice of defining non-performing exposures, Ukraine had the highest historical NPL level in the world, exceeded only by Cyprus and Afghanistan. And if the volume of the nationalized Privatbank's NPL was included, Ukraine had the highest level of NPL in international experience.

Exhibit 29. Countries with the largest historical maximum of NPL, %

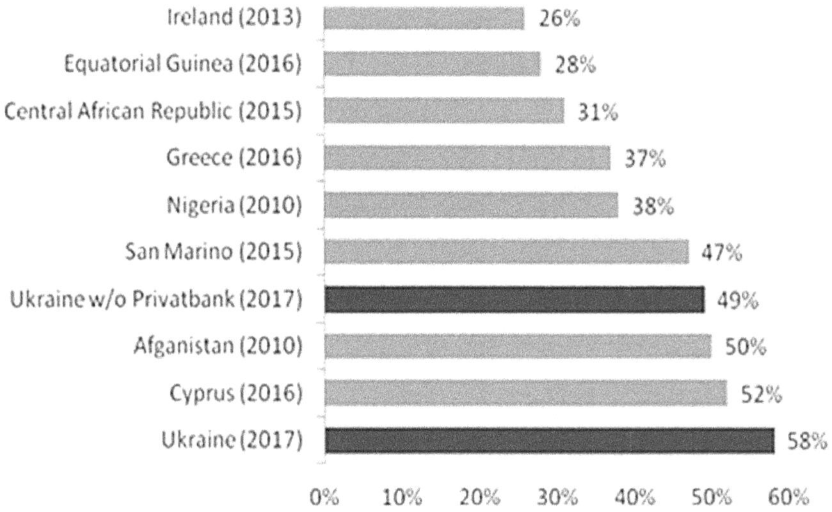

Country	%
Ireland (2013)	26%
Equatorial Guinea (2016)	28%
Central African Republic (2015)	31%
Greece (2016)	37%
Nigeria (2010)	38%
San Marino (2015)	47%
Ukraine w/o Privatbank (2017)	49%
Afganistan (2010)	50%
Cyprus (2016)	52%
Ukraine (2017)	58%

Source: IMF Financial stability indicators, NBU

It should be noted that in absolute terms *the majority of NPL belonged to the corporate segment*. This segment suffered most from deterioration of macroeconomic conditions, devaluation of the exchange rate, and military actions in the east of the country. Further, this same segment had the *highest share of loans to related parties* (or, in the case of state banks, loans to politically influential individuals), with about 40% total NPL, and for which there was no or fictitious collateral. Together with corporate NPLs, which were related to loans provided to enterprises located in the temporarily-occupied territory of Crimea or in the area of the anti-terrorist operation (about 7%), the share of non-performing debts that could be potentially resolved was about half of the total portfolio (UAH 250 billion or approximately USD 10 billion).

In the balance sheets of insolvent banks, whose assets were managed by the DGF, there were additionally about UAH 300 billion of non-performing assets, the market value of which, according to Fund's estimates, were not more than 25% of the book value, and actual sales showed an recovery rate of less than 5%.

In addition, Ukrainian NPL had a ***high concentration within the major business groups***. The TOP-20 business groups accounted for about 37% of Ukraine's total non-performing debt, and if looking at the TOP-40, that number rises to about 44%.

I believe there is a 100% correlation between the amount of NPL and rule-of-law principles in a country. Without proper judicial and court reforms, progress in NPL resolution is limited.

A significant proportion of large corporate borrowers had difficulty in terms of collection of bad debts / foreclosure of collateral, due to significant resistance by borrowers in the courts and during the enforcement processes. This, in turn, contributed to a low level of recovery on these loans (only about 1%), and low demand for these assets by potential investors.

Such a high concentration of problem debts in business groups necessitated a ***consolidated approach to resolving the NPLs***. In some cases, there were different levels of redundancy and quality of distressed debt coverage of within the same business group, thus uncoordinated activity of creditors could lead not only to an ineffective solution for the banking system as a whole (where a secured creditor would get everything, and the rest, nothing at all), but would be also detrimental for the future recovery of lending, since a potentially viable business could be sent into bankruptcy if one of the creditors insisted on that option.

Several episodes in this regard illustrate the problem and show how the central bank took on the unusual role of moderator between problem borrowers and banks.

Case 1: Mriya Agro Holding

One case that gained international notoriety was the agricultural company Mriya. Started in early 1990s as a small-sized family farming business in Western Ukraine, by the mid-2000s, it had grown to a mid-sized business, and then entered a phase of explosive growth in 2006. From 2006 to 2008, the company beefed up its land holdings to 150,000 ha, primarily by snapping up idle farmland across the West of Ukraine. After a hugely successful (much more so for the founders than for investors) private placement of shares in mid-2008, Mriya continued to expand aggressively, and doubled its land bank by the end 2011 to 295,000 ha, which made it the third largest land operator in Ukraine.

To develop its newly acquired land, Mriya tapped into global capital markets. The company positioned itself as a well-managed large-scale family business with an impeccable track record and huge growth opportunities. Those marketing efforts were largely successful, bringing in $90mln through private placement of shares in Frankfurt in June 2008, and $250mn through issuance of Eurobonds in March of 2011.

Mriya's financial performance seemed stellar. On top of 10x growth in the planted area and a favourable pricing environment, the company boosted its sales by 16x in 2011 over 2007. Despite this explosive growth, margins remained consistently better than competitors. Beginning in 2008, Mriya's EBITDA margin averaged 63%, which was twice that of other agricultural holdings with comparable business models.

Meanwhile, market analysts found numerous inconsistencies in Mriya's reported operational results, including fictitious cost leadership, misstated production volumes, and undisclosed related-party transactions. Concerned about questionable acquisitions and dubious ventures outside the company's core competency, analysts raised serious doubts about the validity of the company's supposedly terrific performance.

In October 2014, the company failed to pay off its debt, though this did not come as much of a surprise since official announcements about financial difficulties had been released two months earlier. Following that announcement, the bonds in question then plummeted from 80% of par to around 30%. Negotiations between bondholders ($71 mln were due in 2016 and $400 mln were due in 2018) and the company started immediately but have not been easy, since Mriya Agro Holding continually postponed the launch of formal restructuring procedures. The resignation of the company's international legal and financial advisors, coupled with the departure of the company's two independent directors and the recent replacement of the company's CEO and CFO, has not brought comfort to the process.

So, what was the central bank's role here? Actually, resolving the company's debts and protecting the rights of its creditors was quite important for stability of the banking system given the significant credit exposure of banking and financial institutions had because of the company. The loss of investor confidence in the local market could have led to the withdrawal of investments and cessation of lending throughout the Ukrainian economy.

Moreover, Mriya's restructuring would have been the first restructuring of Eurobonds issued by a Ukrainian business in the last four years. Therefore, the fair treatment of international investors was a test for the Ukrainian authorities in the light of the major upcoming refinancing needs for the Ukrainian state and Ukrainian corporations, and the ongoing negotiations with the International Monetary Fund.

We were approached by an ad hoc committee of large international investors holding more than 50% of the senior notes, as well as an unofficial coordinating committee of major banks with a total exposure of USD 1.3 billion to the company, and we tried to facilitate an organised and transparent process to coordinate all creditors with the aim of mitigating adverse effects on banks' loan portfolios.

For that to happen, we held several general and bilateral meetings with the company's creditors, which led to creation of a regular creditors' committee that was able to take over management of the company in February 2015.

We also initiated a letter to law enforcement agencies drawing their attention to the fact that the company's management actions indicated an abuse of power and fraudulent misrepresentation that had led to significant losses by investors and creditors.

The final point in this case was that only 3 years later, the company was bought by a major strategic investor from Saudi Arabia. The amount of that contract was the largest in the agricultural sector in the history of Ukraine.

Unfortunately, despite the default that became known all over the world and negatively affected the image of Ukraine, to this day, no one has been held accountable. The founder of the company was put on Interpol's "wanted" list, and the extradition to Ukraine was raised, but he continues to live abroad.

Case 2: Creative Group

Oddly enough, a second illustrative case also involved a company in agriculture -- one of the pillars of the Ukrainian economy. This company in this case, though, was not as spectacularly successful as Mryia.

Creative Group was a vertically-integrated agribusiness company specializing in the production of sunflower and soybean oil, oilseed meal, fats and margarines. The company owned 9 factories and 8 elevator complexes, and was among the top 3 Ukrainian processors of sunflower and soybean seeds. Its revenue before the 2014 crisis exceeded USD 1 billion, of which 80% was in foreign currency.

As the result of a private placement in 2007, its main owners were the founder's family (66%), top management (11%) and foreign creditors (24%). It should be noted that the company's founder was a member of parliament and its largest shareholder, was a member of the prior leading party. Therefore, this case illustrates the perniciousness of politically-related lending.

With a questionably profitable business, the company stopped servicing debts in June 2015. It started working with toll materials and leasing its production capacities on the rationale investing in working capital during the litigation process would be too risky. That meant its cash flows were not sufficient to service its debt, which amounted to USD 630 million. Of the total, $ 520 million (83%) was owed to state banks, $ 75 million to the syndicate of foreign banks, and about $ 35 million to other creditors.

At that time, -one commercial bank had its debt provisioned by 99%. In other banks, the level of provisioning did not exceed 15%, while the cost of collateral, taking into account liquidity and sales cost, barely reached 40% of the amount of debt.

The Creative Group's main asset (a new oil extraction plant) was pledged to one of the state-owned banks with the lowest exposure amount.

We understood that foreclosure of the main secured creditor (a state-owned bank) would stop the business by depriving other banks any opportunity to recoup their losses in the future. At the same time, we understood that from the point of view of secured creditors, it would be more profitable to sell the debt claim or collateral. Resolving the issue on non-performing liabilities of the company in that way would mean net losses for the banking system as a whole.

Therefore, we tried to coordinate creditors' actions through the central bank's platform with the aim of creating a level playing field for all participants and maximizing satisfaction of creditors' claims. We also secured the Ministry of Finance, as a shareholder of state-owned banks, to negotiate a common position between the interests of the state and the banking system.

Unfortunately, attempts to agree on debt restructuring were not successful.

Further events developed in a pattern already familiar to us. In September 2015, the Creative Group, whose asset value was significantly lower than its net debt, was sold to a new owner -- masked via offshores -- and in May 2016, the company asked the commercial court permission to declare bankruptcy.

Shortly before, the government had agreed to the state bank's sale of the claim on the loan, which was collateralized with a key asset (oil extraction plant) of the Creative Group. Over the next several years, several criminal cases were initiated against the owners and management of the company, as well as against senior officials of state banks that had been responsible for granting loans to the company. The courts considered more than a dozen claims by banks against borrowing companies. Eventually, the remaining assets of the group were sold through auctions by the state enforcement agency.

The bottom line of this case is that with proper cooperation of creditors, there is a better chance to get a good result than if everyone acts alone. Nevertheless, effective coordination requires both trust between the parties and adherence to the rule of law. I am convinced there is a 100% correlation between the rule of law in a country and progress on NPL resolution.

The conclusion we learned from painful experience in these and similar cases was such that without judicial, law enforcement, and executive reforms, it is impossible to find a systemic solution to a bad debts problem. Without reform, tackling the problems of the past brings no guarantee that problems will not recur in the future.

As referred to in the IMF's paper on the dynamics of non-performing loans during banking crises, it usually takes 5 to 6 years for the resolution of NPLs after the crisis[27]. That said, at the beginning of 2020, the share of non-performing loans in the banking system of Ukraine

[27] Anil Ari, Sophia Chen, Lev Ratnovski, 2019. "The Dynamics of Non-Performing Loans During Banking Crises: A New Database", IMF Working Paper 19/272, International Monetary Fund

remained unacceptably high, accounting for about half of the banks' credit portfolio. However, I would like to point out that this is already a **problem of the past**. Three-quarters of all non-performing loans are **concentrated in state-owned banks**, namely, the three largest banks. In two of them, NPLs were originated well before 2014 and were the result of politically motivated lending decisions, and in one bank, which accounts for 45% of total NPLs, it was the result of the coordinated fraud.

Exhibit 30. Volume of non-performing loans in TOP-20 banks, as of 01/02/2020, UAH bn

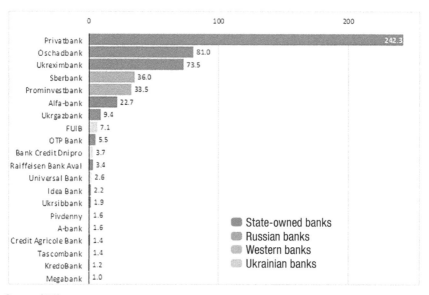

Source: NBU

Exhibit 31. The share of non-performing loans in TOP-20 banks by credit portfolio, as of 01/02/2020, %

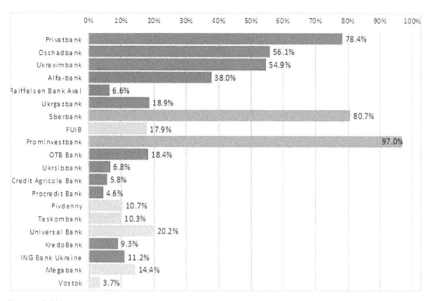

Source: NBU

Today, these loans are almost fully (95%) provisioned, and therefore no longer put pressure on banks' financial results and capital. Their resolution is a matter of time and the decisiveness of the banks' management in working-out the distressed debts. Instead, in most private banks with both Ukrainian and foreign (except Russian) capital, the NPL's share in the loan portfolio is already moderate 10-20% and clearly paving the way to less than 10%.

In order to accelerate the resolution of bad debts in banks' portfolios, the National Bank in February 2020 adopted a regulation[28] (effective from 2021) on the introduction of a gradual deduction from banks' regulatory capital of the value of the property that is not used in their core banking activities. These changes will intensify the disposal of non-core assets by banks, which will free up the resources that can be used for lending and other banking operations.

---

[28] NBU Board Resolution No. 22 dated 27.02.2020

c) Kiev approach to debt restructuring

One of the main obstacles to lending in Ukraine was Non-performing loans (NPL). In international practice, NPL are usually resolved, among other ways, using voluntary out-of-court debt restructuring in which the credit conditions are changed so that a viable borrower can restore solvency. This helps avoid spending time and resources on legal delinquency in case the debt is restructured according to general rules.

The prior practice of corporate insolvency in Ukraine has not produced positive results: there were almost no successful cases of enterprise rehabilitation, and liquidation procedures were ineffective, yielding very poor economic returns for creditors. Abuse by debtors and creditors was common. In essence, the insolvency system contributed to a massive destruction of economic value instead of assisting in the recovery of viable companies and minimizing losses incurred by creditors. According to the Doing Business Ranking of the World Bank, Ukraine's recovery rate (the amount of money secured creditors recover from an insolvent firm at the end of insolvency proceedings) was less than 10 cents per dollar (compared with more than 70 cents per dollar in OECD countries), and the cost of the proceedings was over 40% of the underlying value of the debtor's estate (compared to less than 10% in OECD countries)[29].

However, the biggest hindrance to effective debt resolution in Ukraine was the institutional framework. The challenges in Ukraine's judiciary have been widely flagged. On insolvency, stakeholders' most frequent complaint was that the judicial system ineffective and inefficient because of (i) the length of procedures due to frequent opportunities for appeal and the use of procedural maneuvers, (ii) the poor quality of judges, who were seen as unknowledgeable, and overly "debtor-friendly", and (iii) wide- spread corruption by judges and, to a lesser extent, insolvency administrators. These very significant vulnerabilities of the courts limited the possibility to introduce more advanced rules and practices because they would require that judges and insolvency

---

[29] https://www.doingbusiness.org/en/data/exploreeconomies/ukraine#DB_ri

representatives have some standards of integrity and diligence. Until those basic standards were met, it was necessary to have a system with highly prescriptive rules that do not leave a lot of discretion to the courts and insolvency representatives.

An **out-of-court voluntary restructuring tool** should have allowed banks and borrowers to agree on new loan conditions that would enable the company to resume its full-fledged activities. This practice became widespread in Asian countries after the 1990s crisis. It combined the principles of the London Approach and *international debt restructuring principles* (i.e., the "INSOL principles"[30]). For example, as of 2003, Thailand restructured 48% of its corporate sector debt, South Korea restructured 95%, Indonesia restructured 56% and Malaysia restructured 77% via out-of-court work-out mechanisms. In Turkey, after the 2001 currency crisis, the Istanbul Approach was implemented, focusing on the debts of large companies. As a result, as of August 2003, the debt of 220 Turkish companies worth $ 5 billion was restructured. In several South-Eastern Europe countries (Romania, Serbia, Slovenia, Croatia), similar mechanisms of voluntary restructuring were introduced from 2010 to 2015.

Thus, we started developing an out-of-court restructuring framework with great promise in consultation with the World Bank, EBRD and IMF, and in close cooperation with the MoF, DGF and banks. We called this the "**Kiev Approach**," and it was modelled after the "Istanbul Approach" used in Turkey. It institutionalized out-of-court restructuring based on international best practice and cross-country experience, and covered foreclosure procedures, corporate and personal insolvency, and tax incentives.

The approach envisaged an inter-bank creditor agreement banks would that laid out the terms of engagement with respect to themselves and their debtors in reaching a restructuring agreement; and a law that

---

[30] The INSOL Principles are international standards for a global approach to Multi-creditor Workouts. They are called *"Statement of Principles for a Global Approach toMulti-creditor Workouts"* and were published in 2000.

would authorize this framework agreement, with amendments to tax, enforcement, bankruptcy and related laws. A working group of experts from the private and public sector started working on implementing the approach. The elaboration of the Law "On Financial Restructuring" was put into the IMF cooperation program and adopted in June 2016 for the period through October 2019. Its main objective was to encourage the reorganization of enterprises facing financial problems, allowing problem debtors access to financial resources and, ultimately, the maintenance of financial stability. For the purposes of applying the Kyiv Approach, a Secretariat was established in December 2016 to provide informational, analytical, organizational and administrative support for financial restructuring.

The Law did not specify the parameters of restructuring plans, interest rates or the amount of liabilities subject to restructuring, but left those issues completely at the discretion of creditors and borrowers.

The law had the following benefits:

- It helped loyal borrowers who were solvent or able to become solvent in the future, but were having temporary difficulties servicing debt, to restructure their obligations within a few months. Debtors who were in a critical financial position could reduce their risk of bankruptcy and restore solvency.
- It obliged coordinated actions among all creditors who agreed to restructure debts of a particular borrower. This eliminated competition between lenders over who would be first to recover their loans, even if the borrower subsequently went bankrupt. At the beginning of the restructuring process, a moratorium on the fulfilment of creditors' claims by the debtor was put in place.
- It provided that state-owned banks and the DGF (on behalf of banks with a temporary administration or those in the process of liquidation) could restructure their loans. The Law "On Financial Restructuring" actually set an exception to Article 53 of the Law of Ukraine "On Banks and Banking", which prohibits the setting of interest rates lower than the cost of

banking services in this bank. This exception allowed banks to change the terms of the loan in the restructuring process, when the debtor becomes able to perform during the crisis. Such an opportunity was especially important for state-owned banks and the DGF, which were not able to carry out restructuring on market terms.

The authority responsible for coordination of the restructuring processes was the *Supervisory Board*, which created a *Secretariat* and an *Arbitration Committee*. The Supervisory Board was also involved in the supervision and methodological support of the restructuring. The role of these bodies in promoting the process was extremely important, given that there were almost no standards of restructuring in Ukraine, and often a lack of trust between borrowers and lenders. Without proper coordination, and freedom from the influence of the political factors and corporate interests, financial restructuring cannot be effective.

To initiate the restructuring process, the debtor had to submit an application to the Secretariat together with consent to restructure its liabilities to one or more financial institutions that owned at least 50% of the debtor's total amount of claims (Article 18). The start of an out-of-court financial restructuring procedure was the condition for halting the bankruptcy procedure and a moratorium on the activities of creditors involved in debt collection (Articles 20 and 21). Due to the wide distrust of the court system, all disputes arising during the financial restructuring procedure between the debtor and the involved creditors were examined by an arbitrator appointed by the Secretariat (Article 16). The debtor submitted a restructuring plan for which creditors needed to vote at a meeting of creditors (Article 25). The plan was considered approved if all the borrowed creditors, or borrowers who owned more than two thirds of the claims to the borrower, voted for its approval, with subsequent approval of the decision by the arbitrator (Article 25). The approved restructuring plan did not create legal obligations for those creditors who did not sign the restructuring agreement (i.e., did not provide written consent for the application of the Kyiv Approach).

Initially, it was envisioned that the restructuring under the Kyiv Approach would also have *binding effect* for lenders who voted against the approval plan and for unrelated lenders. However, the relevant proposals were subjected to widespread criticism from some stakeholders, in particular, those creditors who did not want to be forced to participate in the restructuring.

Although a wise concept and the introduction of the Kiev Approach has been a positive step, Ukrainian practice showed that it was not powerful enough. To date, since the introduction of the mechanism, the amount of out-of-court restructured debt is approximately. *USD 1 billion, or less than 5% of total non-performing loans* that could have been potentially restructured using this mechanism. This low participation reflected *embedded weaknesses and should be noted by other countries* interested in introducing out-of-court restructuring mechanisms.

The *disadvantages of the Kyiv Approach* were:

- The legal system did not create real risks for borrowers who were not prone to co-operation.
- The Kyiv Approach did not establish a predictable framework for negotiating with creditors. Banks had the right to decide whether to use it on a case-by-case basis. The more successful approaches tested during the East Asian crisis or the "Istanbul Approach" defined a predictable set of rules that encouraged application of the relevant provisions, and provided that each case was matched by certain predetermined characteristics, thus eliminating the need for negotiation on an individual basis.
- Notwithstanding the provision that state-owned banks had the right to partially forgive debt, in practice, state-owned banks' management was very reluctant to agree to such conditions, fearing they would be prosecuted.
- Good borrowers were not able to resort to operational restructuring with lenders, as it required radical changes to the debtor company.

- Coordination between creditors was incomplete under a combination of the Kyiv Approach and the norms of the Bankruptcy Law (on reorganization before the opening of proceedings).
- The tax incentives provided by Kyiv's Approach were not fully implemented.

Thus, in order to effectively implement out-of-court restructuring mechanisms, countries need to pay attention to:

- **Proper coordination between creditors,** in particular, suspension of a run for assets by individual creditors, and the creation of incentives for lenders to decline to participate in the restructuring. Since individual incentives are very powerful, a moratorium on debt collection, legal action has to be introduced in order to facilitate negotiations. In addition, since lenders may prefer to avoid restructuring in order to transfer the corresponding restructuring costs to other lenders, the bankruptcy laws of the various countries should adhere to the principle of decision-making by a majority, which makes it possible to impose conditions on lenders who do not agree to the restructuring plan, if certain criteria are met. Financial restructuring should not provide uninvolved creditors an opportunity to collect debts from the debtor while other lenders are negotiating a restructuring.
- **Providing appropriate incentives for financial restructuring.** In order to ensure financial restructuring as early as possible, debtors and lenders should have appropriate incentives to negotiate. Debtors should feel the persuasive threat of coercive measures and the risk of bankruptcy proceedings. Regulatory incentives for creditors (including tax incentives) should also be effective and predictable. These conditions in Ukraine were only partially fulfilled. Bad debtors found legal and institutional ways to delay proceedings. Finally, since regulatory requirements did not oblige banks to create provisions for expected losses on credit operations, unless there was a problem with servicing a

debt to such a bank (that is, banks were not obliged to create provisions in the event of non-fulfillment by the debtors of liabilities for loans from other banks), banks were not inclined to take the initiative in solving the problem of joint actions of several lenders.

- **Ensuring identical terms for all market participants.** As public institutions, state banks are subject to strict rules to prevent fraudulent operations to the detriment of the state, which usually limits state banks' ability to negotiate restructuring. Given this fact, and the desire to ensure participation by state-owned banks in out-of-court restructuring procedures, the Kiev Approach directly allowed state banks to participate in financial restructuring and to partially write-off debts of their borrowers (Article 8). However, the management of state-owned banks still doubted the expediency of out-of-court restructuring procedures. Despite the obvious permission under the law, they were usually afraid they would be prosecuted for a partial write-off of debts through a financial restructuring. Still, it is important to note that, in many cases, a partial write-down of a debt could become a prerequisite for reaching a restructuring agreement.

- Last but not least, **creation of a favorable tax regime for financial restructuring.** The Kyiv-based financial restructuring envisaged introducing specific provisions related to the financial restructuring procedure into the Tax Code. Such an approach (i.e., the establishment of tax incentives) had been used in other countries (in particular, Turkey and Indonesia) to create incentives for out-of-court settlements. However, tax incentives available in Ukraine were not consistent with the expectations of the banks and borrowers. In fact, the interpretation of these operations by the fiscal authorities was not favorable to resolution of debt distress.

Namely, the main tax impediments to financial restructuring in Ukraine that were partially resolved at later stages were:

- **Debt forgiveness gave rise to taxable income for the debtor.** According to the tax authorities, if a creditor agrees to write down the principal amount of a loan with respect to a corporate debtor, the amount of this write-down is subject to corporate income tax in accordance with the Tax Code. Debt forgiveness for an individual was also counted as taxable income.

- **Debt forgiveness was not deductible by the creditor.** The amount of principal that was forgiven in a loan was not allowed to be deducted in creditors' tax returns. Due to these negative tax consequences, banks were less likely to restructure a loan.

- **The tax code placed severe restrictions on the write-off of bad debts.** According to the Tax Code, banks could only write off debt of a corporate entity once it had been declared bankrupt and the bankruptcy process had been concluded. This overly rigid rule prevented banks from cleaning their balance sheets by writing off loans that were uncollectable.

- **The tax implications of the sale of loans at a discount were unclear.** The Tax Code did not directly address the issue of sale or assignment of bank loans at a discount. It was not clear whether the sale of a loan at a discount would give rise to a deduction for the difference between the nominal value of the loan and the price at which it was sold. Therefore, stakeholders indicated that they were afraid to sell their exposures due to potential tax consequences. This uncertainty prevented banks from ridding their balance sheets of nonperforming assets.

- **The tax treatment of debt-to-equity swaps also gave rise to uncertainty.** The exchange by banks of debt for ownership shares in a company did not give rise to a taxable transaction. However, the tax authorities could question the valuation of the acquired shares, potentially creating a tax liability if they were assessed to be of a higher value than the exchanged asset.

- **The sale of collateral could give rise to VAT.** According to stakeholders, the sale of collateral as a result of an enforcement action might give rise to VAT liability of the banks, even if the proceeds from the sale of collateral did not cover the full amount of the loan. While the tax authorities had previously issued a clarifying opinion on this matter, it was not clear whether this opinion was invalidated by the new changes to the law.

In the case of Ukraine, a working group on tax clarifications was set up to solve the problem of tax impediments. This group submitted proposals to the Ministry of Finance for approval of several new tax clarifications, which added certainty to the treatment of tax authorities.

To put it in a nutshell, the introduction of out-of-court practices and ancillary procedures provided authorities and market participants with an additional and potentially effective instrument for resolving bad debts. However, the insolvency system was part of a broader legal environment for credit, which was characterized by lack of information on debtors, a general mistrust in commercial and consumer credit relationships, and considerable difficulties in the enforcement of claims. These factors undermined the protection of creditor rights, prevented the development of a payment culture, and contributed to the difficulties in accessing credit.

The law on financial restructuring proved successful in Ukraine, with 25 procedures completed by the end of 2019 in accordance with the law, with the total amount of debt restructured at UAH 36.5 billion (about USD 1.5 billion). It was supported by important amendments to the legislation regarding the protection of creditors' rights[31] and a completely new Bankruptcy Code[32], which among other things, introduced personal bankruptcy in Ukraine, and lifted the moratorium on the foreclosure of FX mortgage loans.

Among the legal impediments, the weak judicial system, ineffective

---

[31] Law of Ukraine "On amendments to legislative acts of Ukraine on recovery of lending", № 2478-VIII as of 3 July 2018

[32] Law of Ukraine "Code of Ukraine on bankruptcy procedures" № 2597-VIII as of 18 October 2018

enforcement practices, and insufficient level of protection of the rights of creditors were the most significant. In the context of information supporting the workout of existing NPLs and preventing the accumulation of new ones, it is important to introduce a central credit register. Ukraine did so in 2018, and by 2019 had accumulated information on 80,000 borrowers, as well as provide banks with access to fiscal and social databases that allowed them to more effectively assess borrowers' creditworthiness.

d) The dilemma of bad banks versus AMC or DGF

The gradual recovery of the Ukrainian economy underscored the importance of resolving the legacy of non-performing loans in the banking system. A huge load of NPLs in banks' portfolios was (and still is) a serious impediment to the recovery of bank lending in Ukraine, especially as the bulk of them were concentrated in state-owned banks.

Since the GFC, most countries are concerned with tackling the NPL problem and a number of different approaches have been introduced across the board. What became evident is that *more radical reforms are needed than merely adjusting the supervisory tools and national legal frameworks*.

Based on international experience, a comprehensive approach to addressing the problem of NPL involves combining measures at three main levels:

    i.   **Internal work-out of the NPL.** At this level, measures are based on the creation of a separate bank unit that independently, or through the involvement of external consultants, develops the bank's strategy for resolving non-performing assets, starting with the process of identifying the NPL, developing a plan of action, provisioning, collateral valuation, debt write-offs, and implementation of an effective system for managing the distressed assets.

ii. **Transfer of bad debts to third parties.** This approach allows separating bad assets from the performing part of the bank's assets, thereby reducing operating costs associated with management and redundancy of low-quality assets, and avoiding further deterioration of the bank's capital and profits from the performing assets. In the end, this approach contributes to increasing the trust of depositors and investors in the bank. In international best practice, there are three main mechanisms for splitting-off distressed assets: direct sales to the investor, securitization mechanisms, and creation of asset management companies.

iii. **Legislative environment.** Creating favourable conditions for clearing bad assets from banks' balances and developing a secondary market for non-performing loans includes the need to address a number of legal issues and bring local standards in line with best international practices.

According to a World Bank survey in May 2017, Ukrainian banks in most cases only transferred NPL resolution function to internal units; in many fewer cases, NPLs were sold to specialized non-bank companies where the role of "specialized companies" was played by factoring companies, which contradicts the classical understanding of factoring. The fact that most Ukrainian banks got stuck at this level did not allow our banking system to significantly resolve the problem of bad debts.

In the case studies previously presented (Mryia, Creative Group), as well as in hundreds of other cases not covered in this manual, banks were forced to transfer assets pledged as a collateral for loans onto their books. In fact, bank acquisition of the ownership of property, though one option for satisfying banks' interests, is *not optimal from an economic point of view*. Taking into account that the bank does not have sufficient expertise in the area of industry, agriculture, or real estate management, taking over such assets would increase the operating costs of banks and deteriorate its financial performance.

Even if NPLs are fully provisioned, capital tied up in NPLs generates low or no returns while the work-out costs are a drag on earnings. It also distracts management focus from core business NPL, and requires expertise generally not available within a bank.

Therefore, international practice suggests that the creation of *specialized companies*, whose main activity is managing the portfolios of distressed assets, is an effective way to unload non-performing loans from bank.

In Ukraine, the largest "AMC" was the DGF, which managed the assets of insolvent banks with book value of approximately USD 15 billion. However, due to rigid legislative framework, the DGF was neither able to provide an effective solution to NPLs of insolvent banks nor to consolidate portfolio debts that were partially owed to solvent banks.

The DGF's introduction of electronic platform to sell assets of insolvent banks (see section 10g. for more details) was a significant step forward in terms of transparency of sale procedures, but it was not effective enough, given the absence of a liquid secondary market for non-performing loans in Ukraine.

The high level of concentration of bad debts of corporate borrowers in Ukraine, and banks' differential treatment of borrowers' financial condition, which affected the different levels of provisioning for such loans, led us to favour creation of specialized financial companies that could consolidate the debt owed to different banks and more effectively use resolution mechanisms.

The advantages of using AMCs to clean up bank balance sheets are that it allows bad debt burden-sharing with a bank and provides for more effective use of the bank's capital (i.e., AMC are not subject to banking CAR, thus allowing debt-to-equity swaps). AMCs can provide economies of scale in hiring professionals with turnaround skills or negotiating with private equity firms, thus contributing to higher recovery values. For these reasons, the creation of specialized companies for managing distressed assets, thereby allowing banks to continue banking business, was justified.

It is important to note that in this initiative, we were in line with the Ministry of Finance, which, with the help of foreign consultants, prepared a project for the creation of a *state-owned asset management company* to which the non-performing assets of state-owned banks could be transferred. The idea was justified by the fact that as of December 2016, state-owned Ukrainian banks held $15.8 billion gross loans on their balance sheets. Of these gross loans, 74% (or $11.7 billion) were characterised as NPLs, with the nationalized PrivatBank maintaining the highest NPL ratio.

In our opinion, it was possible to create a centralized state AMC to work with non-performing assets of state-owned banks. However, the key issue was to ensure its *effectiveness* to minimize budget expenditures. This required answering several questions:

- Was the legislative field favourable enough for the AMC?
- Would the company have a sufficient level of expertise to work with NPLs?
- Were there sufficient financial resources for the company's operational activity and buying-out of bank assets?
- Would it be able to transfer assets from the DGF to ensure the consolidated management of assets of a common borrower?
- Did the concept allow involvement of foreign professional investors into the capital of AMC at any stage?
- How would the losses of state-owned banks be absorbed if assets were transferred to the AMC at a fair value?

In our view, a company appropriate to work with non-performing assets of state-owned banks should have a *high level of corporate governance* and a *professional staff with international expertise* in dealing with NPLs. The experience of some EU countries in establishing AMCs (Ireland, Spain, Germany, and lately Italy) was rather encouraging as the professional work-out of NPL in these countries yielded high recovery rates and minimized losses of bank creditors, as well as taxpayers (in the case of state-owned or nationalized banks).

Moreover, the company that manages bad debts should be provided with a *sufficient toolkit*. In particular, the company should be endowed with the right to:

- write off debt (without tax consequences for the borrower whose debt is subject to the write-off)
- take measures for the collection of bad debts through judicial and extrajudicial instruments
- restructure the debt
- invest in assets that are collateralized for bad debts in order to obtain a cash flow in the future sufficient to service and repay the debt
- entry into the capital of the borrowing company for the purpose of managing the assets of the firm and securing the interests of creditors

As the quality of Ukraine's NPL resolution framework posed a major obstacle to an efficient NPL workout, and as legal, judicial and extrajudicial issues remained critical for the asset management function, we proposed to look more broadly and try to *solve the problem systemically*, including for non-state banks, and created a *legal framework for the functioning of a new category of companies – asset resolution companies* (ARCs) -- that had all the necessary powers and tools to manage and restructure non-performing debts. The idea also included developing a *liquid secondary market for non-performing loans,* which would bring new investors and increase the recovery rate on NPLs.

A corresponding project on the *reloading of NPL resolution framework* was developed with the support of the EBRD and the banking community. The result was a draft law, "On Debt Resolution Activities". According to its provisions, banks would be able to sell distressed debts to specialized ARCs, which would need to meet stringent requirements as to the size of the authorized capital and sources of funding, and which would have limited ability to attract funds from individuals. Such companies would directly negotiate with debtors to resolve issues and conditions for debt repayment.

ARCs could be both private and state-owned. The draft law provided for equality of market participants regardless of ownership.

The Law on Debt Resolution Activities envisaged:

- A new legal framework (only as LLC or PJSC) for the establishment of an **ARC, a separate financial institution dealing with NPLs.**
- Prohibiting banks and their related parties **from being shareholders of the ARCs**
- ARC focus on **purchasing, restructuring, managing and selling loan portfolios, both performing and non-performing.**
- Permission for ARCs to attract funds by all means permitted under Ukrainian law, except deposit collection.
- **Licensing, supervision and regulation of ARCs** by the Financial Services Commission.
- A proposed minimum share capital of **UAH 30 million (USD 1 million); with** more serious and institutional investors expected to arrive in Ukraine.
- Creation of a **public asset resolution company by the state** to deal only with NPLs of state banks.
- Permission for the Deposit Guarantee Fund to sell assets under its management to ARCs.
- Permission for ARCs to sell purchased loans to a bank or another ARC.

An ARC would be able to carry out the following activities:

- **Purchasing** loan portfolios from a bank by an assignment-of-rights agreement
- **Proper notification, though not necessarily consent, of the debtor.**
- **Resolving** loan portfolios by:

- o Collection of debt (voluntary and mandatory)
- o Debt restructuring (both new financing and forgiveness)
- o Investing in the debtor's assets (capital, management, rent)
- o Participating in financial restructuring of the debtor

Adoption of legislative amendments would create **a transparent and investor-friendly legal framework** thus removing inconsistencies and other obstacles in existing regulations. As a result, "toxic assets" would be acquired and managed by ARCs focused on **cleaning NPLs and other bad debts from banking sheets** while banks would be able to accumulate appropriate resources for the introduction of new banking products and **ultimately resume their core business – lending.**

e) Bail-in issues for banks resolution

The concept of bail-in mechanism for bank liabilities is relatively new worldwide. At the global level, an attempt to share the financial responsibility in the event of bankruptcy of systemically important banks was made by the Financial Stability Board, in collaboration with the Basel Committee on Banking Supervision, by publishing in November 2015 a report on "Total Loss-Absorbing Capacity (TLAC) Principles and Term Sheet". In fact, the Report set the standard for requirements for G-SIBs to ensure sufficient resistance to losses, and set the goal of minimizing risks to financial stability, ensuring the performance of critical functions and avoiding loss of taxpayers' money. The report identified requirements on instruments and liabilities (TLAC-eligible instruments) and their share in assets, which can be used in a bank's bail-in procedure.

In the EU, despite the textbook example of using the bail-in mechanism to resolve the insolvency of the Bank of Cyprus in 2013, new rules for restoring a bank or declaring it insolvent did not go into effect until January 2015 with the 'Bank Recovery and Resolution Directive' (2014/59 / EU). Its main purpose was to shift the burden of financial losses in the event of bank insolvency from taxpayers (as occurs in the case of bail-out) to shareholders and creditors of the bank. At the same time, the bail-in mechanism itself, as part of the toolkit used in the event of bank insolvency, entered into force in January 2016. It provided the regulator with the right to apply the write-off or convert creditors' obligations into the bank's share capital. In order to ensure the availability of such obligations where the bail-in procedure could be applied, the regulator could impose on banks individual requirements for the sufficiency of these instruments of capital. In 2015, the main provisions of the Directive were also implemented in UK legislation.

Understandably, during 2014-2016, the bank recovery and resolution regime in Ukraine placed strong emphasis on crisis management. Still, **Ukrainian resolution laws contained some instances of the "bail-in" concept.** Limited provisions were incorporated into laws on banks and the banking system, and as of 2015, on the DGF to account for situations where the bank has (a) been declared insolvent and (b) is being recapitalised with public funds. The provisions did not permit recapitalisation of a bank without recourse to public funds or a recapitalisation pre-insolvency ("open-bank bail-in"). In addition, the provisions did not define the scope and hierarchy of liabilities to be "bailed in" nor include safeguard clauses that would impose strict standards and ex-ante / ex-post controls to ensure the equitable treatment of creditors.

These provisions were activated during the temporary administration of the nationalized PrivatBank in December 2016 in relation to the conversion of senior notes that were issued by an SPV established in the UK into the bank's capital.

When compared to the BRRD, the current framework in Ukraine does not provide for ex-ante planning tools, such as the mandatory preparation of resolvability assessments, or recovery and resolution plans for individual banks. It also lacks specific provisions that oblige banks to earmark adequate levels of capital and eligible liabilities for resolution, and to remove other known obstacles to resolvability. In short, the instruments for resolution must be improved. *A revised legal framework would cover a bank's resolution while a bank is still operational thereby ensuring performance of bank's critical functions.* In the future, the resolution mechanism is to be implemented without drawing on public funds, e.g., by mandatory write-down and conversion of equity instruments or bail-ins, that is, by conversion of a bank's liabilities into equity, in particular, liabilities to institutional creditors of a bank under interbank loans and to holders of debt instruments. This improved "bail-in" tool should contribute to:

- improving the resilience of the Ukrainian banking sector in the event of a major failure that could destabilise the economy at large and cause sovereign contagion
- reducing the likelihood, and volume, of public backstops required in the event of a banking crisis
- reducing moral hazard and the susceptibility of the resolution process to fraudulent action by insiders

In line with emerging international practice, a system should be developed to ensure that the *public does not bear the main costs of financial stability.* Most costs associated with the resolution or liquidation of banks in Ukraine, until now, have been publicly funded. An effective framework for bank resolution should be able to deal with failing banks of any size. Even the largest, most systemically important institutions, those previously deemed too big to fail, should be able to be resolved without use of taxpayers' money.

Bail-in should be introduced as a generic resolution tool that is applicable, in principle, to *all unsecured creditors* (i.e., not limited to 'related parties') as soon as market conditions allow for building up loss-absorbing capacity, and accompanied by clear legal safeguards. In addition to the write-down and conversion of capital instruments, unsecured creditors' claims would be written down or converted into equity, as appropriate, in order to cover funding needs for loss absorption and potential recapitalization, and to minimize taxpayers' potential exposure to the bank's losses. To support the statutory recapitalization of a failing bank by way of bail-in, all banks would be required to build up, adequate levels of internal loss-absorbing capacity over the course of a suitably calibrated phase-in period. This build up would consist primarily of unsecured, mostly subordinated, financial debt instruments, such as loans and bonds, that may be bailed-in as necessary, shielding the bank's depositors, and preventing adverse impacts on the stability of the financial sector.

In a banking system funded primarily by deposits, as is the case in Ukraine, the availability of eligible, potentially loss-absorbing, instruments is inherently limited and will depend critically on progress in the deepening of domestic interbank lending and the bond market to shield depositors from bail-in. *Improving access to the international capital markets* would be particularly important to avoid the concentration of eligible liabilities in the hands of a few systemically important market participants, which could again lead to unhealthy levels of interconnectedness and could increase systemic risk.

f) Non-banking financial institution reform

Comprehensive financial reform implied not only the internal transformation of institutions, but also revision of the existing models of financial market regulation. Ukraine's current sectoral model of regulation of the financial sector was established back in the 1990s with the support of international organizations, and was the most common model at the time. Back then, each financial segment was assigned a separate regulator: the central bank for the banking system, the state financial services commission for the non-bank financial institutions, and the stock exchange commission for capital markets.

The sectoral approach was probably justified at the time, as it allowed individual regulators to build up expertise in relation to their supervised markets, though it is not clear why regulation of activities similar in nature was distributed to different government authorities. For example, the central bank only regulated banks, but not non-bank credit institutions and credit unions, which, like banks, attract deposits from individuals and firms, transforming them into loans. Similarly, with life insurance companies and non-state pension funds, which were also supervised by two separate commissions. The consequence of this division of responsibility for different market segments was the emergence of different regulatory approaches, which in the economic literature is called **regulatory arbitrage**.

One of the glaring episodes in the Ukrainian market was the case of a relatively small bank, *Mikhailovsky*. Under sanctions from the central bank due to excessive related party lending, it started to attract customers' funds at higher than market interest rates as a contribution to the financial company affiliated with the bank. Since customer contracts were concluded at the bank's offices, many did not even suspect they were giving their money to a financial company, rather than placing it in a state-guaranteed deposit. As a result of the company's bankruptcy, UAH 2.5 billion was lost (approximately USD 100 million). This case proves the truth of the Ukrainian proverb: "Two nurses have a child without an eye."

Therefore, choosing *the right model is important: no market segments should be left out of regulation, and regulatory supervision should not be duplicated because of potential conflicts of interest among several regulators.*

Many countries went through integration of financial sector regulation in the 1990s and 2000's (UK, Germany, US). In Ukraine, despite changes in the names of regulators, actual changes in this direction have not taken place since independence.

At the same time, over the past two decades, *significant technological and structural changes* have taken place worldwide, with the emergence of new, more sophisticated financial products on the market, changes in the channels of interaction between financial service providers and consumers, and the growth in quantity and impact financial conglomerates. Examples of these activities that blur the focus of supervisors include crowdfunding, P2P lending, transactions with virtual financial assets through various types of companies both banks and non-banks. It is obvious that the complication and interdependence of financial markets, and the combination of several activities in one legal entity, creates a need for harmonization of regulation, including structural changes in approaches to state regulation of the financial sector.

From the outset, financial reform in Ukraine with the Comprehensive Reform Program 2020 included a project on *splitting the functions of the Financial Services Commission and their transfer to the National Bank and the Stock Exchange Commission.* Specifically, all non-bank financial companies, including insurance companies, were to come under the supervision of the central bank, while non-state pension funds would come under the supervision of the Stock Exchange Commission.

Within the framework of this project, we developed amendments to legislation and a detailed roadmap for the transfer of supervision functions for insurance companies, credit unions and other financial institutions under the auspices of the National Bank.

The advantage of this approach was obviously clear if looked at through the eyes of a market analyst: more than *85% of total assets of the financial sector was in banking,* while the other segments accounted only for less than 15%. However, in terms of the number of companies participating in the market, the situation was exactly the opposite. The number of banks amounted to about 5% of all companies in the financial market, and after strengthening supervision and clearing the market from insolvent banks, that number decreased to about 3%. At the same time, the number of non-bank financial companies began to grow like mushrooms after rain. We saw former bank owners, having left or been withdrawn from the banking business, "hover" customers' deposits in order to lend to the owner's business; and establish financial companies, with much less stringent prudential requirements, in order to continueusing the familiar business models.

Exhibit 32. Ukrainian financial sector by assets, share in % (as of 3Q2018)

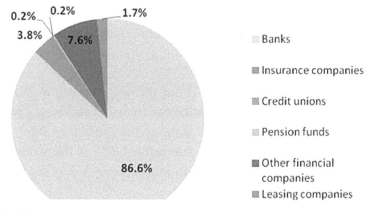

Source: NBU, NFSC, own calculations

Financial reports of non-bank financial institutions generally did not reflect their true liquidity and solvency. It was therefore impossible to track systemic risks in this segment. Moreover, the NBU lacked the power to adequately react to threats in this segment. The recommendations of the Financial Stability Council, of which the National Commission on State Regulation of Financial Services was a member, typically were not sufficient to mitigate the risks.

Concurrent with the beginning of implementation of this project, problems addressed by the draft law have become aggravated even more. Although 2015 changes to the Law on the National Bank strengthened its independence and institutional capacity, making it possible to fully implement the entire banking sector reform package and completely reload the banking sector, due to limited authority and funding, both commissions were only able to punctuate the rules for market participants under their supervision. As a result, the quality of regulation of these segments continues to lag behind best international standards.

During the reform period, the insurance market did not become cleaner and more transparent. Of nearly 300 companies, 50 held about 90% of all insurance premiums. What the other 250 companies do remains an open secret for both market participants and the regulator! It is enough to say that nearly 10% of insurance companies simply did not submit reports to the regulator. According to reports of other companies, about 100 of them were in a "frozen state", with extremely low sales and capitalization.

I should note that Ukraine is not the only country in the world that reviewed its model of regulating the financial sector. According to the 2018 Report of the Financial Stability Institute of the BIS[33], *the biggest global trend of the last decade (after GFC) is the strengthening of central banks' role in the prudential supervision of the non-banking segment of the financial market.*

The key is to ensure institutional and financial independence of the regulator. With clear objectives, the regulator must have sufficient levels of authority, resources, and operational autonomy to be able to implement a professional and unbiased policy for financial market agents.

Obviously, the National Bank, which has the largest institutional and financial capacity among all financial sector regulators in Ukraine, has the clearest goals (including being responsible for financial stability) and operational independence, and is the most resistant to political influence. For this reason, integrated (totally or partially) models are implemented in 70% of European countries, including 15% that are integrated in the central bank, and 12% of countries that are partially integrated based on the Two Agency model.

Reducing the number of regulators in the financial sector would not only save taxpayers' money, but would also affect the quality of regulation and protection of consumer rights. This result would be

---

[33] "Financial supervisory architecture: what has changed after the crisis?"; FSI Insights on policy implementation No 8, April 2018. https://www.bis.org/fsi/publ/insights8.htm

achieved through unified approaches to regulation and supervision of financial market participants.

The model envisaged for Ukraine was similar to the Two Agency model, which belongs to a family of partially integrated models, in which one of the regulators is responsible for the regulation and supervision of banks and insurance companies, and the other for setting general rules for the market and supervision of capital markets. According to this model, both regulators are also responsible for regulating market conduct in their respective market segments. This type of model has been introduced in Italy, France, Greece, and Serbia, and China has started a transition to this model as well.

In the context of the National Bank, it should be noted that the proposed model of *distribution of regulatory functions corresponded to the functional organizational structure of the central bank itself*, in which separate units would carry out the functions of licensing, supervision, inspections, etc. The potential conflict between the goals of monetary policy and prudential supervision would be minimized by institutionalizing the adoption of relevant decisions by various internal committees subordinated to different Deputy Governors.

In September 2019, the Ukrainian Parliament finally passed a Law splitting the Financial Services Commission's functions and transferring responsibility to the two regulators. In July 2020, the NBU will effectively become the regulator of insurance, leasing, factoring companies, credit unions, pawnshops, and other financial companies --in total, almost 2,100 institutions. In turn, the Securities Commission will further regulate the activities of private pension funds.

Obviously, adoption of this draft law will lead to further organizational changes in the National Bank, aimed at attracting the best expertise in the field of supervision of non-bank financial institutions. To this end, the National Bank and the Stock Exchange Commission have already developed a detailed roadmap for the transfer of functions, which will be implemented during a nine-month transition period.

For each of the financial segments a new legislation, in line with European regulations, has to be developed, since legislation has not been updated in years. The same risk-based approach that was applied to banking regulation is expected to be applied to the non-banking sector. Those non-bank companies that carry the lender's risk will fall under general supervision – for example, organizations that attract funds from their customers to support their activities such as insurance companies and credit unions. Financial companies that do not bear the creditor's risk, such as pawnshops, leasing, factoring, and other financial companies, will not be subject to prudential supervision. The result will be that only market behaviour is regulated, in terms of protecting consumer rights.

In conclusion, I repeat that the right design of supervisory architecture is an important factor in the effective functioning of the financial system and of maximizing the synergy of functions and minimizing conflicts of interest between them.

Today, my opinion is that the *transition to an integrated model of regulation and supervision of the financial market is not just a tribute to fashion, but a reasonable necessity*. The fact that even countries with developed market economies are moving in this direction suggests that the embedded flaws of sectoral models cannot be compensated even in the case of historically mature institutions. For developing and transformational economies that do not have sufficiently mature institutions, there are few alternatives to transiting to an integrated model of financial market regulation and supervision. Given that in most developing countries, it is the central bank that has the greatest institutional capacity, independence and expertise, integration of financial market supervision in the central bank is the most reasonable course of action.

g) State bank concentration, strategy and proper corporate governance

Even prior to the nationalization of Privatbank, Ukraine's state-owned banks represented about one-third of total banking assets, and historically lacked operational independence. Lending to companies of politically exposed persons was common and undermined banks' financial soundness for many years. To keep state banks afloat, the government was generous in providing fresh capital solely to cover huge credit losses pertaining to unwise lending decisions. These banks were a source of significant systemic risk for the financial sector.

The reliance of state-owned banks on budget funds gave rise to a problem of moral hazard and did not promote better corporate governance or introduction of efficient risk management. As a result, total fiscal expenditures on additional capitalization of state-owned banks exceeded UAH 74 billion from 2008 to 2015, or 6.4% of combined GDP during these years. Based on the NBU diagnostics of banks of 2015, the government again provided budget funds to increase the capital of Oschadbank and Ukreximbank in January 2016 by almost UAH 14.3 billion in total.

The key burden for public finance came from re-capitalization of the banks, including nationalized banks (Ukrgazbank, Kyiv Bank, and Rodovid Bank) from 2008 to2011. A total of 30% of that capital was used to bail out Rodovid Bank and Kyiv Bank, which, despite the bail outs were never able to resume normal operations. The decision to nationalize these three banks during the 2008-2009 crisis was an example of non-optimal policy decision making. Fiscal expenditures were several times higher than the losses that would have been incurred if the banks had been liquidated in due course.

During the crisis, *state-owned banks played a positive role of safe haven* for retail depositors, and even more so, for corporate funds that were not covered by the deposit guarantee system. The main reason for funds' inflow to state-owned banks was confidence that the government would support such banks under any circumstances, and therefore the risk of losing funds was very low. This created a major competitive advantage for state-owned banks as their funding base was (and remains) more stable compared to private banks.

Meanwhile, state-owned banks remained inefficient for a long time because of ***poor corporate governance, lack of clear business models,*** *and historical reliance on objectives set by public authorities.* State-owned banks were actively engaged in lending and actively provisioned for impaired loans to poor-quality borrowers. As of the end of 1Q2016, the rate of provisioning for loan portfolio at state-owned banks significantly exceeded the rates of private banks. This was largely the result of prior loan portfolio build-up under pressure from politically exposed persons. For instance, decisions made in the areas of alternative energy, chemical, construction, and real estate were extremely risky. The success of projects in those sectors depended critically on the business owners being close to the authorities. Once the owners of such enterprises lost political influence, the financial standing of the corporate borrowers deteriorated significantly. Moreover, some corporate borrowers that fell into the business interests of politically exposed persons refused to service their loans, even though they were operating efficiently.

An additional risk factor for state-owned banks was *active lending to state-owned enterprises.* Often, loans were extended to enterprises that could not borrow from private banks because of poor financial standing. Lending to state-owned enterprises by state-owned banks was limited in practice only by the covenants in loan agreements with international financial institutions that set a maximum share of state-owned companies for the bank's loan portfolio. This allowed limiting further extension of lending to the public sector. A large proportion of the loan portfolio of state-owned banks was formed on non-market terms. In particular, Naftogaz obtained a loan at below market interest rates. Lending to Naftogaz by major state-owned banks was actually used as a tool to solve fiscal problems and significantly hurt the interests of banks.

Thus, poor risk management and lending to bad borrowers was undermining the quality of the credit portfolios of the state-owned banks. Since 2008, state-owned banks began requiring additional capital. *From 2008 through the first quarter of 2016, a total of UAH 88.5 billion, or USD 8.7 billion at historical exchange rates, of additional capital was injected into the state-owned banks.*

The nationalization of PrivatBank was a key event that took place in December 2016 and led to an even more substantial participation of the state in the banking sector. As the risk of the shareholders failing to increase the bank's capital and restructure related-party loans materialized, the government spent the equivalent of nearly 7% of GDP to recapitalize PrivatBank and protect financial stability.

The PrivatBank nationalization resolved one systemic problem, but resulted in a long-term challenge: it meant that the state's share of the banking sector now exceeded 50% by net assets, and reached 62% by retail deposits.

International experience shows that during unfolding crises, an increase in state participation in banks' capital is a common anti-crisis measure. An increase in the share of public banks in the total assets of the banking sector was typical among neighbouring countries (Slovenia, Poland, Romania, Bulgaria, and Serbia). Promptness and timeliness of state intervention was the key to success. In theory, during a subsequent period of economic growth, the state gradually divests from banks' capital and rolls back its role in the financial sector. In some CEE countries, the public share in assets of the banking sector had returned to pre-crisis rates by 2014 (Poland, Czech Republic). In the former Soviet area, two countries (Armenia and Georgia) completely rejected the idea of developing state-owned banks. In Russia, the share of state-owned banks in the assets of the banking sector is over 50%. However, the Russian government intends to reduce its share in the largest state-owned bank, Sberbank of Russia JSC, to 25% over the next few years.

However, the experience of neighbouring countries shows that state-owned banks are almost never used as a tool for implementing the state's economic policy. Their positive role in the economy is reduced to smoothing credit cycles in the economy in times of crises. Almost all state-owned banks are public companies; their shares are listed on stock market, and the state's share in the capital is declining. The capital of the banks is increased through transfer of earnings or private capital injections, which gradually erodes the state's share in the authorized capital of banks.

The main weakness of Ukrainian state-owned banks was that their operational efficiency was extremely low: most of their interest income came from coupon payments on domestic government bonds, the quality of their credit risk management was inadequate, and there were not clear business models. Therefore, the key task in terms of reforming state-owned banks was the adoption of new legislation introducing independent supervisory boards and protecting the banks from political influence.

The National Bank shared its vision with the Ministry of Finance on a strategy for state-owned banks. As a part of Comprehensive Program 2020, the NBU outlined the *following strategic directions for banking sector development:*

- **Reducing the state's share of the banking sector.** The key objective was to gradually (within 3 to 5 years) reduce the state's share in the banking sector to less than 30% (in terms of assets) with a future exit of the state from the sector.
- **Effective corporate governance** by introducing effective corporate governance through independent Supervisory Boards and optimal corporate structures
- **Shaping banks' business models by** encouraging banks to choose a specialized business model and target specific customer segments.
- **Dealing with banks' distressed assets by** creating effective approaches to dealing with NPLs in order to achieve maximum recovery of non-performing loans.

In our view, the Strategy should support the principle of no preferential role or status of the SOB in relation to private market participants. This will ensure a level playing field for all banks and promote investment value and attractiveness of the SOBs for future privatization. Their specialization has to be enhanced and SOBs have to move toward business based exclusively on principles of maximization of return on invested capital. We wanted the Strategy to provide a plan for attracting strategic investors as minority shareholders in the systemically important SOBs in the medium term, and it should include guidelines for reducing the state's share to a minority stake, and full privatization in the long run. An important goal was to have the SOBs listed on one of the major European stock exchanges in the medium term.

Our proposals became the *Guidelines of the strategic reform of state-owned banks released by the Ministry of Finance in February 2016.* They were aimed at reconfiguring the principles and mechanisms of corporate management at state-owned banks and building up a management system for them that would be immune from political influence. One of the key points of the Strategy was adjustment of the corporate management system to OECD recommendations. This would contribute to more stability in state-owned banks' operation, which would lead to improved performance and better assessment by potential investors.

The ultimate ownership goal of the state for the core banks was to gain the highest possible risk-weighted income and to manage its investments in a way to increase their value.

In the short-term, the core banks had two key strategic objectives:

- to implement fundamental changes in corporate governance that would ensure their independence from political and administrative influence
- to implement changes in business and operation models with a view towards achieving the highest efficiency and maximal commercial orientation

To implement the updated strategies for core banks, the state intended to to sell at least 20% of its shares in core banks to a qualified investor or IFI via transparent tender by the mid-term.

In the long-term, the state would consider the possibility of full privatization of SOBs, as it did not intend to maintain its ownership share longer than needed to maximize value for taxpayers.

In order to achieve both short-term and long-term goals, the key was to ensure that state-owned banks' management stays outside politics. Thus, the corporate governance system of SOBs had to be brought in compliance with the recommendations of the OECD, the European Commission, and the Basel Committee on Banking Supervision.

The respective changes to the legislation were developed with active NBU participation and technical assistance from the IMF, the World Bank and other international financial institutions. Parliament adopted the respective legislation in mid-2018, and it opened a way for a *radical review of the principles and mechanisms of corporate governance of state-owned banks* since independent supervisory boards became mandatory for state-owned banks.

According to the Law, ***state-owned banks had to implement these new features in corporate governance***:

- Each state-owned bank should have a supervisory board of nine members. Of these, six members should be independent and three would be representatives of the state (one from the President, one from the Government and one from the Parliament)
- Applications for the positions of Supervisory Board members should be reviewed under a competitive selection process with a list of criteria to be met by each member
- The shareholder (i.e., the Government) should have no right to make decisions on matters that fall within the competence of the supervisory board. (This included criminal liability for unlawful interference with the activities of state bank officials, which was foreseen.)
- Members of the Supervisory Board should carry out their functions on a fee basis with a term of three years.

In order to adapt the legislation in its regulations and to extend the innovations in corporate governance to the whole banking sector, the National Bank developed **Recommendations on the organization of**

corporate governance in banks[34]. The main objective of the document was to increase the level of corporate governance in the banking sector, taking into account the adopted legislative changes and the recommendations of the Basel Committee on Banking Supervision on Corporate Governance and best international practices.

To sum up, the State spent over USD 10 billion on recapitalisation of state banks during the last 10 years. If Privatbank is taken into account, the total amount reached USD 15.5 billion. We had to stop this and to significantly increase the efficiency of these institutions.

At the time of writing, independent supervisory boards have already been formed in all state-owned banks throughout Ukraine. This creates the preconditions for changing the principles of the operation of state-owned banks, and will eventually bring them out of direct influence of existing and future political elites.

Key tasks for supervisory boards were to clear banks' balances from non-performing loans, to develop strategies and business models, to increase operational efficiency, and ultimately to maximize profits for the state. At the current stage, the ultimate goal of the new supervisory boards is to make state banks attractive to investing. The effective work of supervisory boards will be a guarantee that state-owned banks no longer incur losses to the state, as happened in previous years. I hope that their independent and effective work will enable achievement of the strategic goal to reform the state-owned banks.

h) Banks with Russian Capital

Ukrainian banks capitalized by Russian-capital gained signs of systemic risk with the onset of Russian aggression on the territory of Ukraine.

It should be noted that Ukraine's banks capitalized by Russian-capital were the first to suffer when the war began in the East. After all, those

---

[34] Approved by the NBU Resolution #814 dated 03.12.2018

banks' loan portfolio for the most part consisted of loans provided to industrial and infrastructure companies located mainly in the territory that was occupied or located on the front line. Due to the physical destruction of production capacity, the ability of companies in the region to service their loan portfolio was significantly reduced.

Those banks were also the first to encounter significant outflows of deposits, and the first to whom the debtors stopped repaying loans. Other than herding behavior of depositors, it is rationally impossible to explain the reluctance of individual borrowers who were not affected by the military actions to repay their debts to banks that had Russian capital. However, under the guise of patriotic slogans, like "you cannot pay the banks of the occupying country", some borrowers, even those in strong financial condition, stopped paying banks. Politicians of all colors and stripes supported this nationalism, and "Russian" bank branch offices in Kyiv and other cities were vandalized.

For us, as a regulator of the banking system, the problem looked different. In all my public and non-public comments, I was always careful to urge that we call things by their proper names: *there were no Russian banks in Ukraine -- there were Ukrainian banks with Russian capitalization.* That is, while the capital was of Russian origin, the rest of the bank's balance sheet consisted of liabilities to Ukrainian depositors and investors, and assets invested in Ukrainian business.

From 2010 to 2013, banks with Russian capitalization actively expanded their presence in Ukraine, lending to businesses and state-owned companies (including strategic ones), with funds provided by parent banks. The main focus was on lending to commercial, machine-building, transport companies and construction / real estate, and alternative energy projects.

Table 4. Share of Russian capitalized banks

	Net assets	Total assets	Credits (gross)	Deposits of households	Equity capital
2013	8.2%	8.1%	9.3%	6.7%	9.1%
2014	10.8%	10.3%	11.7%	5.2%	11.7%
2015	10.1%	12.0%	15.8%	5.3%	24.2%
2016	8.5%	10.3%	15.1%	4.5%	21.2%
2017	5.6%	7.6%	11.0%	3.0%	20.8%
2018	3.2%	6.1%	8.9%	1.4%	15.3%

Source: NBU

Russian-capitalized banks represented 12% of our banking system during the perfect storm time of 2014 to 2015. This presented an additional danger for Ukraine because we could not predict what the aggressor country would try to do on our territory with its subsidiaries.

Those banks found themselves in a difficult situation and became hostages of the war due to their model of aggressive interbank funding from their mother banks. They were "in a cage". From one side, there was a significant outflow of deposits of individuals, and from other side, the quality of the loan portfolio deteriorated significantly since the lion's share of their loan portfolio was in Crimea and industrial part of Donbas.

As NPL in these banks with Russian capital surged, their capital instantly became negative, and they were forced to write off or restructure non-performing loans and increase their capital through debt to equity swaps – a conversion into capital of debts from parent banks.

We were lucky. I should acknowledge that banks with Russian capital strictly followed the rules of the NBU, and were recapitalized more quickly and in larger volumes than, was required by the diagnostic study conducted in 2015. Three banks with Russian capital during the years 2014 and 2015 increased their capital by UAH 36 bln, and submitted plans for capitalization at UAH 39 bln over the following three years.

Since 2014, the National Bank carried out enhanced daily monitoring of banks with Russian capital in order to take measures in the event of force majeure. However, there were no attempts to withdraw capital from them: on the contrary, there was an inflow of capital. The percentage of deposits withdrawn from banks with Russian capital was 40 to 50%, which was twice as high compared to other Ukrainian banks. But the Russian-capitalized banks did not take a penny of refinance from the central bank. Instead, each of them obtained large refinancing lines provided by their parent banks.

To our understanding, there was no future for banks with Russian capital in the medium term in Ukraine. So, we proposed two options: sell their subsidiaries to reliable international investors, or start a gradual deleveraging process: that is, repay deposits and leave the market. Initially, there were a few attempts to artificially sell these banks to new owners, but these were window–dressing exercises. Given the stringent requirements of the National Bank to potential owners of banks, the situation with Russian-capitalized banks followed the second pattern. After introduction of US sanctions, the first option was not applicable anymore, so only deleveraging was the workable solution.

In March 2017, the National Security and Defence Council decided to impose sanctions on Russian-capitalized banks in Ukraine as well. In pursuance of this decision, we also introduced a number of restrictions concerning the activities of these banks. The sanctions banned capital outflows; and prohibited financial transactions involving the transfer of funds to parent banks, including asset-related transactions, dividend or interest payments, repayment of loans or deposits from correspondent accounts, repayment of subordinated debt, profit distribution and allocation of capital.

Thus, these banks had to leave the market, or, at least, cease being banks in the classical meaning and become asset management companies, gradually resolving their non-performing assets.

With sanctions in place, our task was to calm the market and let Russian-capitalized banks exit the market in a civilised manner, gradual shrinking their balance sheets while fulfilling their obligations to clients.

As Table 3 shows, banks with Russian capital continue deleveraging, with net assets representing only 3.2% of our banking sector in 2018. One of those banks lost liquidity and was unable to restore it due to imposed sanctions, and finally was withdrawn from the market in 2018.

i) Prudential regulation for FinTech, P2P, cryptocurrencies

The problem of the "shadow" economy is faced by all developing countries. Ukraine is no exception, with a "shadow" economy, according to various estimates, historically at the level of 30-50% of GDP. This means that almost half of the country's business life falls beyond the regulatory field. Accordingly, tax is not paid, thereby increasing the burden on the "white" businesses and putting them in unequal conditions compared to those who work in the shade.

It is generally accepted that central banks, like real "white knights", cannot significantly influence this process, which, as a rule, is caused by structural and legal problems in the country. However, our experience shows that the level of the shadow economy can and should be decreased, including through the policy of the central bank! Just as the operations of banks with fake securities were terminated due to actions of the central bank, so too can existing tools of the central bank counter the shadow economy. In the case of the securities market, even though the central bank was not a regulator of the securities market, it forced banks to create 100% reserves for holding fake securities, thereby killing that "market". Similar action is possible with the shadow economy. The most important thing is to act decisively and consistently.

Considering that payments in the shadow economy occur outside the banking system, our solution was to develop a cashless economy, since cashless transactions in banks, by definition, bring transactions to light. That is, banks are responsible for due diligence of their customers and compliance with AML rules. Our goal was to simplify the availability of financial services by promoting the development of remote channels for bank services, promoting new innovative solutions, and introducing international standards in the field of payments. Presumably, the migration of transactions to non-cash would also improve the quality of the transmission of monetary policy due to improved central bank control over monetary aggregates.

Like many developing countries, Ukraine has been historically characterized by low penetration of non-cash payments, especially in the retail payments of individuals. The ratio of cash (M0) to GDP in Ukraine in 2014 exceeded 18%, significantly exceeding the corresponding ratio in other countries in the Central and Eastern European region. A high level of cash in circulation has slowed economic growth, reduced transparency and inhibited the development of up-to-date services and technologies.

That is why we have launched a set of initiatives that were integrated with the **Cashless Project**. Within the framework of this project, we developed and implemented a set of measures aimed at stimulating bank card payments. These included introducing a system of remote identification of bank clients to facilitate their provision of remote financial services (BankID), stimulating the development of payment infrastructure (POS), and many others that are elaborated below. These steps helped to decrease the cash penetration in the economy by nearly half (to less than 10% of GDP in 2019), and to increase the share of non-cash payments two-fold, from 25% to 50% of all bank card transactions, and to almost double the ratio of POS penetration, from 4,700 up to 8,400 terminals per 1 million of population, with 90% of POS terminals providing contactless payment.

But the time for extensive solutions is rapidly passing. One of the most important challenges now facing all developed and developing economies is the rapid diffusion of technologies in the financial sector that are changing the nature of banking. Virtual currencies, block-chain applications, crowdfunding and peer-to-peer lending -- together with high capital costs and extensive regulation – shifts banking business to a new uncharted territory.

I remember that at the 2015 Davos Forum, I argued to my peers that so-called **shadow banking** would be soon a mainstream banking business because banks have to increase efficiency and introduce new innovative business models.

Although financial innovations offer a number of benefits to customers, they blur boundaries between financial products and cause real disruption in applicable business models for traditional banks and other financial institutions. Currently, the share of FinTech is relatively small if compared with the assets of the conventional banking system; however, Fintech firms are rapidly gaining traction in the market. The proliferation of FinTechs in the immediate future will become even more prominent since their target audience is the new generation, who are the most digitally active. FinTech is even more prominent in emerging-market and developing economies as innovations help leap-frog stages of technological and business development without extensive investments in infrastructure.

Despite its obvious benefits for consumers, from the regulatory point of view, the rapid expansion of FinTechs raises a number of serious concerns regarding privacy, consumer protection, money laundering, and ultimately, financial stability. Their most probable disruptive effect on a traditional financial system suggests even macroeconomic stability repercussions.

All major global financial institutions have already expressed their interest in the area of FinTech: G20, World Economic Forum, the IMF, the BIS and even the European Parliament. It is no wonder since **digital technologies have no borders. The same should apply to regulation.**

Since the GFC, the *regulatory burden on banks has tremendously intensified* with much more stringent requirements to comply with AML and KYC rules, and capital and liquidity requirements. Though important in terms of decreasing the systemic risks, these additional requirements strain banks' flexibility and incur substantial costs that leave the banking sector on the back foot in competition with FinTech companies.

The situation is exacerbated as the FinTechs compete mostly on high margin products and for big wallet customers. The heightened competition could significantly affect banks' profitability and thus could lead to additional risk-taking among incumbent banks in order to maintain margins. By extension, this could undermine the sustainability of the banking business in long-term.

To date, many *FinTechs' shift to building partnerships with banks* and other financial institutions has made their relationship largely complementary and cooperative in nature. Most FinTech firms do not have sufficient access to the low-cost funding or the customer base necessary to pose a serious competitive threat to established financial institutions in mature financial market segments. Thus, their partnership with banks is mutually beneficial: FinTechs can viably operate while still being relatively small and, depending on the jurisdiction and the business model, unburdened by financial regulation while still benefitting from access to incumbents' client base. For their part, banks can benefit from access to innovative technologies that provide a competitive edge.

However, *this is not the case with large technology firms* called **Big Techs**, such as Amazon, Google or Facebook. Once they start providing financial services, they could evolve quickly having access to a wide network of customers and their personal 'Big Data'. Big Techs are already present in banking. And the fact that they don't have deposit licenses is misleading. Indeed, they have already made much progress in processing payments, money transfers, introduction of biometric technologies and experimenting with crypto-assets. Moreover, they heavily invest in IT – twice as much as Bulge Bracket banks. Thus, Big Techs' entry raises new challenges for financial regulators in terms of competition, data protection and financial stability, which cannot be met by countries on standalone basis. **We need decent regulations on a global level, which would be implemented locally.**

Unlike the competition with small and medium FinTechs, Big Techs could be much tougher for banks given they are self-sufficient and have a bulk of liquidity that even exceeds the gross annual earnings of major investment banks.

It is a challenge for regulators to find the right approach to regulating the Big Techs so that market competition is preserved and no monopolies appear. When Big Techs engage in banking activities, they are rightfully becoming an element of critical public infrastructure and should be subject to the same regulations that currently apply to banks. **The aim is to close the regulatory gaps between Big Techs and regulated financial institutions** so as to limit the scope for regulatory arbitrage through shadow banking activities. *That's why we need to concentrate our collective wisdom to create needed regulation.*

Conventional banking models are at risk of being disrupted by the drive towards platform models of banking, such as P2P service providers or crowdfunding platforms. In traditional banks, loans are financed on the balance sheet through the bank's own capital and liabilities (deposits and other sources of funding). The new scenario consists of the disintermediation of these activities by means of peer-to-peer (P2P) lending platforms, in which the assets and liabilities disappear from the balance sheets of the new FinTech companies, and their work becomes the intermediation between lenders investing in every individual loan borrowed.

The appearance of this new type of intermediation has been accompanied in some countries by regulation of alternative financing, allowing the emergence of new FinTech P2P lending companies. Meanwhile in a number of countries, including Ukraine, clear regulatory standards are still lacking. This should be an urgent concern for policymakers as here the tactic of "If I do not see it, it does not exist" will not work.

P2P is already in-place in many countries. It is evolving rapidly in EU and UK with double-digit CAGRs. The market share is still relatively small but rapidly expanding and reaching a significant number of customers across the globe.

In regards to P2P, regulators should support sound practices while paying particular attention to (i) customer protections such as information disclosure, fraud, operational failures, (ii) prevention of systemic effects by monitoring risk build-up, and (iii) money laundering.

Ukraine's recent experience serves to confirm these recommendations and provide an rationale for why sound regulatory practices are much needed for proper development of P2P.

The first case of P2P lending in Ukraine was launched by the country's largest bank, Privatbank, in March 2016. Though it was positioned as an independent initiative of Privatbank's management, the fact that the bank was under the regulatory limitations based on the stress-test of the central bank, made us wonder if the true reason for launching P2P was to avoid the restrictive guidelines of the regulator.

Privatbank positioned its project as an intermediation platform for small businesses and self-employed persons who were able to finance development of their business from other individuals in an amount from UAH 50,000 to 300,000 (equivalent to $2,000-12,000) for a period of 6 or 12 months. The platform announced that the "investments" were insured by the insurance company affiliated with the bank.

It is worth to note that *PrivatBank's P2P model was unique* not only due to an extensive engagement of a systemic bank in platform operations, but also in terms of having features of different P2P models, such as the client-segregated model (for allowing direct contracts between investors and borrowers); the "guaranteed" return model (that provided insurance for credit risks and assurances from the bank to refinance borrowers in case of default); and the notary model, for use on loans initially originated by the bank.

Moreover, the platform was based on the bank's 24/7 service, and the customer was asked while using the service to deposit money whether he/she wanted to obtain a higher interest rate using the platform. Bank clients were not provided with clear information on the risks of "investments" nor that the return on "investments" is not guaranteed). Thus, their business model carried high risks for clients given:

- Uninformed decisions (investors accepted the risks without information about borrowers)
- Borrowers were selected by the bank (separation of credit risk decision and credit risk bearing)
- Misleading assurance of return certainty and low risk profile (insurance by a related insurance company, which was financially incapable of covering the risks; and a promise to re-finance defaulted borrowers

Due to high market share, in just two months Privatbank was able to unload retail loan and deposit portfolios from the bank balance sheet and achieve P2P volumes exceeding the UK and the US in terms of percentage of GDP! After that explosive two-month launch of P2P lending, Privatbank re-distributed P2P to about 15% of total new retail deposits for the period, with the number of platform users reaching 53,000 and the value of P2P loans exceeding UAH 1.2bn.

The National Bank ordered Privatbank to incorporate P2P loans into its balance sheet due to a number of risks pertaining to P2P lending on a systemic bank's platform, including credit (counterparty) risk, risk of fraud, lack of transparency / misleading information, legal risks, liquidity risks, operations risks, money laundering, which were neglected by the bank's P2P platform.

While the old proverb says that the first pancake is always lumpy, our lesson learned was that the *regulator must impose disincentives for banks to run P2P under banking brands and must set strict information and risk disclosure requirements*. For future P2P development to not endanger financial stability, a **clear supervisory responsibility between the regulators for crowdfunding and other "shadow banking" segments should be established.**

Another downside of financial technology is that the proliferation of non-cash payments further complicates the case of countries producing their own cash. A vivid illustration of the case is **NBU Mint**, a structural unit of the central bank of Ukraine responsible for the production of banknotes, coins and banknote paper. Given the decline in global demand for cash, the maintenance of production facilities solely for the needs of a single country and not built into global production chains become unprofitable.

In the case of NBU Mint, the lion's share of the income was provided by the production of banknotes and paper sold for export since the domestic demand for the company's products did not allow loading its capacity, even by 20%. As the global market is controlled by the oligopoly of large companies, it is difficult for individual countries to become global players in this market. This determines how small countries work as sub-contractors for large companies that distribute capacity utilization all over the world.

Open Banking

Open banking is a new global trend that has induced a major shift in regulation facilitated by changes in both technology and consumer preferences. The combined effect of these developments may be far-reaching with greater competition in certain services while also posing new risks.

In the UK, the Bank of England has already opened an access to its Real-Time Gross Settlement system to alternative payment service providers thus making it easier for a broad set of firms to plug in and compete with more traditional financial services providers

In the European Union, the revised *Payment Services Directive (PSD2)* makes it easier and safer to use internet payment services; better protects customers against fraud, abuse and payment problems; and promotes innovative mobile and payment services. PSD2 mandates open access to certain types of customers' banking data for non-bank licensed providers of payment initiation services and account information services.

The National Bank of Ukraine is not standing on the side-lines but together with the other financial sector regulators and state authorities is actively reviewing international experience and local legislation in order to develop a consolidated approach to regulations in the area of FinTech in line with world best practice.

Under Program 2020, the National Bank started major work on a *fundamental upgrade of local legislation in the area of payments and money transfers based on the concept of Open Banking.* The regulator intends to harmonize Ukraine's plans with the EU's PSD2, which would increase competition in the financial market and promote innovative development of the local payment market.

Among other things, the new legislation would introduce secure online access to funds and customer account data for certain categories of providers of payment initiation and account information services; create new regulation in the electronic money segment and provide the right for non-bank financial institutions to issue and acquire payment cards, issue electronic money, and open payment accounts (for purposes of payments and settlements). It would also increase payment service users' rights by setting clear requirements for providers of financial services, limiting the liability for unauthorized transactions, and so on.

To further facilitate the development of FinTech in Ukraine, the National Bank launched the *Expert Council on communications with innovative companies.* This entity would serve as a prototype of *Sandbox,* which in pilot mode allows direct dialogue between the National Bank and FinTech companies. To review companies' business models, experts from different departments of the central bank and, if necessary, from other government agencies, are involved in the discussion. For each of the innovative products, companies are provided with direct feedback and advice on its legal and regulatory support.

I recommend that central banks **be open for innovations but remain aware of the inherent risks**. That means we should not only see the market as it is but also project what it could be in the future in order to have adequate ammunition in place for any adverse circumstances. That requires central banks to proactively lead the market towards the future while maintaining its sustainability in the long-term.

BankID

Increasing the performance of business processes in banks is an important prerequisite for improving the level of productivity, as true for the Ukrainian banking sector as elsewhere. In 2015, McKinsey and Finalta conducted a survey, commissioned by the banking community and backed by the National Bank, which showed that productivity in the banking sector in Ukraine is significantly behind the world's leading countries: 2.6 times behind Poland, 6.3 behind the US, and 9.1 times behind the UK's productivity level. In retail transactions (payments and transfers), this gap was even larger. For example, the number of retail transactions per employee of a relevant bank unit in Ukraine was 13 times lower than in the United States.

Such sobering statistics confirm that Ukrainian banks should spend more resources on attracting new clients and finding the best solutions for them. Instead, banks are spending resources supporting operations. Consequently, an increase in operating expenses results in a deterioration of banks' financial performance and impedes their capitalization. In my opinion, one of the main reasons for such a backlog is the large number of inefficient processes in banks and the excessive amount of paperwork.

That is why, in 2015, we launched BankID Project in order to create a unified public system of remote identification of individuals and legal entities. Its development was in accordance with the Comprehensive Program for Financial Sector Reform 2020, and envisaged three main directions, followed in parallel.

In the first direction, we established an interface for bank clients to receive administrative services remotely from the Unified Public Portal of Administrative Services and other public entities providing administrative services. Subsequently, after establishing connections to dozens of public administrative portals, bank customers were able to obtain a number of public services using their bank data such as register as an individual entrepreneur, apply for a biometric passport, and receive various certificates and extracts from the registers of the Ministry of Justice, etc.

In the second direction (bank-to-bank), BankID was scaled into banking services. Within this framework, the National Bank introduced remote identification of bank customers to obtain banking services (including at other banks), and it allowed banks to create commercial models using BankID, which would encourage more banks to connect to BankID.

Next, the NBU agreed with the Ministry of Finance on draft amendments to the AML Law (adopted in December 2019), which enabled remote identification of individuals. In parallel, the National Bank had amended its regulations in 2018, regarding AML[35] and payment account instructions[36], according to which banks were entitled to use the information on customer identification data received from another bank through BankID. This enabled bank customers to open accounts remotely without visiting a bank. A person's physical presence became necessary only for initial identification by the bank. In the future, a bank client will be able to receive banking services (opening accounts, making transfers, etc.) at any bank using BankID (password and login) and a digital signature to confirm the services ordered.

The third area of development (bank-to-commercial) provided for the possibility of using BankID between banks and commercial companies. Companies (such as mobile carriers) might be interested in identifying and getting better profiles of their customers, both for marketing purposes, and to offer and test new services/products.

From 2016 to 2018, the number of bank customers in Ukraine using remote services of their bank almost tripled. In addition, by the end of 2019, BankID had more than 100 types of administrative and commercial services available.

---

[35] NBU Board Resolution No. 417 dated 26.06.2015 (updated)
[36] NBU Board Resolution No. 492 dated 12.11.2003 (updated)

Introduction of the new generation of RTGS and IBAN

The National Bank was also persistent in the development of a local payment system, adapting it to advanced international standards. In November 2017, a ***new modernized generation of the RTGS platform*** for electronic interbank payments was launched. The System of Electronic Payments (SEP) of the National Bank was established in 1993 and since then has provided over 95% of interbank local currency transfers through accounts opened with the National Bank of Ukraine. The introduction of the 3rd generation of SEP was envisaged by the *Strategic Information Technology Development Program for 2016-2020,* adopted by the NBU Board in August 2016.

The new SEP-3 was upgraded based on modern information technologies, using IBM WebSphere application servers, industry JEE standards and a system of data transportation based on WebSphere MQ. The key characteristic features of the new RTGS system were:

- Increased productivity achieved through horizontal and vertical scalability
- Modern industrial solutions for back-up and recovery
- High resiliency based on cloud technologies of the National Bank
- High security and integrity of data

During 2019, the NBU SEP processed approximately 1.5 million initial payments in an average amount of UAH 130 billion per day. That said, the system is capable of processing about 10 million payments on a single banking day. At the same time, the introduction of a new generation of SEP laid the preconditions for further development, namely transition to **international financial messaging standards** and the introduction of new innovative tools for cashless payments. First and foremost, this is about the implementation of IBAN (ISO 13616) and ISO 20022 standards, which include advanced technological tools (XML), end-to-end payment processing, new functionality, and harmonization with European and international payment infrastructures, directives, and standards.

Among the next priorities for the SEP are introducing instant payments; switching to the 24/7/365 operation mode; updating the cryptographic information security system; extending functionality; and an informational messaging component.

The introduction of the **24/7 operation mode** of SEP is planned to be implemented in *two stages*. The first step is to extend the current mode for making interbank payments to 23 hours a day, 7 days a week (23/7), taking into account a technological break of one hour for the transition to a new day. With this step, the current SEP technology, as well as the accounting and statistical reporting procedure, will be maintained. The extended operation mode of SEP is planned for Q2 2020.

During the second stage, a "seamless" mode of operation (24/7) is to be launched with the transition from the current to the next banking day done immediately, without suspending payments during the transition to the new day. This mode of SEP is planned to be implemented within the framework of the next generation of SEP (SEP-4). The availability of payment facilities 24/7 will increase customer access to financial services and enable banks and their clients to make time-sensitive payments.

The 4th generation of SEP will be consistent with the international standard **ISO 20022**. The National Bank has begun to implement the new standard, which is used for payment infrastructure worldwide, particularly in Europe (for example, SEPA and TARGET2-Securities) in partnership with SWIFT. The transition of SEP to the ISO 20022 is to be completed by the end of 2021, and will further facilitate interaction between Ukrainian and international payment systems.

In parallel, in August 2019, the National bank launched a new process for introducing an **international bank account number in accordance with the requirements of ISO 13616 (IBAN)**. In November 2019, the use of IBAN became obligatory for clients of all banks in Ukraine when making transfers in both national and foreign currencies, in particular for cross-border transfers. It was important that all payment cards issued by banks to the client's account remained valid, and maintained a continuous opportunity for the client to initiate a transfer of funds from a bank account.

The introduction of IBAN made it possible to harmonize the Ukrainian payment environment with the European one, and due to the reduction of the payment credentials, made the settlement of documents easier. Because to this, bank clients can easily identify the payer and recipient of the funds, as well as the servicing bank. They can also avoid mistakes in account details by reducing the number of details in settlement documents, and can make transfers faster. Among other benefits for bank customers, the National Bank plans to introduce a standard for making payments using QR codes. The use of QR codes containing IBAN information will facilitate the payment of bills and the exchange of billing information.

Digital assets

In a short period, digital assets without a central ledger (we still prefer not to call them digital currency), such as BitCoin and many others, have gone the classic evolution from denial to interest to, in many cases, acceptance.

BIS General Manager Augustin Carstens' comments are well known: that cryptocurrencies are a combination of a bubble, a Ponzi scheme, and an environmental disaster. Similar comments by Bulge Bracket bank CEOs can be summarized by JPMorgan's Jamie Dimon, who called bitcoin 'a fraud' and 'worse than tulip bulbs'.

The National Bank of Ukraine, too, took a *cautious position* on this issue, and issued a *statement* in November 2017 in conjunction with other regulators of the financial sector saying that the complex legal nature of crypto assets does not allow them to be recognized either as cash or currency and means of payment of another country; nor as currency value, electronic money, securities, or money surrogates.

The biggest challenges are not technology such as blockchain or the like, but the absence of proper corporate governance applied to these instruments.

Having said that, we continue to work on the legal status and regulation of crypto asset transactions, taking into account the position of regulators in other countries and the latest trends in technological development with the aim of protecting consumer rights, and counteracting money laundering and other unlawful actions. In our statement, we warned that any activity related to buying, selling or exchanging crypto assets carries a number of risks that individuals and legal entities must be aware of before carrying out those transactions. Anyone planning to invest in crypto assets should realize that they do so at their own risk.

In past years, the level of understanding of the nature of digital assets created via the distributed ledger technology did not change significantly. However, the *digital ecosystem has become considerably wider*, entering the immediate mandate of central banks.

Leading global banks are actively preparing for the issuance of 'utility settlement coins' for clearing and settling financial transactions over blockchain and digital versions of major currencies backed with reserves in central banks. Moreover, in May 2019, the central banks of Canada and Singapore held the first successful trial of swapping digital currencies using blockchain technology. Thus, regardless of our attitude, crypto assets exist and many investors are experimenting with them.

The *regulation of operations with digital assets* is another tricky issue. As long as the capitalization of the market is low, regulators may not notice it, but when it grows to the extent of becoming of systemic importance, regulators attitude will change. As the proverb says: Do not **wait until the rain starts to think about having an umbrella in place.**

In my view, the question is not whether it is necessary to regulate operations with digital currencies, but how to do so properly. Here I rely on the fact that regulation of these operations at the country level is ineffective. As with most financial technologies, **regulation of digital currencies can only be global.**

This is the way to go for global trendsetters in regulation, such as the BIS and the IMF. **The prudential regulation of digital innovations has to**

be consistent across the globe to be effective. A new framework akin to "Basel III" is needed for FinTech. Legal and regulatory issues on preventing the usage of crypto assets as a vehicle for money laundering and financing terrorism, as well as privacy and risk management issues must be resolved.

j) Central Bank Digital Currency (e-UAH)

One fairly strong response from central banks to the challenges associated with the proliferation of digital assets may be to issue their own digital currency.

A number of banks have already made significant advances in this matter. Canada launched Project Jasper Singapore has Project Ubin, and Sweden has its E-krona Project. On the other side, the ECB rejected Estonia's plan to launch its own state-run digital currency and indicated that the ECB will not allow other EU member states to introduce their own currency. *A consensus has not yet been reached.*

I am pleased to note that during mytenure, the National Bank launched a **pilot project on the issuance of a digital currency of the central bank (called e-UAH) in 2016.** The project was launched under the umbrella of a set of "cashless" initiatives, aimed at creating preconditions and providing tools for increasing non-cash payments.

During the pilot, we did a thorough analysis of international experience, researched legal aspects and macroeconomic effects, and designed an optimal business model. Importantly, in parallel with the theoretical study of the CBDC, our project included a practical part. While testing the technology of the blockchain platform "E-hryvnia", a limited number of e-hryvnias were issued in circulation, and transactions were tested in a productive mode.

For the study, the scheme selected a central bank digital currency (CBDC) as the equivalent of cash with assumptions that e-hryvnia:

- was considered a digital form of money issued by the NBU
- was characterized a national currency, which is fiat money
- could be exchanged for cash or deposited without restrictions in the ratio of 1:1
- was not an interest-bearing tool, therefore it was a means of payment, not a store of value

The National Bank considered the CBDC as an alternative tool for instant payments of small amounts by individuals. The benefits of the CBDC were simplicity of use, safety (payments were guaranteed by the National Bank), quick acquisition of user status, and speed of settlements.

In order to run the pilot project, *two working groups were set up*: an internal working group (consisting of representatives from NBU structural divisions) and an initiative group, which included representatives of payment companies on a voluntary basis. The National Bank chose the private distributed ledger technology for the pilot project, which was run by internal resources and the IT infrastructure of the National Bank, as well as participants of the initiative group.

For the period of the pilot, zero commission rates were applied to all operations using e-hryvnia. The e-hryvnia business model will be further elaborated along with the payment market participants.

The small-scale pilot project (the limited number of operations and range of users, as well as the small amount and volume of transactions carried out) did not provide an opportunity to analyse all the advantages and disadvantages of e-hryvnia in terms of macroeconomic impact. In particular, it was difficult to predict how many customers would become e-UAH users if implemented on a national level.

Only if most of the population and businesses switch to e-hryvnia instead of cash and bank accounts can this significantly change the banking system's role as a financial intermediary. A definitive conclusion will have to wait.

I believe that before a launch of CBDC, central banks should seriously consider two main aspects: customer identification (ID) via different market participants, and banks' role since banks as intermediaries will no longer be needed, as all transactions will be done directly between central banks and customers.

We did not assume the risk of inflation as highly probable, since a distribution of e-UAH would be under the central bank's control if it were introduced as the national digital currency. At the same time, in the long run, there might be risks such as loss of the central bank's ability to effectively influence macroeconomic, primarily inflationary, and processes as a result of changing banks' role as financial intermediaries, losing their money creation function and, thus, changing the efficiency of the channels of monetary transmission.

If liquidity spilled over from the banking system, it would be kept at the central bank. At the same time, in there were significant volumes of liquidity flows, especially during periods of crisis, the transfer of funds from customers' bank accounts to e-hryvnia could create or deepen the liquidity crisis of both individual banks and the banking system as a whole. This would have a negative impact on banks' resilience and financial stability. In order to prevent liquidity crises of the banking system, restrictions on the exchange of deposits into e-hryvnia should be established.

The impact of e-hryvnia on monetary indicators depends on whether it will compete with cash or non-cash transactions, as well as on what proportion of transactions using e-hryvnia will be P2P transfers and payments for goods and services.

The full-fledged introduction of the CBDC in Ukraine will require significant investments in the respective retail payment infrastructure, including integration with the existing infrastructure. This should be preceded by the creation of a business model that takes into account the interests of all market participants: individuals, traders, distribution and settlement agents, banks, etc., and that stimulates development and further use of the e-hryvnia. Popularization of CBDC to make this tool truly a mass product is another open question that could be answered with additional analysis of existing user preferences.

If central banks are unwilling to enter the uncharted territory of having their own digital currencies, one IMF suggestion[37] is to use a synthetic approach, which is in essence a public-private partnership, and might make sense. Under the regulations of the central bank, e-money providers would perform all functions, including customer due diligence, managing of transactions and personal data, ensuring cyber security of the underlying platforms, dealing with customer complaints and requests, marketing of services, etc. If all the requirements were met, the central bank would provide settlement services for the authorized e-money providers in the central bank's reserves.

Although central bank digital currencies partially eliminate the drawbacks of private virtual currencies, such as riskiness and instability, a number of questions remain: Should there be a state-backed token, or perhaps an account held directly at the central bank, available to people and firms for retail payments? How would it affect monetary transmission? Would that mean that commercial banks lose their clients? How could risks to financial stability be accessed? How private should transactions with digital currencies be? Should central banks embrace a role of an emission centre or provide e-money providers and trading platforms access to their reserves?

Those questions are most relevant for emerging economies in which the risk of a bank run in a crisis would be enormously exacerbated if CBDC could be considered as a safe haven for depositors, and must be answered before CBDCs gain traction. The cross-border implications of CBDC requires a close cooperation of central banks, in both advanced and emerging markets and developing economies, preferably under the auspices of international financial institutions.

---

[37] The rise of digital money / FinTech notes/ International Monetary Fund, July 2019.

CHAPTER 12

Recommendations for other countries starting comprehensive reform of financial sector

BEFORE STARTING COMPREHENSIVE reform, you should clearly understand what you are going to do, where you would like to start, what your time horizon is, and what resources (human, political, financial, and advisory) you need to successfully implement changes.

Therefore, my first recommendation is to build the right and effective reform infrastructure in which all government agency and officials know their responsibility for specific areas. Build a platform where you can discuss projects and take decisions. Create an effective monitoring system, where red flags are raised in a time fashion in case gaps appear in the management system or project implementation.

The lack of proper and timely execution of planned reforms is a key weakness in most developing countries. But reforms are valuable not when they are planned on paper, but when they are fully implemented. However, in most of countries, including in Eastern Europe and Central Asia, transformational reform became a long and difficult process with erratic results. This is due to a lack of experience in reform conceptualization, delivery, process management and donor coordination.

My second recommendation is to start by setting a solid legal foundation for reform. Ensure that sufficient powers for decision-making are available to key institutions and to the policy-makers in charge of reform.

You need not only to do reform quickly and efficiently but you also need to immediately start building safeguard mechanisms to protect your reforms and reformers in the future.

And here we come to the most important problem of all reforms in any country. A sustainable rule of law, a reliable judicial system, and an effective and transparent law enforcement system are "musts" for sustainability of reform.

In this regard, I would like to answer the question that I have been asked many times over the past three years: How to make reform irreversible? Unfortunately, nothing is irreversible in life, even the course of rivers can be reversed. Rather, our task as reformers is to create safeguard mechanisms that do not allow something to later destroy all our achievements. If, as in the case of Ukraine, through the decision of a small district court that you have never even heard of, any government decision can be cancelled, then what kind of sustainability does reform have? In that case, no matter how much you reformed, it does no good if you cannot protect it.

Therefore, my recommendation is to start by ensuring the basic principles of the rule of law. After all, **where there is the rule of law, there is also the rule of common sense.**

That is why we started reform of Ukraine's financial sector by gaining legislative support for the independence of the central bank, and for strengthening its institutional powers. Looking back, we see that we could have done more in this direction, especially protecting the employees of the central bank who enacted all these reforms.

Delay in key reforms or even steps to reverse previous achievements, in particular through judicial and legislative decisions, can significantly increase the vulnerability of the economy, and prevent continued cooperation with IFIs. In the end, this endangers the macro-financial stability of the country.

Political factors will always influence the financial sector. There is simply no escaping this reality. Proof of this reality can be seen in the pressure on central banks in India, Turkey, and the United States.

Despite the fact that during five years of reforming the financial sector in Ukraine, we did not have national elections, this does not mean that our path was smooth. All our activities were accompanied by pressure from politicians who did not want to lose their influence on the country's main financial regulator or their vested interest in state-owned banks.

In June 2019, Stanley Fisher said that accusing the central bank of wrongdoing is a one-way bet for politicians. If inflation is too high or an economy falls into recession, they can claim to be correct; if the prediction does not pan out, they can be silent. Though Fisher's comment was in respect to the Federal Reserve, which was facing an assault from the White House on the independence of monetary policy, I am convinced the same is true for any central bank in today's world.

Politicians have to understand that their attacks on central banks' independence are like shooting themselves in the foot: if the central bank is not able to carry out an independent monetary policy in the best interests of people, the macroeconomic instability that will follow will end politicians' careers.

My third recommendation is to attract to your side all the healthy forces of society within the country and abroad. Working with opinion leaders is very important to ensure public support for reform. And cooperation with international organizations will allow bringing in the best international expertise, which is usually not available in the country, as well as funding that allows the banks to "buy time" for reforms.

After my visit to Tunisia as an advisor in 2019, it became clear to me that international assistance and strategic consultations happen only sporadically in developing economies. However, in the process of implementing reforms, it is important to have coordinated and sustained support from international partners and donors. Their initial support of Ukraine during the turbulent period of 2014 to 2015 was essential to lay the foundation for reform.

Cooperation with IFIs is crucial for reforms' success. Financial support here is important, but not the key. The main thing is the opportunity to obtain expertise based on the world's best practices, which is usually not available in developing countries.

In the modern world of trade wars and geopolitical conflicts, risks are always present. *Our task is to provide ourselves with sufficient ammunition to meet those risks fully armed.*

This ammunition, which will enable reform of the financial sector, can be provided by continuing cooperation with the IMF and other international organizations, especially as in the case of Ukraine, during a period of peak payments for external debt. Constructive cooperation with the IMF, within the framework of the new financing program, allowed Ukraine to receive other official funding, improve conditions for access to international capital markets, and support investors' interest in Ukrainian assets.

In the case of Ukraine, the IMF also became a factor uniting heterogeneous political interests in the interests of the country. The fact that Ukraine's memorandum with the IMF was signed not only by the Governor of the central bank and the Minister of finance, but also by the Prime minister and the President, highlighted the fact that the general efforts of all branches of government were directed at fulfilling the conditions of the memorandum. This led to successful results. That is why, even three years after my departure from the central bank of Ukraine, macro-financial stability remains still in place, despite the fundamental absence of the rule of law and the ongoing political turbulence.

My proposal for International Financial Institutions

Many of the world's emerging economies lack practical experience in systemic transformation to fully-functioning market-oriented economies, including strengthening of institutional capacities, introducing better governance of public authorities, and ensuring reform delivery and its sustainability. International assistance and strategic consultations are provided sporadically by IFIs, but the coordination of technical assistance and donors' activities is insufficient. Given that most developing economies I've visited during my tenure at the NBU and later on have similar challenges in the financial sector, I believe there must be a **unified approach** to provide a rapid response in order to build on reform momentum and amplify reform waves in a given country, whenever it appears.

Expertise in reforming the financial sector is rather unique as it is not a regular exercise, and in many countries, it may take place only once in generation. In my view, however, such expertise could be accumulated in **International Financial Institutions (IFI)**, which have a keen sense of the pulse of each country in a region, and understand their current and future needs.

I believe that IFIs should take a more proactive role and become Leaders of Reforms. I am sure that establishing a **Centre of Excellence of Reforms** could be a focal point for reform support across the globe – it would offer analytical excellence and expertise, a set of pre-developed reform tools, and the financial support to jumpstart the operation. It could enable a rapid response to the need of reforms in a given country by delivering a comprehensive reform concept and infrastructure, dedicated teams of experts and project managers, and proper coordination of TA and donors.

Such a centre's **main objectives** could be to provide:

- **Analytical excellence** to help assess the situation and recommend what type of intervention is needed / likely to succeed, in coordination with donors
- **Expertise, that is** mobilization and maintenance of a network of experts on call, who have the personal stature and experience necessary to be "field commanders"

- **A toolkit, so that although** each situation is specific, time is not wasted "reinventing the wheel". The Centre would create and manage knowledge on reform implementation, including a practitioners' Reforms Implementation Toolkit (RIT)
- **Support for the start-up** of operations in selected/approved situations. In practice, the Centre should have enough rapidly deployable resources to support the initial six to twelve months of effort, which is generally the time it takes most donors to mobilize resources

I have already proposed such a **Centre of Excellence of Reforms within the EBRD for the ECC region as part of a very good initiative** -- the EBRD's Ukrainian Reform Architecture (URA), a real example of the coherent approach to reforming the priority areas of a country. The URA was funded by the creation of a specific donor fund, a multi-donor account established to support Ukraine's reforms in 2016.

CHAPTER 13

Ad hoc policymaking

WHEN THIS BOOK was already finished, an unprecedented crisis erupted on planet Earth. This is a real Black Plague, the 21st century coronavirus pandemic, COVID-19. The shock is severe even compared to Great Financial Crisis of 2008. It simultaneously hit households, businesses, financial institutions, and markets everywhere around the globe. We observe now unprecedented business disruption, collapse of some industries, broken supply chains, falling commodity prices, and weak health care systems unprepared for the challenges facing them.

Unprecedented crisis requires unprecedented measures! We need an incredible amount of public finance and resources. **We must treat this situation as wartime.** "We must act like any wartime government and do whatever it takes to support our economy", said Boris Johnson, Prime Minister of the Great Britain.

Thus, all possible sources should be used now: enormous military spending, accumulated foreign currency reserves and savings, capital buffers of banking systems, etc.

The burden of this crisis will not be equally distributed among rich and poor countries. While advanced economies may be able to meet the forthcoming challenges with large financial envelopes, most emerging economies might find themselves guideless. The challenge is even greater for low-income economies.

But **a wartime is no excuse not to do reforms!** My experience in leading a central bank during wartime demonstrates that the only option for developing countries is to consider the ongoing crisis not as a disaster, but as an opportunity to carry out needed reforms. No need to be afraid of the word "reform". The simple definition of reform is to make changes in order to improve efficiency. When governments and central banks spend enormous money to save lives and jobs, they can in parallel improve processes and eliminate inefficiencies.

As I track events around the COVID-19 pandemic, I am reminded of mid-2014, when I started my tenure at the central bank against the background of the active phase of war in the east of the country. Now, the fight against a pandemic is exactly a global war with an enemy attacking from the inside. "We are at war," French President Emmanuel Macron repeated six times during a speech on COVID-19: "The enemy is there—invisible, elusive—and it is advancing."

This Practical Manual is precisely about how to accomplish drastic reforms in a wartime. As stated in Chapter 1, any disaster or war should only accelerate efforts at comprehensive reforms. Ukraine lost 20% of GDP, spent 15% of GDP to clean up the banking sector, 10% of GDP for support of unexpected military expenses, and 10% of GDP for support of state-owned monopolies during 2014-2015. This book has shown that not only did we survive, we completed comprehensive reforms in our energy sector, banking sector and public finance. Wartime is exactly the moment when decisive reforms should be launched across the board in the public policy, and first of all, in the area of public finance, which is liaising among other economic sectors.

Thanks to a decade of relatively steady growth in the global economy, many countries approached 2020 with a certain margin of safety. My country, Ukraine, was no exception, even though the period of macroeconomic stability in Ukraine was much shorter.

I would like to remind my colleagues that macro-financial stability can be quickly wiped out if reforms are not continued, or, even worse, if they are reversed. We should not forget how costly it was to get the country away from the fault line in 2014-2015, and therefore not repeat the vicious practices that led us to the precipice. Today, when the ice breaks not where it is thin, but at once on all fronts, one has no time to hesitate. Only joint and decisive actions of governments and central banks will allow nations to enter a crisis turn, and as car racers say, get out of it by flooring the economic accelerator.

Paradoxical as it may seem, *a severe crisis, like no other, is the right time to carry out overdue reforms.* The reason is that in a crisis, there is no room for manoeuvre. When "the sun is shining", even if we observe clear signs of macroeconomic imbalances, we often doubt the timeliness of reforms. But in wartime, with heavy expenditures on essential needs, the public sector plays a key role in prioritizing and taking decisive actions to bring the situation under control. This can entail large budget expenditures and an increase in government debt. It is necessary to resort to this temporary measure to be able to normalize your policy subsequently, after the alleviation of shock.

Today, the world's largest economies spend trillions of dollars to maintain the health and safety of their citizens. Fiscal stimulus and safety nets could reach unprecedented 10 to 12% of GDP. Fortunately, they can afford it. In the COVID-19 crisis, monetary policy will not be an effective mechanism as it was in 2008. At the time of the outbreak, the space of conventional and unconventional monetary policies was already utilized, key rates were already in zero territory or even negative and balance sheets of the US Federal Reserve and ECB had increased 3 to 4 times since 2008.

Moreover, monetary policy itself could not solve the current crisis. Rather, what are needed are complex measures, such as fiscal relief, financial support, direct support of businesses and households. Governments need to work out the most ambitious fiscal rescue program of our times: wage subsidies and job retention schemes, tax relief via differing taxes, tax holidays and tax benefits as well as credit guaranties. I am not talking about large-scale injections and direct spending in healthcare and public services, because the authorities need to quickly arrange subsidized credit to support the production of health equipment and other critical activities.

The United States already announced a USD 3 trillion rescue package, the European Union has agreed EUR 500 billion coronavirus rescue package. The United Kingdom has already applied fiscal measures for nearly GBP 40 billion. These packages even envisaged possible direct state financing of enterprises through entry to their capital or nationalization of the most affected sectors of economy.

Of course, Central Banks can ease market liquidity problems and stabilize long-term yield curve via large-scale asset purchases. The US Federal Reserve has already committed to unlimited balance sheet expansion for the foreseeable future. The ECB has announced a EUR 750 billion Pandemic Emergency Purchase Program, and the Bank of England has launched their joint HM Treasury-BoE Covid Corporate Financing Facility which, together with the Coronavirus Business Loans Interruption Scheme, makes GBP 330 billion of loans and guarantees available to businesses (15 % of GDP).

Banking system face this crisis in a much better condition than they were in 2008. According to BIS, the largest 106 international banks increased their Tier 1 capital from EUR 1.95 trillion in 2011 to EUR 3.72 trillion in 2018 to comply with tougher rules introduced by regulators.

Moreover, central banks have already freed up USD 500 bln as banks' capital around the world, which can add USD 5 trillion credit to the real economy. The biggest part of this relief was attributed to cutting of extra capital buffers. These buffers were designed to strengthen banks after 2008 crisis. Central banks have also recommended freezing dividends, management bonuses and share buybacks.

Now we will look at the main difference in policy responses by developed countries and emerging markets.

Despite generous economic stimulus measures in the United States, US Treasury bonds remain the main "safety asset" for the whole world, just as the US dollar in cash continues to serve as an airbag for many citizens of the developing countries, including Ukraine. Thanks to US Federal Reserve actions, the yield on short-term US government bonds is currently below 0; the yield on bonds up to 10 years does not exceed 1%. Moreover, significant demand for these "safe havens" is still there. Thus, it is much easier for the US and other major economies, such as the EU, to finance their contingencies. This is involuntarily helped by the fact that the inflation rate in developed countries is close to zero, and, therefore, the extraordinary measures taken by these nations to increase demand will not lead to disruption of the macroeconomic balance.

However, in emerging markets, the opposite is true. Since the beginning of the crisis, investors have removed USD 100 billion from emerging markets. This is the largest capital outflow ever recorded. That means that emerging economies face completely different challenges. Most of them lack a significant manoeuvre for the increase of fiscal expenditures due to budgetary constraints, which has only intensified due to protective measures and the resulting slowdown in economic activity. Further, this group of countries is often characterized by a high level of government debt, including denominated in foreign currency. Consequently, the turbulence in the financial markets will certainly affect emerging economies as a result of the reversal of capital flows to the safe havens. The outflow of capital from emerging markets and the resulting pressure on the exchange rate of local currencies leads to an increase in public debt and its service cost, which, in turn, leads to even greater impairment of these countries' ability to take costly anti-crisis measures. The outflow also creates pressure on foreign exchange reserves, which central banks are using while attempting to smooth out this outflow.

This chapter is dedicated to urgent policy response for emerging markets.

Ninety percent of developing economies have no fiscal space for maneuver when GDP fell by 10% on average in 2020. Moreover, they will have a large debt burden and budget deficit to support urgent pandemic measures that could reach 15% of GDP. The key question here is how unforeseen expenses will be financed. Pressure on central banks to keep the economy afloat by monetizing government debt is inevitable.

Therefore, for central banks, an episode related to the COVID-19 crisis is a test of their willingness to consider applying tools not found in their traditional arsenal. With that, central banks should keep in mind their primary mandate, namely maintaining price and financial stability. When using non-conventional measures, central banks should think about how to get into normal operation mode after the crisis is over.

Chapter 2, "Our Rapid Response Measures", has many valuable insights about Ukrainian–style QE, consequences of fiscal dominance and lessons learnt. 45% inflation in 2015 was caused by significant expansion of the money supply and 3x devaluation of local currency. At that time, the country was at war with enormous accumulated misbalances in all economic sectors and nobody in the world could help us to finance unexpected military expenditures. Nonetheless, in parallel, we started to do large-scale reforms. Using the printing presses and avoiding real reforms can only delay the inevitable and worsen the economic costs of dealing with inflation. Who doesn't recall World War I when countries financed the war by excessive amount of monetary emission? The result was the highest inflation and even hyperinflation the world had ever experienced. Overall price levels more than doubled in every country involved in the war.

Now is a different time! The correct step in this situation is to seek financial support from international financial institutions, including the IMF, World Bank, EBRD, and others. Therefore, I am pleased that the IFIs were among the first in early 2020 to announce their readiness to use all possible financial, technical and human resources to combat the global epidemic with the IMF securing $1 trillion of its lending capacity. The IMF immediately launched its flexible and rapid-disbursing emergency response toolkit for $50 billion and up to $10 billion is available for low-income countries with zero interest rate.

In my view, it is important to ensure that the relevant programs are front-loaded and allow supporting fiscal spending. Against the background of a sharp deterioration in the economy and unforeseen government spending on healthcare and other government programs supporting business activity, expanding the fiscal space will be more essential than ever for many developing countries. To avoid negative effects of fiscal dominance, EM need to use IFI money to cover budget deficit, at the same time they start reforms and give commitments to IMF and WB for an exchange of their support via Extended Financial Facility (EFF). As we see already, 95 countries have already applied to IMF for emergency assistance via Rapid Financing Instrument (RFI) in the amount of USD 27 billion. RFI program is very fast and effective tool for budget support to finance medical expenditures and social security, payable in a single tranche without any pre-conditions. I am sure that with the help of international financial organizations, using various assistance programs, this can be done very effectively. In order to control a usage of IMF funds under RFI framework it is better to have post-factum audit of expenditures for countries. This will allow IMF to analyze the effectiveness and transparency of this instrument and will warn some countries against the misuse of RFI money.

The second important task for central banks is to *maintain liquidity of the banking system and the flow of loans into the economy*. For this, central banks are already actively easing their monetary policy and making their regulatory requirements more flexible. The current crisis is also a good opportunity for them to test their prudential toolkit, including additional capital buffers formed during the period of macroeconomic stability.

In its recommendations on policy actions to address the pandemic of COVID-19, the IMF encouraged central banks to support the demand and confidence by easing financial conditions, ensuring the flow of credit to the real economy, and fostering liquidity in the markets[38].

Therefore, let me start with my views on what could be done on a fiscal side, and then switch to monetary and exchange rate policy, and banking regulation.

---

[38] Policy Steps to Address the Corona Crisis, IMF Policy Note, 2020. https://www.imf.org/~/media/Files/Publications/PP/2020/English/PPEA2020015.ashx

Fiscal Policy

As noted earlier, many countries have tight fiscal constraints that limit their abilities to finance contingencies for the pandemic. However, an additional fiscal stimulus may be necessary to provide well-targeted support to affected households and businesses and to prevent a long-lasting economic recession.

Due to the erosion of the tax base stemming from the loss of incomes in the private sector, the rise of public debt is inevitable. That said, it is important to keep the process of debt accumulation under control by active balance sheet management of the state and central bank. We should remember that any crisis will eventually end, and public authorities should be ready with their homework on the exit plan.

In Ukraine during the period of hostilities of 2014-2015, we were forced to support budget expenditures by monetizing government debt. Understanding the deleterious consequences of this practice in the long-term, we developed and agreed with the Ministry of Finance a plan to exit the fiscal dominance, which was implemented within a year and a half (see section (a) in Chapter 2).

However, before applying emergency measures, other options for refinancing public debt should be considered. My experience as a central banker indicates that one way out of the vicious cycle is the *restructuring of external and domestic public debt*, which allows delaying debt payments and thereby expanding fiscal opportunities. If countries have non-sustainable debt profile (debt/ GDP of 70% or higher), they need to do a restructuring of external debts and re-profiling of internal debts. Otherwise, if they don't, there is a risk that official assistance will end up paying off private holders of the country's debt. That means, bilateral and multilateral debt relief will not be used to finance the emergencies of the economy. Ukraine's respective decision was part of the package of our early response measures in 2014-2015 (see section (a) of Chapter 2). Together with the Ministry of Finance, we even took aboard state-owned banks and enterprises that followed the sovereign in the restructuring of their external debt.

Work on the terms of the respective programs should be started immediately, as this will help to achieve better conditions with creditors and meet the most urgent financing needs while easing the debt burden of the public sector.

Governments may decide to establish a special budget vehicle to finance pandemic contingencies. This could be funded with targeted government bonds and with the support of international financial institutions. The advantage of such a vehicle is that it allows minimizing the risks of violating financial stability in the country that would exist if the central bank was the only source of financing.

Now world leaders are discussing such an opportunity for emerging markets. They proposed so called "standstill" on Eurobond debt payments for a few years because of global exogenous shock. They use the word "standstill" instead of "moratorium" to avoid a negative connotation. I think it is a very good idea for countries with non-sustainable debt profile. I have no doubt if it is done on global level it will make life easier for all these countries.

Banking Sector and Macro-Prudential Regulation

Banking supervision around the world is based on IFRS and Basel principles; therefore, general recommendations are very well suited for emerging markets. No doubt, in extraordinary situations, central banks should act quickly and efficiently.

While in normal times central banks aim to achieve their primary mandate of keeping inflation close to target by setting the policy interest rate, in time of major distress, central bankers should deploy more comprehensive measures to stabilize markets and to ensure that the financial system continues to operate smoothly. A contingency plan should already be in place and be activated as soon as possible. As banks may encounter an outflow of liquidity due to impaired confidence in the banking system, central banks should be ready to provide liquidity support via open market operations and asset purchase programs.

In sum, the following generic recommendations are important actions during the crisis:

1. Use capital buffers

2. Support liquidity

3. Lower the amount of mandatory reserves

4. Encourage banks for loan prolongation and modifications

5. Lower the requirement for the ratio of liquid assets in a bank's balance sheet

6. Temporarily introduce flexible credit risk management based on former performance of the borrower and not forward looking

7. Introduce capital and FCY control measures if necessary (see Chapter 5)

8. Stop dividends payment, management bonuses and shares buybacks

9. Simplify and transfer on-line all possible official procedures and communication with regulators

At the same time, banks should not be forced to lend new loans to businesses in distress. This is a task for the state to introduce fiscal stimulus and a safety net.

Central banks could review their regulations on credit risk assessment to allow for a temporary leeway in setting up provisions for potential losses when assessing the risk of borrowers affected by the crisis. This would be helpful in allowing banks to accommodate restructuring of loans to borrowers facing financial difficulties due to the impact of the COVID-19. With that, general provisioning rules and loan classification should not be compromised. Banks should be urged to meet minimum capital and regulatory capital requirements. Depending on the fiscal space, governments could provide the capital to banks in the form of state guarantees to cover the risks of temporarily distressed borrowers.

Unfortunately, problems of business disruption will soon affect the banking sector, and the shock associated with the pandemic will potentially significantly affect the capital of banks due to the rapid deterioration of asset quality. The additional capital buffers under the framework of Basel III could be released (if already in place) or delayed to absorb losses and to ensure that banks have a sufficient amount of capital to maintain their lending capacity. However, this may not be enough. In my opinion, there is a high risk of that scenario. In many developing countries, bank capital may fall below minimum requirements. In this case, it is important for regulators not to change the rules, but be prepared to give banks time to meet the rules by developing and approving individual recapitalization programs, analogous to our decisions during the "recovery" of the banking system in 2014-2016 (see section (d) in Chapter 8). During that period, we granted banks a 4-year term to bring their capital level in line with the requirements of the regulator. Only banks that did not cope with this task were withdrawn from the market. The others continued to work successfully and enhanced their capital efficiency metrics.

Chapter 8 has applicable insights about the recapitalization plan of the Ukrainian banking system when Tier 1 capital was allowed to be zero for some period of time and gradually increase when recovery was in place.

I would like to stress that the main principle should be transparency – do not hide the problems and NPL in the banks' balance sheet. With that, I should note how important it is to ensure that insolvency of banks is not hidden under the cover of a liquidity mismatch. To verify this, the regulator should have an adequate risk assessment system that is sufficient to provide a clear picture of the quality of banks' assets.

Exchange Rate Policy and Monetary Policy

Under the inflation targeting regime, exchange rate flexibility can offset external shocks, but foreign exchange intervention may still be necessary if market conditions become disorderly.

Meanwhile, as my experience in diagnosing the external sustainability of many developing countries shows, huge balance-of-payments imbalances hang over them like Damocles' sword because of the artificially fixed exchange rate. Instead of allowing the exchange rate to accommodate shocks, and thereby to reduce pressure on the real sector, many countries continue to bend the line and hold the nominal exchange rate anchor. Due to the ongoing outflow of capital, this is becoming unbearable, and if taken to extreme, can result in major disruption.

Therefore, when switching to a floating exchange rate in a turbulent period, central banks need to have their own contingency plan, which can be used when certain triggers are activated (see our experience on contingency planning in section (b) in Chapter 2). This will allow the central bank to maintain confidence in its actions, even if the behavior of the markets does not correspond to the basic scenario of the transition.

My own experience shows that an artificial fixation of the exchange rate by setting an official value different from the market one, does not make sense, since the official exchange rate will rapidly lose its legitimacy, and the FX market may fall into the grey area outside the control of the central bank.

Section (a) in Chapter 5 describes instrumental insights into how to switch to a flexible exchange rate.

I see no other alternative for small open economies of emerging markets than a monetary policy of inflation targeting. Chapter 6, "New Monetary policy framework", provides a real, practical toolkit for transition to a new monetary policy of inflation targeting. Do not waste valuable time; start the transition while under the umbrella of IFI financing.

Finally, *international cooperation among central banks is crucial.* Given the scarcity of foreign reserves of the central bank, swap lines with leading central banks can help maintain market liquidity in foreign currency (see section (e) in Chapter 6). This facility provides the central bank with additional flexibility to address rapidly evolving developments in financial markets. The costs of servicing these lines can be offset by the public benefit of the smooth market operation.

In crisis or near-crisis situations, central banks may need to resort to capital flow measures for a temporary period. I should note that for these measures to be effective, the respective restrictions should be imposed immediately across the whole range of capital flows. If not, the motivation for capital outflow is strong enough that selective restrictions run the risk of being ineffective (see section (b) in Chapter 5).

Other Black Swans

Unlike many previous crises from economic history, the recent crisis did not come from the financial sphere, but the health sector. This is an inherent feature of our time. Churchill is credited with saying that 'Generals are always prepared to fight the last war'. Similarly, economists are always ready with an antidote for past crises. In my opinion, central banks should be prepared for unexpected challenges. Specifically, their policies should be flexible enough to be able to adapt to new realities. The COVID-19 pandemic may have outpaced the global crisis associated with global climate change, but it does not obviate future crises.

Moreover, even in the best case, least painful, way out of the current crisis, we will come out of it with significant indebtedness, both of the public and private sectors. Given the prolonged recovery of economic activity, this could lead to a global debt crisis, which was projected long before the pandemic. These harsh realities validate the fact that in the future we will need truly strategic thinking in order not to be taken aback by events whose occurrence we can neither control nor anticipate.

I N MY FINAL address to Parliament in April 2017, I said that my mission at the NBU was complete.

First, the country switched to a flexible exchange rate and launched a new monetary policy for inflation targeting. Secondly, the banking system had been cleared of insolvent banks and had strengthened its stability for the future. Thirdly, the National Bank was completely transformed, all processes were rebuilt, and our central bank had become a powerful modern institution.

IMF findings[39] have proven that, unlike real sector reforms, financial sector reforms have detrimental electoral costs, regardless of whether they are carried out under strong or weak economic conditions. Our team learned this lesson first-hand, as we were ostracized by both politicians and fellow citizens who had suffered losses in failed banks. Despite the resistance to reforms, my team succeeded however, primarily because we were not politicians, and did not count on electoral dividends. We were driven by understanding the need for changes that in the long run will lead to a better future for our country.

My resignation was my personal choice rather than a political decision. Of course, it was caused by incredible pressure and even death threats from criminal oligarchs. But it was my personal decision. For the first time in the history of the NBU, this decision had nothing to do with politics. My decision was yet another proof that our country has embraced true democratic values. I tenaciously fought for the NBU's independence during my three-year tenure. With this decision, I once again proved that the National Bank is out of politics. This is the norm and standard for all developed countries, which Ukraine aspires to be. The central bank must remain independent.

---

[39] The Political Costs of Reforms: Fear or Reality? / IMF SDN/19/08, October 2019

It may still sound unbelievable that we managed to stabilize the macroeconomic situation, radically change the "landscape" of the banking sector, and build a modern central bank in the wake of war and political instability, a deep economic crisis, and an empty state treasury.

I can tell you that if I had tried to do everything myself, it would not have worked. Leaders take people who share their vision and drive, and they start doing the reforming – that's why in respect to banking reform I say that our team did it.

Our experience transforming the banking sector and central bank has been recognized as a tremendous success by all of our international partners and local stakeholders. But *it did not happen by chance*:

1.   We had a mission and a vision.

2.   We had a detailed strategy and an action plan.

3.   We had values and leadership.

The implementation of strategic goals was carried out by a professional and dedicated team at all levels of the central bank, and was facilitated by implementing changes using project management approaches consistent with best international practice. The reform was supported and trusted by international partners and donors, and we've been always honest and transparent in communications with stakeholders, and ready to acknowledge and correct our mistakes.

The results are that Ukraine now has:

- A truly independent modern central bank
- A transparent and well capitalized banking system that generates the highest profit in history
- Sound monetary policy that contributes to sustainable economic growth

- International recognition as a role model for a modern and transparent central bank

Upon completion of Program 2020, the question will be to determine the future priorities of the National Bank. In my opinion, after the stages of market clearing and reloading are gone, the new priorities of the *National Bank should be aimed at the development of the financial sector as a whole*, not only the banking sector, though banking will continue to remain the central pearl of Ukraine's financial system.

I am thankful to the international community: the IMF, World Bank, EBRD, European Union and the US government helped us to survive and stabilize Ukraine's macroeconomic situation.

There are many people I have never seen to whom I am grateful. I can only guess who launched the campaign #SaveGontareva in late 2014, which got thousands of likes on Facebook amidst a sea of hatred. I never learned the name of the person who wrote -- in the midst of war and destruction of our industry -- "Blaming Gontareva for the collapse of the hryvnia is as fair as blaming a stewardess for a plane crash".

Today, international institutions hold the NBU as an example, sending central bankers from other developing countries to the NBU for training.

The NBU's new structure underpins the central bank's independence. No one at the central bank will be able to make decisions at their own discretion anymore. One-man shows are gone forever.

The reform of the banking sector, which is the circulatory system of the economy, was part of, and a very important part, reforms in Ukraine. In our case, we had a limited central bank mandate with respect to many related areas of activity, which once properly reformed, helped strengthen the positive outcome of the banking sector reform. I hope this practical guide will help implement reforms in other sectors in Ukraine and in other countries as well.

Finally, not long ago, some colleagues from other central banks told me that central banks are "White Knights". They begin reforms by safeguarding macro-financial stability and end up cleaning up the market, and delivering the right conditions for a country to grow. Let's continue to believe in that!

REFERENCES

CMU Resolution No. 961 dated 18/12/2016

Daniel Calvo, Juan Carlos Crisanto, Stefan Hohl, Oscar Pascual Gutiérrez "Financial supervisory architecture: what has changed after the crisis?"; FSI Insights on policy implementation No 8, April 2018.

Davide Furceri; Jun Ge; Jonathan David Ostry; Chris Papageorgiou; Gabriele Ciminelli, 2019. "The Political Costs of Reforms: Fear or Reality?", Staff Discussion Notes No. 19/08, International Monetary Fund

Decree of the President of Ukraine No. 170/2015 dated 24.03.2015

Law of Ukraine "Code of Ukraine on bankruptcy procedures" No. 2597-VIII dated 18.10.2018

Law of Ukraine "On amendments to legislative acts of Ukraine on recovery of lending", No. 2478-VIII dated 03.07.2018

NBU Board Resolution No. 314 dated 12.05.2015.

NBU Board Resolution No. 315 dated 12.05.2015 (updated);

NBU Board Resolution No. 328 dated 21.05.2015 (updated)

NBU Board Resolution No. 369 dated 15.08.2016 (updated)

NBU Board Resolution No. 411 dated 14.12.2016

NBU Board Resolution No. 417 dated 26.06.2015 (updated)

NBU Board Resolution No. 492 dated 12.11.2003 (updated)

NBU Board Resolution No. 540 dated 29.08.2014

NBU Board Resolution No. 587 dated 18.09.2014

NBU Board Decision No. 627 dated 20.09.2018

NBU Board Resolution No. 732 dated 26.10.2015 (updated);

NBU Board Resolution No. 806 dated 11.12.2014

NBU Financial Stability Report, June 2018

NBU Macroprudential Policy Strategy, December 2018

NBU Resolution No. 351 dated 30.06.2016 (updated)

NBU Resolution No. 64 dated 11.06.2018

NBU Resolution No. 863 dated 25.12.2014

Policy Steps to Address the Corona Crisis, IMF Policy Note, 2020.

Šarūnas Černiauskas, Vlad Lavrov and Michael Nikbakhsh, 2019 The Vienna Bank Job, OCCRP

Stankova Olga, 2019. "Frontiers of Economic Policy Communications", Departmental Paper No.19/08, International Monetary Fund

Tobias Adrian; Tommaso Mancini Griffoli, 2019. "The rise of digital money", FinTech notes, International Monetary Fund.

Volcker, Paul A., 1984, "The Federal Reserve Position on Restructuring of Financial Regulation Responsibilities," Federal Reserve Bulletin, Vol. 70 (July)

Valeria Gontareva, 2019 Research for EBRD "Comprehensive Banking Reform in Ukraine".

Valeria Gontareva, 2019 Research for IGA "Banking Reform in Ukraine. Lessons learnt and generic recommendations for other countries".

Valeria Gontareva

Senior Policy Fellow, Institute of Global Affairs
London School of Economics and Political Science
http://www.lse.ac.uk/iga/people/Valeria-Gontareva

Valeria Gontareva joined LSE in 2018 in the capacity of Senior Policy Fellow. Before that she served as the Governor of the National bank of Ukraine from 2014 to 2017. She was the first woman to lead Ukraine's central bank and oversaw vital reforms to implement a new monetary policy of inflation targeting and flexible exchange rate regime, to clean up Ukraine's banking sector, to strengthen regulatory supervision, and to ensure the independence of the National Bank. Mrs Gontareva started her career in financial services in 1993 and gained two decades of private sector experience at both Ukrainian and international financial institutions before her appointment as Governor of the central bank. Between 1996 and 2000 she worked at Bank "Societe Generale Ukraine" as Capital Market Division manager, member of the management board. Between 2001 and 2007 she was First Deputy Chairman, Managing Director at ING Bank Ukraine. From 2007 to 2014 she led Investment Capital Ukraine as Managing Partner, the leading financial service group in Ukraine. Mrs Gontareva graduated from Kyiv Polytechnic Institute in 1987 and also obtained a master degree in Economics from Kyiv National Economic University in 1997.

Yevhen Stepaniuk

Yevhen Stepaniuk served as an Assistant to the Governor of the National Bank of Ukraine in 2014-2016 and a Head of the Financial Sector Reform Office of the National Bank in 2017-2019. In this capacity, he coordinated the development and implementation of the strategy for the financial sector reform in Ukraine and managed the portfolio of cross-ministerial projects. He was also responsible for dialogue with stakeholders and public communications. Over 2006-2013 Mr. Stepaniuk worked at the central bank of Ukraine in the field of macroeconomic research and analysis, contributing to the bank's reports in areas of inflationary development, exchange rates, capital markets, monetary and macroprudential policies. Mr. Stepaniuk holds a Ph.D. from the University of Banking (2013) and an MSc from Kyiv National Economic University (2006). He has taught macroeconomics, monetary policy, and financial stability at leading Ukrainian universities and has published extensively in economics and finance.

Lightning Source UK Ltd.
Milton Keynes UK
UKHW010637280720
367298UK00001B/20